ANARCHISTS, BEATS
AND DADAISTS

ANARCHISTS, BEATS AND DADAISTS

JIM BURNS

PENNILESS PRESS PUBLICATIONS

www.pennilesspress.co.uk

Published by

Penniless Press Publications 2016

ISBN 978-1-326-44654-3

Cover: The cabinet of Michel Gherlerode – Royal Library Brussels

CONTENTS

ACKNOWLEDGEMENTS

Personal Modernisms, *Northern Review of Books* (on-line), June, 2015

Alger Hiss, *Northern Review of Books* (on-line), February, 2014; *The Crazy Oik 23, Warrington, Autumn, 2014*

Blood on Steel, *Northern Review of Books* (on-line), March, 2015

British Writers and MI5, *Northern Review of Books* (on-line), May, 2013; *The Crazy Oik* 18, Warrington, Summer, 2013

Woody Guthrie, *Tribune,* London, 27th March, 1981

Edward Dorn/Amiri Baraka, *Northern Review of Books* (on-line), May, 2014; *Beat Scene* 73, Coventry, Summer, 2014

Alan Ansen, *The Kerouac Connection* 19, Bristol, Spring, 1990

Lawrence Ferlinghetti, *The Kerouac Connection* 17, Bristol, Spring, 1989

Bob Kaufman, *The Kerouac Connection* 10, Bristol, April, 1986

Kerouac and the Beats, *Tribune,* London, 28th November, 1969

Catching Up With Kerouac, *The Kerouac Connection* 7, Bristol, July, 1985

Writing Beat, *Northern Review of Books* (on-line), January, 2015

Brion Gysin, *The Kerouac Connection* 12, Bristol, November, 1986

Exodus, *Beat Scene* 77, Coventry, Summer, 2015

Janet Richards, *Beat Scene* 71, Coventry, Autumn, 2013

Discovery, *Beat Scene* 75, Coventry, Winter, 2014

The Beat Scene, *Beat Scene* 79, Coventry, Autumn, 2015

Between Worlds, *Beat Scene* 78, Coventry, Summer, 2015

Fielding Dawson, *Poetry Information* 14, London, Autumn/Winter, 1975/76

Destruction was My Beatrice, *Northern Review of Books* (on-line), July, 2015

Tristan Tzara, *Northern Review of Books* (on-line), July, 2015

Joan Gilbert, *The Aylesford Review*, Volume 1, No 1(new series), Aylesford Priory, Maidstone, Summer, 1968

Two American Poets, *Ambit* 190, London, 2007

Eddie Linden, *Ambit* 79, London, 1979

Malcolm Cowley, *Northern Review of Books* (on-line), March, 2014

New Fiction, 1972, *New Statesman,* London, 19th May, 1972

Walt Whitman, *Northern Review of Books* (on-line), January, 2015; *The Crazy Oik* 25, Warrington, Spring, 2015

The Hosanna Man, *Northern Review of Books* (on-line), October, 2014

The Street of Wonderful Possibilities, *Northern Review of Books* (on-line), July, 2015

The Taste in My Mind, *Northern Review of Books* (on-line), July, 2015

An Unholy Row, *Northern Review of Books* (on-line), September, 2014

Tubby Hayes, *Northern Review of Books* (on-line), May, 2015

Underground London, *Beat Scene* 76, Coventry, Winter, 2015

Bopper, *Jazz Monthly,* St Austell, August, 1968; *The Little Word Machine* 10, Bradford, 1979; *Ragged Edge Magsheet* 2, Appliance Books, Ipswich, 2003

Border Trouble, *Tribune,* London, 29th August, 1969

Love From Uncles Bert and Joe, *Weekend Guardian,* London, 4th March, 1989

Are You Sure it's Tonight? *Smiles Above the Platform: Poets in Public,* edited by Diane M. Moore, Marc Goldring Books, London, 1996

My thanks to all the editors concerned, and to Ken Clay and Joan Mottram.

INTRODUCTION

This seventh collection of essays and reviews follows on from the previous six in bringing together what I like to think is largely a survey of mostly lesser-known writers, poets, artists, musicians, and related people and their publications. Some names in the list of contents will be immediately identifiable, but it could be that certain aspects of their work may not be familiar to most readers. Walt Whitman's links to a group of early American bohemians is an example of what I'm suggesting.

As with the previous books, the Beats have a central role, though I hope I've looked at a few lesser-known poets, such as Bob Kaufman, along with pieces on Kerouac and Lawrence Ferlinghetti. And the magazines that published them, like *Exodus,* and *Between Worlds*, seem to me worth writing about in order to record their contributions towards circulating interesting literature. I doubt that little magazines now have the importance they once had, but prior to the arrival of the internet they were key methods of communication. They were, also, the organs of expression for bohemia, and that, too, no longer exists in the way it once did. I'm perhaps beginning to sound like an old man lamenting the decline of everything he once loved, and there may be some truth in that. I do miss the magazines and the bookshops where you could find them.

What might be called "fringe figures" have always fascinated me, and the short pieces about Alan Ansen and Brion Gysin deal with a couple of them. Both were linked to the Beats, for one reason or another, but had much more to recommend them than that. Eddie Linden edited a magazine called *Aquarius*, that published a lot of good poets, including some who were unfairly overlooked for many years. Janet Richards knew a lot of poets and others around San Francisco, and her book, *Common Soldiers,* is a neglected account of the 1940s and 1950s. Joan Gilbert was a young poet who tragically died young. She showed promise, though it was unfulfilled, and her work is worth recalling.

There are a few items about jazz in Britain, all of them mostly relating to the years between 1945 and 1960. I bought my first bebop records in 1950 and still find the period fascinating. There has been a tendency to dismiss the 1950s as a dull, dismal decade in many ways, but that's far from the truth. Jazz was in a very buoyant state, and literature had much to offer, if you knew where to look for it. The essay on the magazine *Discovery* indicates how much good writing there was appearing in print in the 1950s. Also, enthusiasts for the Beats might care to reflect on the fact that some of the best work by Kerouac and Ginsberg was produced prior to 1960 or so.

The politics of the Left in Britain and America continue to fascinate me, and several items concern the events of the 1930s and the intrigues of the Cold War. The case of Alger Hiss and his encounters with Whittaker Chambers still arouses strong feelings, though the evidence appears to show that Hiss had been involved in some form of subterfuge, if not outright spying. He was never convicted of that and only served a prison sentence for perjury. The character of Whittaker Chambers – was he a liar and a fantasist? – is something that deserves continued study.

Finally, I've included a handful of short, personal pieces that hopefully fit in with what has gone before. "Love from Uncles Bert and Joe," "Border Trouble," "Bopper," and "Are You Sure It's Tonight?" might provide a sketchy autobiographical picture if anyone is interested. An element of humour creeps into a couple of them. Like Bulwer-Lytton in his novel, *Pelham*, I take exception to the notion that "whatever is gloomy must be profound and whatever is cheerful must be shallow."

PERSONAL MODERNISMS

In the late-1950s I started to collect little magazines and some small-press publications, largely from the 1940s. I was lucky because there were plenty of second-hand bookshops and one way and another I managed to build up a complete set of *Penguin New Writing,* together with an almost-complete set of *Modern Reading,* and lots of individual issues of *Poetry Quarterly, New Writing and Daylight, Selected Writing, Bugle Blast, Writing Today,* and *Focus.* There were others, and I admit to probably having overlooked many things simply because a glance at them hadn't immediately aroused my interest. And I didn't have unlimited funds at my disposal. Not that a lot of the magazines and books were expensive if one didn't mind their often battered appearances. I didn't, provided all the pages were there and the texts of the poems, stories, and articles were intact. And so I got those magazines referred to, along with two books by Wrey Gardiner, a copy of the original edition of Elizabeth Smart's *By Grand Central Station I Sat Down And Wept,* the 1945 anthology drawn from issues of *Personal Landscape,* a couple of Julian Maclaren-Ross's books, and the five issues of Denys Val Baker's anthologies of writing from little magazines.

As I read the little magazines and the anthologies I came across names that, in the late-1950s, weren't exactly well-known in Britain. Or if they were, it wasn't always for the right reasons. Henry Miller might be a good example. A book like *Tropic of Cancer* didn't get its official British publication until 1963. Other names I noted were Kenneth Patchen and Kenneth Rexroth, and the fact of them being American probably meant that their work wasn't accorded much attention here. But what about Nicholas Moore, George Barker, George Woodcock, Alex Comfort, David Gascoyne, J.F.Hendry, Henry Treece, and D.S.Savage? Despite being British they certainly weren't in the forefront of the local poetry world in the late-1950s. I doubt that many people even thought of Woodcock and Comfort as poets, and it was only later, when Woodcock published a key text on the history of anarchism, and Comfort's *The Joy of Sex* brought him fame, that they became better-known. Philip Larkin was attracting attention, and it was the poets publishing under the label of The Movement who were garnering all the plaudits at that time. And critical surveys tended to often skip over the 1940s and put their emphasis on what was known as the Auden generation of the 1930s.

James Gifford mentions books by Stephen Spender and Bernard Bergonzi and says: "Each of these works has as a defining trait a strong tendency to view Modernism and late Modernism through a perspective developed from the High Modernism and the Oxford Poets (MacSpaundays), and by and large limited to their ideological and theoretical scope."

It's Gifford's contention that works like those by Spender and Bergonzi ignored, or played down, "Tambimuttu's *Poetry London*, the preceding Villa Seurat group, or the New Apocalypse and the subsequent New Romantics." Elsewhere, he adds poets in California (the key players in what became known as the San Francisco Renaissance) and wartime Cairo, to his list of those who can be seen as functioning in opposition to what Auden and his followers represented. Anarchism was a prime factor for many of these poets and provided a conduit through which they communicated with each other. Anarchism and little-magazines.

The early influence on most, if not all of the poets grouped under the loose label of New Apocalypse, was Henry Miller whose books, the best known of which in the 1930s was *Tropic of Cancer*, had a major impact. As Gifford puts it: "The conceptual, political, and aesthetic background for the New Apocalypse grew directly from the Villa Seurat network's influence on English post-surrealism." Miller had challenged the surrealists then-alliance with the Communist Party and his 1938 "An Open Letter to Surrealists Everywhere" became a key document for those poets who preferred not to be associated with any political creed, and especially not a doctrinaire one like communism. Miller's concern was for the individual: "The brotherhood of man is a permanent delusion common to idealists everywhere in all epochs: it is the reduction of the principle of individuation to the least common denominator of intelligibility. It is what leads the masses to identify themselves with movie stars and megalomaniacs like Hitler and Mussolini." It's easy to see that such an attitude would not be looked on kindly in the 1930s, when political allegiances of one sort or another were paramount, or in the 1940s when patriotic pressures were insisting on a spirit of common interests and togetherness. Miller and the writers associated with the New Apocalypse, New Romantics, Personalists (all descriptions applied to poets standing aside from the MacSpaunday group) were often attacked for what George Orwell described as their "nihilistic quietism." And Kathleen Raine referred to "defeatism" in relation to these same poets.

Developing the question of how the "association between the 1930s, as a decade of poetry, and four Oxford graduates, W.H. Auden, Stephen Spender, Cecil Day-Lewis, and Louis MacNeice has become axiomatic and naturalised," Gifford refers to two Penguin anthologies, *Poetry of the Thirties* (1964) and *Poetry of the Forties* (1968) which, he asserts, "had a significant influence" in terms of what was seen as the canon for those decades and so was taught in the classroom. Robin Skelton, he says, does include some New Apocalypse poets in *Poetry of the Forties*, though in his introduction to the book he is quite dismissive of the group, and his selection of the poems he does use, and the placing of them in relation to other work, tends to reduce their interest and importance: "George Barker appears only twice, Bernard Spencer appears only with his works most heavily influenced by Auden rather than poetry after his break from the Auden school of thought, and Dylan Thomas's works focus on his least surrealist and syntactically complex poetry." Any anthology is always open to criticism relating to its contents, and Gifford's questioning of Skelton's inclusions and exclusions seems to rest on the way he "collapses the opposition many 1940s poets felt towards Auden as a stylistic issue related to Romanticism and the function of the symbol rather than a political difference that drove the stylistic choices."

Gifford also opens up the question of social differences between the MacSpaundays and at least some of the poets associated with the New Apocalypse. He quotes Peter Childs as claiming that the "canonisation of Auden" came about because of "his appeal to a 'liberal middle-class conscience' which has constructed the decade's value and significance." And Childs pointed out that "Dylan Thomas and George Barker were from lower middle-class backgrounds and entered neither public school or Oxbridge." Gifford himself adds that neither "Barker nor Thomas cared much for the easy accessibility of their work to the class from which they arose; nor do they turn to their art as a means of changing the world, as Auden had until the war years." This reference to the New Apocalypse poets perhaps not knowing, or even caring, who their likely audience would be is further accented by Gifford quoting G.S. Fraser who, in his introduction to an anthology of their work, acknowledged that they were "not likely to have the same immediate popularity as the generation that immediately preceded them, the generation of Auden, Spender, and MacNeice."

I think it is obvious that little magazines and small presses were of importance to the poets of the New Apocalypse. And the 1940s were boom years for such publications, though not everyone agreed that the "democratisation" implied by a more-open access to publication was necessarily a good thing. Robin Skelton, for example, was dismissive of the "amateurish near-poems" produced by most of the contributors to the "overseas anthologies and the many little magazines that appeared during the war years," and he went on to say that editors and publishers appeared to believe that "a new romanticism" had arisen and that it "made the acceptance of pretentious and sentimental attitudinising extremely easy." Henry Treece, who Skelton described as the founder of the New Apocalypse school, was taken to task for his role in encouraging this situation to develop. Even Gifford has to acknowledge that it's unlikely that any of Treece's own poems are ever going to be revived. And I have to admit that my own reading of his work in some of those old 1940s publications, and in Kenneth Rexroth's *New British Poets* anthology, published by New Directions in 1949, and a good source for lesser-known 1940s poetry, has never inclined me to think of him as an important poet in any way. But in context he's readable and not necessarily worse than many other poets of his period. Saying that may make me appear to agree with Skelton's statement about the weak nature of much 1940s poetry. But I incline to the view that most poetry at any time is usually less than memorable. And looking back at it rarely makes it seem better than it was. This, of course, does not invalidate the requirement for a correct historical record of its existence to be established.

The same can be said about the little magazines and related books that provided a means of circulating the work of the Personalist poets (the term seems interchangeable with New Apocalypse and New Romanticism) located in London, San Francisco, Cairo, and other places. Gifford's long account of the various publications is particularly valuable as information about them is often difficult to come by. A.T. Tolley's *Poetry of the Forties* (Manchester University Press, 1985) has since its publication been seen as a major source of information, and Gifford acknowledges that while disagreeing with some of Tolley's interpretations of the relationships among poets associated with the New Apocalypse and the importance of those poets within the 1940s literary world as a whole. Gifford, in fact, spends quite a lot of time disagreeing with other academic critics about their accounts of what New Apocalypse added up to. However, he does offer a lively narrative of the role of little magazines in disseminating new work by such poets as Lawrence Durrell, Nicholas Moore, David Gascoyne, and others. Several of the poets had been involved as editors of little magazines at one time or another, and it's no surprise to read that they appeared in each other's publications. The same names crop up in *Delta, Seven,* and *Kingdom Come. Delta*, incidentally, followed on from *The Booster*, which was officially the magazine of the American Country Club in Paris but had been taken over by Henry Miller's friend, Alfred Perles, who transformed it into a vehicle for work by Miller, Durrell (an excerpt from his notorious novel, *The Black Book*), Anais Nin, and David Gascoyne. The good times lasted until the American Country Club threatened legal action if the magazine didn't revert to its original function. I sometimes think that any history of little magazines is best based on anecdotes and reminiscences relating to the struggles to see them born and then kept alive. Academic accounts usually can't capture the spirit of the little magazine world.

The anarchist connection was clearly of importance insofar as the exchange of ideas and publications was concerned. Alex Comfort edited *New Road* which published Americans like Kenneth Rexroth and Kenneth Patchen. And there were links to *Arson*, an anarcho-surrealist magazine produced by Toni del Renzio, and to *Now,* which George Woodcock edited from Freedom Press and published work by George Barker, Herbert Read, W.S.Graham, and William Everson. Gifford discusses the anarchist element among the New Apocalypse poets in some detail. Anarchism has always lent itself to a variety of interpretations, but perhaps the dominant aspect in relation to many of the people involved was the individualist anarchism espoused by the 19th Century German philosopher, Max Stirner. This isn't the place to analyse Stirner's *The Ego and its Own*, but it does seem to have had a degree of influence on the thinking of poets who were concerned to promote the personal in preference to the collective. I've perhaps made this appear to be simpler than it was, and it did occur to me to wonder whether all the poets always shared similar interests and ideas.

I mentioned having come across a copy of the *Personal Landscape* anthology published by Poetry London in 1945 and Gifford analyses the background to the magazine. It was started in Cairo by Lawrence Durrell, Bernard Spencer, and Robin Fedden, with some involvement from Terence Tiller. I doubt that, with the exception of Durrell, these names will mean much, if anything, to many contemporary readers. And it may be that even in Durrell's case his poetry is mostly forgotten. He did make a name for himself later with the *Alexandria Quartet*, but in 1941 his novel, *The Black Book*, was only available in the edition published by Obelisk Press in Paris, and a combination of censorship and the war meant that few people had read it. Those who had, and they included the American poet Robert Duncan, viewed it in the same light as Henry Miller's *Tropic of Cancer*. Gifford has a fascinating chapter on the way in which Duncan, soon to be a major figure in the San Francisco Renaissance, was influenced by Durrell: "I contend Duncan's anarchism informs his mysticism and poetics, and his fascination with Durrell, Miller, Barker, and the other Personalists is both a consequence of his anarchism just as his increasing interest in anarchism is a consequence of his interest in their verse and prose." It's possible to see that Duncan's concerns, like those of others in the United States, were in accord with the intentions of many of the contributors to *Personal Landscape*, to keep to "the same well-trod paths and avenues away from 'propaganda' and 'outside national and political frontiers.' It's a temptation to bring such publications as *Circle* and *Ark* in the USA and *Transformation* in London into a discussion of what Personalist poets were doing, and Gifford does devote space to them, noting that *Circle* "immediately endorsed an anarchic surrealism akin to English surrealism."

When the war ended the Cairo group inevitably split up. And there were various alterations to relationships and activities as the post-war situation changed. It has been noted by Tolley and others that the network of little magazines and small-press publishers that had thrived during wartime, and supported the poets loosely grouped with the New Apocalypse, had virtually collapsed by 1950 or so. And Kenneth Rexroth, writing in 1957, had some interesting things to say about the decline of contacts between British and American poets:

"Anarchism, conscientious objection, war resistance, were more popular with young English writers than with the Americans, and there was considerable contact during and just after the war between San Francisco and London. Writers like Alex Comfort, D.S. Savage, George Woodcock, Herbert Read were widely read. The first magazines to publish the new San Francisco school were *Horizon, Poetry Quarterly, Poetry Folios.* This has all died out, not because the Californians have changed, but because the British have. A kind of hopeless inertia – atomphobia – has settled upon the British avant-garde."

I suppose, too, that the fact of some of the writers – Alex Comfort, George Woodcock, Lawrence Durrell – tending to drift away from an active role with poetry, and some of them – David Gascoyne, W.S.Graham, Nicholas Moore – physically moving away from places where they had contacts with other poets, and feeling the impact of the decline of magazines and publishers like Poetry London and Grey Walls Press, must have had its effect. Changing tastes may have had something to do with the lack of readership for many of the poets published in New Apocalypse magazines. The 1950s saw the rise of poets associated with The Movement, with its emphasis on what might be called a more direct and down-to-earth approach to writing poetry. Anarchism and surrealism were out.

James Gifford provides plenty of food for thought in his survey of the poets of the New Apocalypse, New Romantics, Personalist movement. Or should it be movements? They are, as he rightly says, mostly overlooked, either by design or accident, in many works of criticism and in university courses. Opinion may differ about the reasons for that, but the historical record of their existence does need to be correctly established, and Gifford's book is a step in the right direction.

PERSONAL MODERNISMS: ANARCHIST NETWORKS AND THE LATER AVANT-GARDES

By James Gifford

The University of Alberta Press. 294 pages. $34.95/£28.99. ISBN 978-1-77212-001-1

ALGER HISS, WHITTAKER CHAMBERS AND THE CASE THAT IGNITED McCARTHYISM

I'm looking at a small pamphlet published in New York in 1932. It's a short story called "Can You Hear Their Voices?" and was written by Whittaker Chambers who was then a member of the Communist Party. He had written four stories for *New Masses*, the Party's literary and cultural magazine, in 1931, the best-known of which was the one reprinted as a pamphlet. It was based on an actual event when hundreds of angry farmers marched into a town in Arkansas and demanded food for their hungry children. The story was turned into a play and translated into various languages and, for a time, Chambers was looked on as a promising revolutionary writer. He also contributed poems to such publications as *Poetry* and *The Nation*, and he was commissioned to translate a number of books, including Felix Salten's *Bambi*, which turned out to be a best-seller.

Chambers remained a member of the Communist Party for some years, though his literary career as a fiction writer and poet never prospered. He later claimed that he'd worked "underground" for the Party, though by the late-Thirties he had become disillusioned and decided to break with communism. He got a job with *Time* magazine, initially as a book reviewer, but soon expanded into other areas, and contacted the FBI in order to provide information about his activities and fellow-conspirators during his supposed "underground" years. According to Chambers his life was in danger and NKVD agents were anxious to eliminate him because of what he knew about spy networks in American government agencies. He changed addresses frequently, used different names, and tried to avoid being traced by anyone who may have known him when he was a communist. Was Chambers a fantasist, as some have suggested, or were his fears justified? It's still an open debate.

In August, 1948, Chambers testified before the House Un-American Activities Committee(HUAC) as an "expert witness on Communist infiltration of government," and named a number of people who, he claimed, had been members of an "underground" group in Washington. Among those he named was Alger Hiss who was what would now be called a "high-flyer." A well-qualified lawyer, Hiss "had joined FDR's New Deal in 1933, advised Roosevelt at the infamous Yalta Conference in February 1945, presided over the founding of the United Nations and personally delivered the UN Charter to President Truman." In the 1930s he had worked for the Agricultural Adjustment Administration (AAA) and the State Department, and Chambers insisted that he had personally handled documents passed to him by Hiss. There was little doubt that some sort of left-wing group had operated in the AAA under the leadership of Harold Ware, and when the Hiss/Chambers controversy erupted one of the people linked to it, the novelist John Herrmann, fled to Mexico in an attempt to avoid being questioned by the FBI.

It's perhaps necessary to say a few words about the general atmosphere in the late-1940s as the Cold War got under way and purges of left-wingers in government, unions, Hollywood, and private industry became common. It could be said that there was a kind of hysteria at work, and right-wing politicians, who had been opposed to New Deal policies since Roosevelt's days, saw an opportunity to roll back what they said was a too-powerful state which was influenced by socialist ideas. And rising politicians such as Richard Nixon, who would play an important role in the attack on Hiss, made a name for themselves as patriotic anti-communists. It would not be long before Senator Joseph McCarthy jumped on the bandwagon.

When Hiss was summoned to appear before HUAC to answer the charges of being a member of the Communist Party, and of participating in some sort of illegal activities, he indignantly denied that he had ever belonged to the Party, and he said that he had never known anyone by the name of Whittaker Chambers. Chambers had provided details of visits to Hiss's home, some of which sounded convincing, and spoke of cash being loaned by Hiss, a car which was often used by him, and other matters which, to many people and especially those who disliked what Hiss stood for in terms of his background and social standing, had a ring of credibility about them. It has to be said that others were convinced that Chambers was lying, and even Nixon initially had some doubts about the reliability of the stories that Chambers told. Hiss did say that, although he had not known a Whittaker Chambers, he had encountered a journalist named George Crosley who had approached him for information for a series of articles he was writing. This would have been a perfectly open and legal exchange, the information concerned not being subject to any restrictions. However, Chambers denied ever using the name of George Crosley. Later, he could have been shown to have been lying because a publisher was willing to testify that he had been offered some poems by Chambers under the name of Crosley, but Hiss's defence team decided not to call him. The person concerned, Samuel Roth, had convictions for publishing obscene material and it was thought that using him as a defence witness might create a wrong impression.

Hiss continued to deny knowing Chambers or a "Carl," the name Chambers claimed to have used when working "underground" for the Party, and when shown a photograph he thought that it might be of the George Crosley he had met. He then insisted on a face-to-face encounter with Chambers and when it took place he thought the person facing him could be George Crosley, but that he had never known him as Whittaker Chambers. The latter, for his part, immediately knew Hiss, though that in itself meant nothing as Hiss's high profile made him easily recognisable. When Chambers repeated his claims in public about knowing Hiss as a communist the latter decided to sue for defamation. In response, Chambers changed his story to admit that he had been engaged in espionage, something he had previously always denied because he was worried that he could be prosecuted. He said that he had been a courier for Soviet intelligence and he produced documents said to be in Hiss's handwriting, and others which he claimed were typed on a machine owned by Hiss. As matters hotted up various associates of Hiss were alleged to have been involved in illegal activities. One of them said that Hiss was never a communist, but Nathaniel Weyl, who admitted to spying, said that Hiss had been a Party member.

There were claims and counter-claims, and Chambers repeatedly changed his stories, bringing up new "facts" whenever he was in a tight corner. For example, he stated that Hiss's wife knew Maxim Lieber, a literary agent who acted for many left-wing writers, but Lieber said that he'd never met her, and wouldn't know her if she walked into the room at that moment. Would Lieber have been a reliable witness had he been called (he never was)? His own involvements could well have worked against him. Lieber was quite open about his own membership of the Communist Party, but denied ever doing anything illegal and said his contacts with Chambers were totally innocuous. But some of Hiss's stories were occasionally vague enough to have aroused suspicions in the minds of those who wanted to believe in his guilt. There was a car that Hiss insisted had been sold to George Crosley, though he later said that he had given it to him, but which was shown to have been passed to a dealer and later picked up by someone who gave a false address and was identified a communist. Hiss also created something of a bad impression by repeatedly using the phrase "to the best of my recollection" when asked certain questions.

Evidence of how Chambers was totally unreliable when it came to telling the truth is given in detail by Lewis Hartshorn. He claimed to have been fired from a job at the New York Public Library, but the records showed that he lost his job because he had been stealing books. When asked about the books he'd translated he only mentioned *Bambi*, but Hartshorn says that between 1928 and 1940 he actually translated seventeen, and that many of them were "widely reviewed." As for his supposed activities as a communist, a fellow-communist, Sam Krieger, didn't believe that Chambers could have done the things he claimed to have done, and described him as "a politically very unreliable individual and the last person in the world to have been entrusted with any kind of official responsibility." The noted art historian Meyer Schapiro, a friend of Chambers for many years, thought that he was acting out a "mystification" when he joined the Communist Party, and recalled that during their three month tour of a Europe beset with radical politics of one kind or another, Chambers had shown no interest at all in communism. Hartshorn lists so many lies and contradictions, such as Chambers' statement that he was once the editor of *New Masses*, that it would be impossible to mention them all here. He also quotes various people, like Alexander Trachtenberg and Charles Dirba, both high up in the American Communist Party hierarchy, as refuting claims made by Chambers about meeting them. It could, of course, be argued that, as communists, they would not want to admit to knowing Chambers, but as so much else he stated has been shown to be untrue it's perhaps best to believe them.

The libel case was delayed when the Justice Department intervened on the grounds that a trial for perjury was likely to take place, though there were at first some doubts about who would be the accused. Hartshorn quotes someone as saying that J. Edgar Hoover wanted to see both men charged with perjury. In the event it was Hiss who stood in the dock accused of lying about not knowing Chambers, and of denying that he had passed documents to him. It needs to be noted that HUAC hearings had continued, with supposed fresh evidence in the shape of some microfilms produced by Chambers, and with arguments about the validity of evidence relating to a typewriter supposedly used to copy documents that Hiss had taken from his office. With regard to how Chambers had obtained material if it had not been given to him by Hiss, there is evidence that indicates that some government employees did pass information to him. Julian Wadleigh admitted doing just that. And other people testified to the fact that security at the State Department was so lax that anyone could wander around the building and enter offices without being challenged in any way. Harrison Salisbury, a reporter for the *New York Times,* recalled that he saw "no guards at the doors, no plastic identification cards, nothing to prevent Chambers or anyone else from poking into just about any office he pleased.....Such a world seems impossible today and no doubt it was fearfully insecure."

Alger Hiss was tried twice, the jury at his first trial being unable to agree. At the second trial he was found guilty and sentenced to five years in prison. Was he guilty? Obviously, Hartshorn doesn't think so and he works hard to show that Chambers was a liar and a fantasist, and that some evidence was certainly rigged so as to suggest that Hiss was not telling the truth. It's interesting, too, that his brother and wife were never charged with anything, despite Chambers having named both of them as communists and conspirators in the plot to pass documents to the Russians. It's hard not to think that the authorities had got what they wanted when they saw Hiss sent to prison. He had seemed to represent the kind of liberal establishment they distrusted, and in demonstrating that someone like him could lie and engage in treasonable actions they were making the point, important at a time when the nation was encouraged to condemn anyone who wasn't obviously a right-wing patriot, that conformity was essential. Hartshorn quotes Charles Brennan as saying: "There was never any substantive understanding of what Communism meant. The word was just used as a general category for that which was foreign, unfamiliar, and undesirable."

Some years ago when writing an article about John Herrmann I remarked that information that had come to light with the fall of communism made it almost certain that Alger Hiss had been involved in some form of illegal activity, if not actually that of spying. The late Gael Turnbull wrote to me to dispute what I'd said. He had been in the United States as a medical student in 1950 and had followed the Hiss/Chambers confrontations closely, and he was convinced that Hiss was innocent and that Chambers had really been the one who had committed perjury on a grand scale. We exchanged a few letters on the subject, but eventually agreed to hold to our own opinions. Not that mine was a fixed one and I had to admit that it was based on what I'd read. And I've now read Lewis Hartshorn's book and it has convinced me that Whittaker Chambers was a liar and a fantasist. But I still can't shake off the feeling, and that's all it is, that Alger Hiss had something to hide. He may not have passed any documents to Chambers, and he may have known him only as George Crosley, but was there something he wouldn't admit to? Did he know about other people who may well have been doing things they shouldn't have done? I don't think Lewis Hartshorn has said the last word on this subject, and I doubt that it will ever be settled satisfactorily unless someone manages to track down documentation that provides a definite solution. The question is, does such documentation exist?

When writing this review I've had to select just a few examples of the kind of stories Whittaker Chambers came up with to justify his naming of Alger Hiss as a communist. And I've equally had to limit what I could quote from Hiss's denials of any involvement with so-called "underground" activities. Hartshorn's book is so packed with details from both sides of the argument that it's easy to become confused at times. This isn't because of his writing, which is clear enough, but simply a comment on a case that was bound to be complex and prone to confusion as memories of what had taken place ten and more years before consistently clashed.

ALGER HISS, WHITTAKER CHAMBERS AND THE CASE THAT IGNITED McCARTHYISM

By Lewis Hartshorn. McFarland & Company Inc., 218 pages. $38.95 ISBN 978-0-7864-7442-4

BLOOD ON STEEL

On the 30th May, 1937 (Memorial Day in the USA) hundreds of striking steelworkers gathered at Sam's Place, located not far from Republic Steel whose management had taken a hard-line position with regard to recognition of the Steel Workers Organising Committee (SWOC) as representing union members at its factories. An agreement had been signed with US Steel, the major operator in the industry, but Republic Steel and some other relatively smaller operators (collectively known as Little Steel) had refused to negotiate on the matter, so a strike had been called. The workers who came together at Sam's Place, many of them with their wives and children, intended to march to the gates of Republic Steel to assert their right to picket, protest against police brutality in earlier encounters, and perhaps persuade non-striking workers to join them outside the gates. The exact number of people present isn't known, but Michael Dennis says it was possibly between 1,500 and 2,000. By the end of the day four strikers had died, six more succumbed to their injuries later, and over one hundred were injured, some of them seriously.

Violence during strikes in America in the 1930s was frankly not unusual, but what singled out the Memorial Day encounter for major attention was not only the level of deaths involved, but also the fact that a newsreel unit had been present and film was shot of the encounter between police and demonstrators. It's perhaps misleading, in fact, to suggest that the "battle" was anything but one-sided. The police were heavily armed and there is little evidence that the great majority of the strikers did more than turn and run when they came under fire. All ten of those who died had been shot in the back or the side which appeared to indicate that they had been fleeing or turning away from the police.

It's necessary to look at the general situation in American industry to fully appreciate what was at stake in 1937. The economy was showing some signs of recovery, and major industries like autos, steel, and rubber were again employing large numbers of people. As circumstances improved there were energetic drives to unionise workplaces. A newly-formed organisation, the Congress of Industrial Organisations (CIO), had broken away from the craft-based American Federation of Labour (AFL) and had set out to recruit union members in industries like the auto-plants, rubber, and steel, which were labour-intensive. At the same time laws had been passed as part of President Roosevelt's New Deal which established the rights of workers to join unions and be involved in collective bargaining. Employers were frequently unhappy with this state of affairs and some continued to refuse to negotiate and sign agreements. Strikes erupted, with sit-down techniques often effectively giving workers temporary control of their workplaces. There was a tradition of anti-union activity in the steel industry going back many years to the Homestead strike of 1894 and the major walk-out in 1919. When SWOC started to recruit in steel in the 1930s the management at Republic Steel took a particularly tough stance in refusing to meet union officials.

As mentioned previously, the Chicago police force had been active from the start of the strike in breaking-up earlier demonstrations. They refused to allow picket lines with more than a token number of pickets, and were known to be disposed to use force against anyone infringing the arbitrary rules they set or otherwise opposing their authority. There was evidence to show that the police acted in collusion with Republic Steel management to the extent that the police operated from company premises and some, at least, used batons supplied by Republic Steel. The company, in addition to any assistance they could expect from the official police force, also had its own security men, though they primarily functioned inside Republic Steel premises. But let me quote Michael Dennis on the subject of how the company prepared to face up to the strikers:

"While SWOC organised, Republic Steel stocked weapons and armaments for an imminent confrontation. The company had spent more than the city of Chicago on tear gas and sickening or vomiting, gas. Its inventory included 4 submachine guns, 525 revolvers, 64 rifles, 245 shotguns, and enough clubs and ammunition to hold off the Illinois National Guard. Republic's contingent of 370 police guards stood ready to use them. The company's escalating layoffs, harassment, and anti-union espionage aggravated an already drum-tight situation."

SWOC, for its part, could count on those workers on strike, along with assistance from some others from different areas who saw the struggle against Republic Steel as part of a wider war to not only obtain union recognition, but also improve working conditions and "humanise" the workplace. Too often people were treated as if they had no rights and could be dismissed at the whim of a foreman or supervisor. Some local churches supported the strikers, as did groups of university students, liberal elements in Chicago, and, of course, the Communist Party. Dennis refers to an agit-prop theatre group which performed plays like Clifford Odets' *Waiting for Lefty* and Albert Maltz's *Black Pit* in union halls and similar locations. On Memorial Day one of their number stood on the back of a truck and sang songs such as "The Ballad of Joe Hill" and "Solidarity Forever" to raise the spirits of the strikers. But support like that didn't alter the fact that the march on Republic Steel did not have overall CIO backing and that little or no help came from other unions. Some United Automobile Workers Union (UAWU) members did want to strike in sympathy with the steelworkers, but were stopped from doing so by their union leadership which threatened them with disciplinary action if they broke the contracts the UAWU had agreed with management in the automobile factories.

When the march to the Republic Steel premises began it's unlikely that anyone anticipated what would later happen. But was it significant that certain key members of both the local Communist Party and the union leadership were not present? Did they realise that a showdown with the police was on the cards and that it would inevitably end in violence? Dennis doesn't investigate this angle (did no-one at the time think to question the absentees about their failure to be there?) but he does say that several rank-and-file activists among the strikers had to hastily assume some sort of leadership of the demonstration.

Who or what triggered the police into drawing their guns and firing into the crowd when the marchers came face to face with them was inevitably a bone of contention later. The police naturally claimed that they'd been attacked and had acted in self-defence. But there appears to be no evidence that any of the strikers were carrying weapons, though it's possible that one or two missiles may have been thrown from the back of the crowd and hit the fence around Republic Steel. And a few demonstrators might have tried to fight back once the shooting and clubbing started, though most, as noted earlier, simply turned and ran. The newsreel from that day appeared to show this quite clearly, as did statements from observers at the scene. And the fact that I referred to - that people were shot in the back or side – likewise points to them moving away from the police.

Michael Dennis devotes several pages to a detailed account of the actions of the police as they used their guns and clubs indiscriminately. Women, including one who was pregnant, and children were among those hurt. What is still shocking is not only the initial shooting but the way in which injured people were viciously clubbed and kicked as they lay on the ground and obviously presented no threat to the police. Demonstrators attempting to help fallen comrades were attacked and requests for assistance for the badly-injured were ignored. When some strikers tried to take one of their friends to hospital in a car the police forced them away and threw the man in the back of an already-crowded police van where he died. It seems clear that certain policemen deliberately delayed driving badly-hurt people to hospital. When someone complained they were told to shut up and that they had got what was coming to them. I've pulled out only a few examples from Dennis's account but they indicate the extent to which the police can be said to have run wild. Four strikers died at the scene and six from their wounds later.

Needless to say, conservative elements in Chicago rallied to the defence of the police and supported their claims that the strikers were armed and determined to break through the police lines. Were any of the police injured in any way? Dennis doesn't look into this question, and I suspect that the answer would have been "no," even if he had. But the *Chicago Daily Tribune*, the city's leading right-wing newspaper, claimed that communists were behind the violence and named one of the dead strikers as a Party member. It was a fact that a handful of the demonstrators belonged to the Communist Party, and it would have been surprising, given the time and place, if they hadn't. But, as noted, Party leaders were noticeable more by their absence. And is it likely that they would have had a planned policy of violent confrontation for the demonstration if they had been present?

In the aftermath of Memorial Day there were mass meetings, an enquiry, and though the newsreel did briefly sway public opinion in favour of the strikers, around the country as a whole there was a growing anti-union mood among many middle-class people. It wasn't that they were necessarily anti-working class, but violence during strikes and the mass sit-ins in the automobile factories tended to worry them. Aggressive union tactics seemed to lead to confrontation in which the rights of property-owners were challenged and some militants wanted to widen their actions to include political as well as purely workplace-based demands. Union leaders responded by becoming more-cautious in their tactics. Dennis quotes steelworkers' union leaders as saying: "We are dealing with organising steelworkers & this only, forget about Spain situation, auto situation, & all other world problems." He also discusses how President Roosevelt took an increasingly detached approach to labour issues as Southern Democrats allied with Republicans to challenge aspects of his New Deal policies. Workers may have seen Roosevelt as on their side, but out of necessity he usually played an impartial role in labour disputes and preferred to let other people deal with issues like that.

The strike for union recognition at Republic Steel was lost and it was only in 1942, when the demands of war production, union activity, and pressure from the federal government, determined how management needed to react, that an agreement was signed with the United Steelworkers of America (USWA). In the post-war years there were less demands from the grass-roots for radical social or economic change. Members largely left it up to the union leadership to negotiate favourable terms relating to pay and conditions. A union's purpose was, for many people, to help them participate in American consumerism. The start of the Cold War and the onset of McCarthyism further reduced the activities of militants in the unions who wanted to shape wider policies. Most American unions purged their ranks of communists and other left-wingers. As Dennis puts it: "By the 1950s, the CIO had lost the sense that it belonged to a larger united front that still had to address fundamental issues of political and economic inequality."

The story of the Memorial Day Massacre is interesting in itself, but Michael Dennis widens his account to consider matters pertaining to the role of unions today. But the fact of it being about unions in the United States needn't limit its relevance for British readers. After all, our unions have similar problems relating to their activities. And they face restrictions on how they go about looking after the immediate interests of their members while attempting to play a role in influencing larger social and economic matters.

BLOOD ON STEEL: CHICAGO STEELWORKERS AND THE
STRIKE OF 1937

By Michael Dennis. The John Hopkins University Press. 140 pages.
£13. ISBN 978-1-4214-1018-0

BRITISH WRITERS AND M.I.5

Some years ago I read a couple of books that dealt with the way in which the FBI carried out surveillance of various American writers. Those books, Herbert Mitgang's *Dangerous Dossiers:Exposing the Secret War against America's Greatest Authors*, and Natalie Robins' *Alien Ink: The FBI's War on Freedom of Expression,* provided extensive lists of authors, ranging from William Faulkner to Allen Ginsberg, and including Theodore Dreiser, Norman Mailer, and William Carlos Williams. I've just pulled a few names out of a large hat. At the time I was reading the books I did wonder how many British writers had been subjected to surveillance by our security services, but there didn't seem to be detailed information that would allow me to come to any kind of conclusion. It did seem obvious that the police and MI5 would have files on certain writers,but who were they?

James Smith's book offers some answers, though they're mainly about a handful of well-known writers. This is not said as a criticism, but instead to show that Smith has chosen to focus on a few specific names in an effort to demonstrate just how much surveillance took place.

The police and MI5 kept a close watch on what they thought of as "bohemian revolutionaries" or "intellectual communists," and Smith says that "Special Branch routinely monitored gatherings of 'Jewish and Intellectual type(s) of communists,' with the result that events ranging from small meetings to public festivals were attended by officers themselves or their details were relayed via a network of secret informants." There is ample evidence to indicate that mail was intercepted, telephones tapped, and premises bugged. Ralph Fox complained to the Post Office about irregularities in the delivery of his mail which he suspected, were due to it being intercepted. Nancy Cunard asked the police why her movements were monitored. And the novelist Ralph Bates had his manuscripts vetted by Special Branch as he passed through the port of Newhaven.

One group of writers of particular interest to the authorities included W.H. Auden, Stephen Spender, Christopher Isherwood, and Cecil Day-Lewis, and Smith devotes a chapter to them. They were, in cultural terms, trend-setters, with their bias towards "poetry and drama deploying Marxist imagery and anti-fascist themes, political tracts such as *Forward from Liberalism* (Spender) and *The Mind in Chains* (edited by Day-Lewis), and contributions to Popular Front organs such as *Left Review*." All that, and their support for the Republican government in Spain, attracted the attention of the police and MI5. It does seem, though, that it wasn't necessarily their literary efforts which bothered the authorities, but rather their links to left-wing organisations or to individuals who were under suspicion. Spender and Day-Lewis had joined the Communist Party. Auden's friendship with Guy Burgess, later identified as one of the Cambridge spies, led MI5 to consider whether or not he had known about Burgess's activities and, in particular, his decision to flee to Russia to avoid being arrested. As for Isherwood, it was largely due to his knowing Gerald Hamilton that he became of interest to MI5. Hamilton, the model for Arthur Norris in Isherwood's *Mr Norris Changes Trains*, was in Smith's words, "a remarkably disruptive individual that even Isherwood's fictionalised representations seem to underplay." Hamilton was involved in criminal activity and suspicious political work, so was always under surveillance.

Smith notes that the members of the Auden group quickly moved away from radical politics and "made a rapprochement with the institutions they had seemingly previously rejected." This didn't mean that MI5 stopped keeping records of what they got up to. As mentioned earlier, Auden's links to Guy Burgess caused some concern. Day-Lewis experienced difficulties in the 1940s when he wanted to obtain work with the BBC and the Ministry of Information in order to avoid being conscripted into the armed forces. Like Spender, he was eventually cleared for employment, though with the suggestion that he be kept under some form of surveillance in case he tried to insert pro-communist propaganda into whatever he was doing. MI5 also wanted to know how Communist Party officials reacted to Day-Lewis's withdrawal from the Party. They obtained information about this from transcripts of conversations which were routinely bugged.

A somewhat different bunch of left-wingers who came to the notice of the police (particularly in the Manchester area) and MI5 included Ewan MacColl and Joan Littlewood. MacColl was known to local police because of his membership of the Young Communist League and his involvements with left-wing street theatre. The police constantly harassed MacColl, who was still then using his real name,

James Miller, though initially MI5 were not all that interested in him. It would appear that he first aroused attention through his work with the British Workers' Sports Federation (a communist front organisation) and his participation in the 1932 mass trespass at Kinder Scout in the Peak District. But even then, the MI5 investigator, Roger Hollis, wasn't concerned about MacColl's theatre work and remarked, "I think Miller may be left to his plays." This was to change when MacColl started to work for the BBC.

Joan Littlewood had moved to Manchester in 1934, looking for work in radio and with local repertory groups. She married MacColl in 1935, and co-operated with him in the Workers' Theatre Movement, Red Megaphones, and Theatre Union. The latter was a forerunner of the more-famous venture, Theatre Workshop, which was established in London in 1953. Smith cites a number of reports to MI5 by local police in which the various activities of MacColl ("communist cultural") and Littlewood (radio programmes) were noted. There was also a report which commented on their social lives: "at weekends, and more particularly when Miller's parents are away from home, a number of young men who have the appearance of Communist Jews are known to visit Oak Cottage." This was the Miller family home where MacColl and Littlewood were then living. The degree of surveillance carried out was quite significant, and another report stated that the detective concerned had been "able to listen to their conversations during the evenings at Oak Cottage," though he did say that he hadn't heard anything relating to communism and related political matters.

Police and MI5 surveillance continued through the war years, and Littlewood was still hired by the BBC, though not on a permanent basis. As for MacColl, who was still using his real name, he was briefly in the army, deserted, went into hiding, and survived until 1945 without being arrested. He then re-surfaced as Ewan MacColl. Both he and Joan Littlewood had, to a large degree, moved away from direct contact with the Communist Party, but Smith says that they functioned with a social framework that included many Party members. And in 1952 MI5 intercepted a letter containing an application from MacColl to rejoin the Communist Party. When Theatre Workshop was set up in Stratford it immediately became the subject of surveillance, and Littlewood later recalled seeing plain-clothes policemen taking notes in the theatre. Smith also mentions that information about Theatre Workshop was passed to MI5 by contacts within the "broader theatre industry." Were suspicions about it really justified? It's worth drawing attention to an incident which perhaps indicated that Littlewood and company were independently minded. Carl Weber, a famous director based in East Berlin, came to England to supervise the Theatre Workshop production of Brecht's *Mother Courage*. But he proved to be "much too German, much too dogmatic, and even much too Communist," and was soon barred from the theatre during rehearsals.

Two political writers known to MI5 were George Orwell and Arthur Koestler, both with a record of involvement in the Spanish Civil War, among other things. Orwell had been watched by the Wigan police when he was in the town gathering material for *The Road to Wigan Pier*. He was suspected of "communist activities," and said to be associating with "undesirable elements," the latter presumably known communists and other left-wingers. He received "an unusual amount of correspondence" and was observed making notes about local industries, etc. The fact that Orwell was already a published novelist and journalist doesn't seem to have come to the attention of the police in Wigan. One of the things that can be seen in reports from police in the provinces is that it was forms of what they thought of as unconventional behaviour that often bothered them. References to casual ways of dressing occur, and interests that didn't fit into an accepted pattern are commented on. This isn't surprising, and anyone who grew up in the towns and cities of Britain in the 1940s and 1950s will easily recognise the kind of thinking behind many police assumptions.

Orwell remained a problem even after publishing his mistrust of communists in *Homage to Catalonia*. He worked for the BBC during the Second World War, and Special Branch officers claimed that he had tried to obtain employment for alleged subversives. A report states: "This man Orwell has advanced communist views, and several of his Indian friends say that they have seen him at communist meetings. He dresses in a bohemian fashion both at his office and in his leisure hours." Fortunately for Orwell, some members of MI5 were a little more sophisticated in their judgements, and James Smith says that the agent checking the police report "did little to hide the sense of scorn felt for the intellectual paucity of the police." Surveillance of Orwell continued but on a diminished scale, and mostly by Special Branch.

With Arthur Koestler the security services had a much more complex problem to deal with. Smith is of the opinion that compared to the "relatively sparse files on Orwell, Koestler's MI5 file narrates what, in many places, seems more like the plot of a spy-thriller than fact." And he adds that Koestler could be legitimately seen as a "plausible security concern." He had been a member of the Communist Party and had engaged in "underground" activities in Europe. He had been involved with the Party in Germany, worked with the propaganda networks of Willi Munzenberg and Otto Katz, two notorious communists, and was imprisoned in Spain when, using the cover of being a newspaper reporter, he tried to gather evidence about how Franco was being supported by Hitler and Mussolini. Further adventures took Koestler to the Middle East, internment in a French concentration camp, a short stint in the Foreign Legion, and a roundabout route to get into Britain. When he arrived he was arrested and almost deported. He had, by this time, severed his links to the Communist Party, and though he was viewed with suspicion by MI5 he managed to persuade enough people in positions of influence that he was genuinely anti-communist. During the Cold War years he could always be counted on to provide an attack on the tyranny that communism represented. He was, for example, one of the contributors to *The God that Failed*, an influential anthology in which Koestler, Stephen Spender, Richard Wright, Ignazio Silone, and others, told how they had lost their faith in communism.

James Smith claims that "Special Branch, and indeed the police forces in general, were manifestly (and sometimes comically) incapable of understanding controversial but legal left-wing political movements and had particular difficulty in judging the security threat posed by intellectuals who involved themselves with dissident causes." And he goes on to say that ordinary policemen were not intellectually equipped to assess the masses of information they gathered. Their response was to harass suspects, gather more information, and invoke security alerts that had little or no basis in reality. Even some MI5 officers were guilty of similar attitudes and behaviour.

Smith does stress that, whatever the nuisance aspect of the surveillance of British writers (and some may well have missed out on work due to MI5 reports on their suitability for employment), the security apparatus did not, on the whole, have the power "to decide what was or was not beyond the pale." What's more, "It is one of the strengths of Britain's political tradition, in an era when HUAC, McCarthyism, and J. Edgar Hoover's FBI were tearing America's cultural life apart, that MI5 and Special Branch remained marginal, and frequently contested, rather than decisive, voices." This is an accurate summing up, and anyone needing confirmation about the contrast with what happened in the USA ought to read the various histories, biographies, autobiographies, and other documents of what has been referred to as "The Great Fear." Writers went to prison for refusing to say whether or not they were communists, blacklists were established, and publishers leaned on to refuse to print work by left-wing authors. What happened in Britain in terms of harassment was minor by comparison.

However, Smith does ask if "the assumption of the presence of surveillance resulted in self-censorship. Did certain authors choose not to write on certain topics, to not publish in certain venues, or to not speak out on certain political causes because of the fear that this was being recorded and potentially held against them?" He thinks this may have been the case, at least with regard to some of the people he has looked at. Joan Littlewood broke off her connection to the Communist Party because she was worried that it was affecting her career with the BBC. Orwell deliberated about whether or not to write for a communist publication. And Koestler made a point of not associating with left-wing groups in Britain.

It's difficult to know about questions of self-censorship unless a writer admits to it, but I do wonder how many of them, not necessarily well-known or widely published, drew back from publishing work that might be looked on as politically questionable? The police probably had files on writers in their respective areas who were known left-wingers. Smith mentions Shelagh Delaney in this respect, and her file refers to her being a "communist sympathiser." The fact that her play, *A Taste of Honey*, was being produced by Theatre Workshop was also noted. We don't know how many other files existed locally, or if some writers backed away from political involvements when they worried that their jobs or their families might be affected by police harassment.

James Smith acknowledges that many files have still not been released, and those that have were subject to "redaction," with many details blanked out. Working with the materials available to him he has written a valuable and well-documented book that will, one hopes, lead to further research into surveillance of writers by the police and MI5.

BRITISH WRITERS AND MI5 SURVEILLANCE, 1930-1960
by James Smith. Cambridge University Press. 206 pages. £55 (US $95).
ISBN 978-1-107-03082-4

WOODY GUTHRIE

THERE is a peculiarly American mixture of rumbustious political activity, travelling and singing that stretches back to the legendary Wobblies, and is perhaps typified in a popular sense by Woody Guthrie's life and music.

Guthrie was never a member of the IWW, though he knew about its philosophy and carried a copy of the famous Little Red Songbook. But I would guess that, had he seen the light of day a few years earlier, he may well have played a part in the organisation's history.

As it was, Woodrow Wilson Guthrie was born in 1912, just at the time when the Wobblies were in their heyday and singing Joe Hill's songs on street corners around the country. His family wasn't working class, but it had its share of ups and downs, and the young Woody was reared on a diet of varied experiences.

An erratic scholar, he nonetheless read a great deal, and gave early evidence of some idiosyncratic skills. At the beginning of the thirties he made a living of sorts by playing music, doing odd jobs, and dabbling at commercial art. The first days of the Depression do not seem to have affected him a great deal, either personally or politically.

But he began to drift, hitching his way from one place to another, riding freight trains, mixing with hoboes, migrants, the unemployed. And with old Wobblies, many still proudly bearing their battle scars and preaching the gospel of the class war. It was through them that he started to get radicalised.

It wouldn't be true to say, though, that he picked up all his politics in the hard school of experience. A lot of his ideas came from books, and from talking with people like the Left-wing actor/activist Will Geer, and with Communist Party intellectuals. Guthrie was impressed by their courage and determination in the face of often brutal opposition.

Once established as a singer, he worked on radio, supported radical causes, recorded extensively, and helped out by performing in union halls and on picket lines. He served in the merchant navy during the war, and came out of it to face, a few years later, the effects of McCarthyism. He might have coped with the political climate, but his personal behaviour was often affected by heavy drinking, and by the onset of the nervous disease, Huntington's chorea, which ran in the family blood.

His final years were sad ones and he died in 1967 more of an influence than a performer of any consequence. A man of many moods, there is little point in denying that he could be disturbingly unpredictable, though the disease may have had a lot to do with that. But he generally stuck by his friends and his politics, and the best of his music will continue to live on record and superbly recapture the tone of an era.

Joe Klein's account of Guthrie's life is well documented, and he doesn't try to gloss over the inconsistencies in his subject's character. I suspect he found it hard to understand Woody's liking for the communists. In this way he misses the point that the thirties were a special time in America, and that it often seemed as if only the party was willing to put up a fight against poverty and injustice. But that apart, it's a fair and accurate book.

Guthrie had a talent for taking old tunes and adding new lyrics to them, and it was something he shared with Joe Hill, the enigmatic Wobbly whose words were in the Little Red Songbook. But Hill usually got his inspiration from popular songs and hymns rather than from folk ballads. He was, unlike Guthrie, an immigrant, relatively new to America and its traditions.

It would be almost impossible to write a biography of Hill. He seems to have made an art out of hiding his real personality. Whether this was, as some old Wobblies suggested, because he wasn't always particular about how he got his money is something that will never be known for sure. And Wallace Stegner leaves the question open in his novel.

First published 30 years ago under the title *The Preacher and the Slave*, it's a vigorous and often moving attempt to get to grips with Hill's character, and the possible reasons for his strange behaviour during his trial for the murder of a Salt Lake City shopkeeper.

Hill wasn't an activist in the sense of directly participating in the strikes and free speech fights. He came and went in his own way, and the standard histories of the IWW say little about him, other than that he wrote some of its best-known songs. The only time he ever drew attention to himself was at the trial - and if he had a past he didn't disclose it to the police, or indeed to his friends and lawyers. He died in front of a firing squad as defiant as he'd been in court.

Stegner brilliantly suggests the strangeness of the man, and sets it against the social conditions of the period. Hard times were all around, and it could have been that Hill wasn't averse to appropriating money from those he thought had too much of it. But could a small-time thief have had the interest and commitment to produce the witty and pointed songs that Hill wrote? If he did, he wouldn't have been alone in those days in seeking a common link between some forms of criminality and revolutionary acts.

Joe Hill is a splendid book, immensely readable, evoking both the individual and the spirited movement he was connected with. It's good to have it in print again.

WOODY GUTHRIE: A LIFE by Joe Klein (Faber)
JOE HILL by Wallace Stegner (Nebraska University Press)

AMIRI BARAKA & EDWARD DORN :
THE COLLECTED LETTERS

Exchanges of letters between writers can offer insights into the characters of the people concerned as well as into their work. And they can additionally throw light on particular periods of literary activity. Amiri Baraka and Edward Dorn began to establish themselves as poets and prose writers at a time when American literature was widening its scope and the "New American Writing," as it was often referred to, was starting to attract attention. This didn't necessarily mean that people like Baraka and Dorn suddenly found it easy to break into print, nor did it lead to their being able to support themselves from their writing. But it may be interesting at this point to say something about them. Not everyone will necessarily be familiar with Baraka's books, nor with Dorn's. Some background information may be useful.

Amiri Baraka, or Leroi Jones as he was called prior to his embracing black nationalism in the 1960s, was born in Newark, New Jersey, in 1934, and grew up in what has been described as a stable, working-class household. He seems to have done well at school and won a scholarship to Howard University in Washington. But he soon rebelled against what he saw as its bourgeois educational ethics and left. He then joined the Air Force, though he was quickly discharged because he was suspected of communist tendencies. This was at a time when McCarthyism was rampant and any sort of deviant behaviour was suspect. It would appear that copies of *Partisan Review* were found in Jones's locker. There's a humorous side to this, *Partisan Review* being anti-communist and even probably supported by the CIA as part of its cultural programme. But the fact of it being an intellectual publication, and not given to the kind of populist anti-communism that Senator McCarthy and his supporters favoured, would probably have been enough for Jones to attract unfavourable attention. He soon moved to Greenwich Village and became involved in the "bohemian poetry, theatre, and music scene." Over the years he established himself as a poet, editor, playwright, jazz critic, and political activist.

Edward Dorn was born in Illinois in 1929 and so grew up during the Depression, something that was reflected in a poem like "On the Debt My Mother Owed Sears Roebuck." Dorn attended Black

Mountain College in the 1950s and got acquainted with Charles Olson, Robert Creeley, Joel Oppenheimer, John Wieners, and others who would play a significant part in "The New American Writing" of the late-1950s and early-1960s. Dorn wrote prose as well as poetry, but was never able to earn a living from his writing alone. He took part-time teaching posts and in 1965 was offered a position as a Fulbright lecturer at Essex University where he remained until 1970. When he returned to the USA he still found it necessary to teach part-time while trying to develop his poetry. In 1977 he was offered a teaching position at the University of Colorado and stayed there until he died in 1999.

The initial contact between Jones (I'll use the name he had during the main part of the time they corresponded) and Dorn was in 1959 when Jones was editing his little-magazine, *Yugen*, and wrote to Dorn to ask him to send some poems. Jones was publishing a wide selection of the new writers, including Beats like Kerouac, Corso, and Ginsberg, Black Mountaineers such as Fielding Dawson and Joel Oppenheimer, and Frank O'Hara who was linked to the New York School. Dorn was going to be in good company. There are notes about most of the people mentioned and it's useful to have them. Kerouac and Ginsberg don't need to be explained, but what about Max Finstein? Unless you're a specialist with an interest in this period of American poetry it's unlikely you'll know anything about Finstein. His name does crop up here and there in the letters, not always in a complimentary way. But he's not alone in that and I'll say something later about how and why Jones and Dorn seem to feel it necessary to be derogatory about many other poets. And not just poets. Joyce Glassman (later known as Joyce Johnson) became a particular hate figure for Jones. Claudia Moreno Pisano says that Glassman "is the target of some of Jones's more vicious misogynist vitriol," probably because in her role as an editor at a commercial publisher she didn't match up to his expectations of publication of Dorn's work.

The exchange of letters became regular once the initial contact had been established. Both poets were experiencing financial problems and they often compare notes on how much, or more likely how little, they're likely to be paid for a reading or whether or not the money can be raised to publish a small book. Publishing their poems in little magazines wasn't ever going to bring in payments of any consequence, or even any payments at all, most magazines struggling to stay alive. Jones's own magazine, *Yugen*, had folded after eight issues, and a mimeographed publication, *The Floating Bear*, that he'd started with Diane di Prima, didn't pay contributors.

By 1961 Jones was becoming increasingly politicised and in September he wrote to Dorn to say that he'd been arrested and charged with "resisting arrest; inciting to riot; disorderly conduct." He'd also attracted the attention of the right-wing Senator Eastland who described Jones as a "Beatnik poet, radical leftist racist agitator." This led to an exchange of ideas about politics and to what degree poets should involve themselves in activism. Jones was obviously an advocate of poets getting involved, but Dorn had his doubts and tended to take the position that it was probably better to stay outside politics, at least in terms of the poet being caught up in direct action on the streets. He had a deep distrust of the State (any State, even a revolutionary one) and thought that they all should be treated with suspicion. As Jones became even more active and moved towards changing his name and abandoning his white friends and even his white wife and their children, they continued to disagree about political involvement. Claudia Moreno Pisano has an interesting quotation from Howard Brick's *Age of Contradiction: American Thought and Culture in the 1960s*: "American thought and culture grew turbulent and rife with contention; the realm of ideas and arts became more subject to instability than the foundations of American social structure itself."

I mentioned earlier that throughout the letters there are frequent derogatory references to other writers. Philip Lamantia is described as "the fastest longest more boringest talker in the East or West," and Michael McClure as "the hugest egotist of us all." There's a reference to "hayseed Kerouac," and Robert Creeley as "simple-minded about socio-political matters." Max Finstein and Marc Schleifer (connected with the magazine, *Kulchur*) are attacked, with Schleifer said to be "the world's worst poet." And women in particular seem to have angered Jones. Denise Levertov, Diane di Prima, Joyce Glassman, and Lita Hornick (who financed *Kulchur*), just to mention the better-known names, come in for criticism, often of a nasty kind. Dorn sometimes joins in, but I had the feeling that his heart may not have been in it and he was just reacting in a way that Jones expected. Perhaps I'm wrong? There are other dismissals, of course, often of established and/or academic poets. I suppose this was inevitable and it happens as any new group of poets starts to fight for a place in the sun. I'm not sure that it adds anything to our knowledge of the poets, new or old, though literary historians may thrive on such material.

Dorn was mostly based in Pocatello, Idaho, during the years covered by the majority of the letters (roughly 1959 to 1965), whereas Jones was in New York and therefore in a position to meet a wide variety of poets. In a letter from March, 1963, Jones reports that several "Deep Imagists" had paid him a visit and names Rochelle Owens, George Economou, and Armand Schwerner. I can't imagine that the Deep Image group will now mean much to many people, other than students of literary movements, but they were active for a time in the early 1960s. And as individuals the various poets carried on writing when the group label lost its relevance. I have to admit that I was never sure just what they represented in terms of their ideas about how to write poems. Jones's brief report on their visit gives the impression that he wasn't too keen on their work. It also gives him the opportunity to once again display his crude comments about one of the women in the group. Another letter, later in 1963, finds Jones sneering at Denise Levertov. The misogynistic strain in his thinking becomes so evident that the reader can't help wondering just what his problem was.

Jones was by 1963 beginning to establish a reputation as a poet, critic, and editor. He edited an excellent prose anthology, *The Moderns,* which featured some of Dorn's work alongside Kerouac, Burroughs, Creeley, and others, and his jazz study, *Blues People: Negro Music in White America,* was published to critical acclaim. His early poems, collected in *Preface to a Twenty Volume Suicide Note,* showed him to be an adventurous and entertaining poet. Dorn, by contrast, was still largely limited to publishing in little magazines, though his collection, *The Newly Fallen,* had appeared in 1962. And that came about largely due to Jones's interventions on his behalf. It wasn't that Dorn's work lacked substance or interest, but the fact of his being away from a major centre of literary activity like New York or San Francisco meant that he wasn't in a position to make contacts and cultivate editors and publishers. He was lucky to have Jones as a friend who promoted his writing.

A letter in 1964 has Jones admitting to "Jew-baiting" while he was "on some powder and drinking my head off," and it perhaps is an indicator of how he would later write poems which contained what Kenneth Rexroth referred to as "vicious anti-Semitic doggerel." In 1965 Jones announced that he would in future be known as Amiri Baraka and he began to distance himself from his white family and friends. The letters more or less come to a halt, partly because of Jones's new involvements but also because it was in 1965 that Dorn decided to move to England and take up a position as a lecturer at Essex University. He remained there until 1970. Claudia Moreno Pisano mentions that Jones says that he and Dorn corresponded in the 1990s, but the letters haven't yet come to light.

I've admittedly moved around the letters and selected certain areas of them for comment. And it may be that in doing so I've overlooked some of their more interesting passages. Leaving aside the tendencies to belittle other poets and to often denigrate women, they do provide a great deal of valuable material for literary scholars. Obviously, much of the information relates to personal matters, such as families and finances (always a problem), and to the whereabouts and activities of mutual friends and fellow-poets. But there are also references to little magazines and small-press publishers. Jones's involvements with *Yugen and The Floating Bear*, are discussed, and Dorn's little magazine, *Wild Dog,* is also referred to. Jones recommends *Yowl*, a magazine edited by George Montgomery, and suggests that Dorn send some prose to *Second Coming*. It seems to me that information like this is useful to an understanding of the period concerned. Little magazines played an essential role in the rise of the new writing. There is, incidentally, a letter from 1960 in which Dorn tells Jones that he'd sent a poem called "Pronouncement" to a Dr Gilbert Nieman in Puerto Rico but had heard nothing further about it. Nieman edited a magazine called *Between Worlds* from the Inter-American University in Puerto Rico and Dorn's poem was published in the first issue which is dated Summer, 1960.

Claudia Moreno Pisano has provided informative notes about many of the people referred to by Jones and Dorn and she efficiently fills in the gaps between letters. There is in, addition, a useful bibliography. This is an essential book for anyone with an interest in Jones/Baraka and Dorn or the wider field of the development of the "New American Writing" of the 1950s and 1960s.

AMIRI BARAKA & EDWARD DORN: THE COLLECTED
LETTERS

Edited by Claudia Moreno Pisano. University of New Mexico Press.
248 pages. $59.95. ISBN 978-0-8263-5391-7

ALAN ANSEN

You would hardly describe Alan Ansen as a well-known poet and, in fact, it's probably true to say that he's more notable for his involvements with other writers (W.H. Auden, William Burroughs, etc.) than for his own work. He was close to Auden for a time and, interestingly enough, also came into contact with some of the Beats during the same period. It may seem surprising that there was, at least in the 1940s, a loose overlapping of the Auden set and certain of the Beats, but it did exist. Chester Kallman, Auden's companion, introduced Ansen to Bill Cannastra in 1947, and from that meeting stemmed Ansen's awareness of Kerouac, Ginsberg, and Lucien Carr. Of course, this didn't mean that Ansen immediately took to the Beats - he was wary of Kerouac for a time, for example - but he did eventually form close friendships with Ginsberg, Burroughs, and Corso. He got to know Kerouac better, too, as *On the Road* makes clear. Ansen appears as Rollo Greb in that book. He crops up in other Kerouac novels, and in works by Burroughs, Ginsberg, Corso, and Irving Rosenthal.

The fascinating outline of Ansen's life is presented in Steven Moore's introduction to *Contact Highs* and it is clear that, for all his links to Auden and to the Beats, he was always very much his own man. In the 1950s he moved away from Auden's influence and went to Europe, where he lived in Venice and Athens, visited Paris and Tangier, and became associated with the famous (and rich) art dilettante, Peggy Guggenhelm. Fated, perhaps, to become a footnote in books about other people, Ansen is mentioned in her autobiography. He went back to the U.S.A. in the late '60s, but returned to Europe and, after Auden's death, renewed his friendship with Chester Kallman. He also kept in touch with Burroughs.

As a writer, Ansen will be best known to Beat enthusiasts for a single poem ("Dead Drunk," reprinted in this volume) about Cannastra's violent death, and some short essays about Burroughs. The latter were published in pamphlet form by Water Row Press in 1986. Ansen also started a novel about the Auden/Cannastra days, though it came to a halt after a few chapters. Water Row Press published the surviving fragments as *The Vigilantes* in 1987 and they have some curiosity value.

It is as a poet that Ansen deserves attention, and it's worth taking a brief look at his career. His first small collection was published in 1959 by the Tibor De Nagy Gallery, and his only book from what might be called a "commercial" publisher was *Disorderly Houses* from Wesleyan University Press in 1961. The difficulty some people had with Ansen's work was hinted at by a comment on the back cover which said, "It would not be accurate to call Mr. Ansen a 'beat' poet, although he has something of the disenchanted attitude and the freedom of language of that school." But Ansen's "gloomy frivolity" must not have appealed to the selectors at Wesleyan and when he presented another collection for their approval it was quickly rejected. After that, Ansen turned to publishing his own work and, over the years, small books have circulated among his friends and literary acquaintances. *Contact Highs* includes poems from *Disorderly Houses* and the privately published books, so gives us a chance to consider Ansen's work over a thirty year period.

I mentioned earlier that Ansen has always remained his own man, and it's equally true to say that he's remained his own poet. That he served an apprenticeship with Auden is obvious from his skilled handling of set forms, but at the same time he moves easily into a looser, more discursive style of writing which does, occasionally, parallel that of some of the Beat poets. I don't want to overstress that aspect of his work, however, because I'm quite sure that Ansen didn't need the Beats to open his eyes to the variety of poetic forms available to him. A well-educated man, he presumably knew enough anyway to be aware of all the possibilities. What the Beats perhaps did was liberate him from a reluctance to explore those possibilities. He never seems to have lost his urge to play, and his poems are full of witty asides, little stylistic tricks, references to books, art, and music, and rhyming patterns which are sometimes almost child-like, though not childish. Rachel Hadas, in a critical exploration of Ansen's poetry which rounds off the book, quotes him as saying, "By instinct and biographical compulsion, I want the naked scream. By training and remembered satisfactions, I utter in patterns," and it's as good a description as any of the way he writes. Ansen may have an urge to let himself go, and even explore the seamy side of life, but he can't help writing poems which are well-ordered and dignified.

It needs to be said, also, that Ansen's poetry has to be considered in its totality, which is one reason why I haven't quoted lines out of context. Being the product of a certain kind of sensibility, it explores a private, though not obscure, world and sets up its own kind of interactions. Not too many of the poems stay in the mind as individual pieces, but as a whole they have a certain appeal.

This is a valuable book, bringing together as it does a wide selection of Ansen's poetry, an informative outline of his life, an interesting critical survey of his work, and a useful bibliography of his earlier books. It should be of interest to those who like to find out about the minor or fringe figures of the Beat movement, but it would be a pity if that was the only reason for reading it. Ansen ought to be considered in his own right as a poet, and my own view is that he has written sufficient poems of note to justify this kind of attention.

There is an 11-page interview of Alan Ansen, by Regina Weinreich, in the Fall, 1989 Issue of *The Review of Contemporary Fiction,* also published by The Dalkey Archive Press.

CONTACT HIGHS: SELECTED POEMS 1957-1987 by Alan Ansen. Dalkey Archive Press, 1817 North 79th Avenue, Elnwood Park, IL 60635, U.S.A., 213pp 1989.

LAWRENCE FERLINGHETTI

Lawrence Ferlinghetti has always been one of the more politically minded Beats, and his work, both in poetry and prose, is scattered with references to his interests and concerns in that area. His leanings are towards anarchism, with a specific emphasis on the tradition that incorporates the notion of the poet as an enemy of the state. He makes direct reference to this in *Inside the Trojan Horse,* and quotes Edward Abbey as saying that "the artist in our time has two responsibilities: art and sedition."

Of course, it's a mistake to assume from this that every piece of writing (by Ferlinghetti or the writers he admires) will necessarily make an overt statement of defiance. A simple love lyric or a humorous poem may not appear to be directly linked to "subversion," though it can be argued that, to quote Kenneth Rexroth, "against the ruin of the world, there is only one defence - the creative act." In other words, writing poems may be considered dangerous in a world where instant success and instant news are the dominant modes. Nobody gets rich writing poetry, and to give one's time to it, instead of making money, might well be subversive of accepted values.

Having said that, I'd suggest that it's sensible to be aware of the effects of publication. Writers like to have their work read and they need to sell books. They make personal appearances, give interviews to the newspapers, radio, and TV, and generally participate in the commercial world that they often want to deny. Some claim that they are only using the system and its technology to attack it, but personally speaking I tend to view such claims with a jaundiced eye. Writers seem to want to have it both ways.

I have a great deal of sympathy with many of Ferlinghetti's views, as expressed in his work and in interviews, and I found his novel, *Love in the Days of Rage*, both lively and likeable, though its general political position might be seen as woolly and sentimental. It is set in Paris in 1968, a year in which the events were, depending on your point of view, either significant or just an outburst of high spirits. It always seemed to me that the only real danger to the French state came about when the workers joined in, and at that stage the government got really tough. I doubt that a revolution was ever truly likely, and even if something akin to one had happened the authorities had ample resources to call on to stop it. The technology of repression can't be defeated by a few slogans and some makeshift barricades.

The story revolves around a love affair between Annie, an American painter, and Julian, a well-heeled banker and armchair anarchist. They meet as the tear-gas drifts through the streets, and fall in love. Annie has a background of the New York art world (abstract expressionists like Motherwell, Kline, de Kooning, though also links with an old '30s radical who worked for the WPA and ran with the *Partisan Review* crowd) and Julian was born in Portugal and has a fund of stories about life during the Salazar dictatorship. They argue about art and politics, with Julian attempting to persuade Annie that his own situation, banker and anarchist, isn't necessarily contradictory. He is, he says, involved with the state at its most vulnerable point, and in due course will act to destroy the French monetary system. The novel ends where he is engaged in such an adventure and Annie is waiting for him in a secret hideout in the countryside.

The story is sketchy, to say the least, and it primarily exists to allow Ferlinghetti to indulge in pages of near-reverie about revolution, Paris, art and literature, and love. The influences are fairly obvious - André Breton's *Nadja*, Djuna Barnes's *Nightwood*, Ferlinghetti's own earlier novel *Her* (even to the extent of using a passage from it in the new book) - and a string of references to other writers point to incorporated interests. Cendrars and Camus are mentioned approvingly. George Whitman's Shakespeare & Company bookshop comes into the picture, and at one point a list, almost along the lines of the guests at a party, brings in a slightly elitist note. If you were around in the 1960s and read the intellectual weeklies and quarterlies you'll know how Genet, Ionesco, Marcuse, Julian Beck, Judith Malina, and others like them, were highly fashionable. I must admit I had to struggle to recall much about some of the people on the list. But no matter, because readers who have a rosy view of the 1960s will probably find it all fascinating and wish they'd been there. Some of us did think more interesting things were going on in Prague, but it might be a mistake to try to completely disassociate the events in the two cities.

Ferlinghetti is good on painting, and the opening pages of chapter 12 are vivid evocations of the effects of paintings by Pollock, Kline, etc.

I particularly enjoyed these passages, though I'm prejudiced in favour of abstract expressionism, having first come across examples in the 1950s and still finding it fascinating. The impact of a good Pollock, Kline, or de Kooning can always make me feel excited. Ferlinghetti is also lively with details of cafe life, and even throws in some ramblings from a character who describes himself as "the last surviving golden tongue of the Lost Generation, the very ghost of Nonstop Fitzgerald or Hairy Crosby himself ..."

So, I enjoyed *Love in the Days of Rage* without thinking it either a major literary work or a wise political document. I did wonder if Ferlinghetti has any real idea of how the monetary system works and what would happen if it did collapse, but the book is a poet's view of economics and politics, rosy and idealistic, and those of a pragmatic turn of mind will possibly not take it too seriously. Still, I wouldn't want to deny Ferlinghetti's genuine concern for the way the world has gone (and is still going) so far this century.

You can get a fairly clear picture of many of the matters covered in the novel though expressed in a more succinct fashion, in *Inside the Trojan Horse*, a small book which contains the text of a lecture given at San Francisco State University in 1987. It brings in references to Paris and to writers like Cendrars, Rimbaud, and Apollinaire, and also mentions Ginsberg, Rexroth, and Kenneth Patchen. It's easy to see how Ferlinghetti links the "outsider" role of the poet over the years and across continents. He's sharp on "the suppression or destruction of the subjective faculty," and notes how "the technocratic mentality is basically amoral and utilitarian, and dedicated to the greatest profit, gratification, and success in the 'real' world." And he quotes Marcuse to the effect that worthwhile art is subversive of perception and understanding. He notes the "general deterioration and bankruptcy of political thinking," and rightly (to my mind) criticises the counter-culture of the 1960s for its failings. Many of its members were, he says, "seduced by power and money, others by other kinds of sensual success or creature comfort, while others made the mistake of thinking that the enemy could be conquered by rock'n'roll and LSD ... and still others 'dropped out' into various bucolic enclaves in which Buddhist 'empty mind' displaced philosophical and/or political thinking, and education or learning per se was generally considered too restrictive a discipline for expanded consciousness."

In many ways this bright little book (and it also contains a few poems) ideally complements *Love in the Days of Rage*, and I'd recommend that they be read together. The novel, the text of the talk, and the handful of poems, show how a creative artist can incorporate a consistent world view into his writing, and though I've outlined a few reservations I have about Ferlinghetti's political romanticism, I wouldn't want to be seen as being on the opposite side to him. His enemies are my enemies, and we are, I hope, in the Trojan Horse together, exchanging ideas while we await an appropriate moment to burst forth.

Finally, a few words about *The Canticle of Jack Kerouac*, a warm and affectionate tribute to his old friend and fellow-writer. It was written early in 1987, following a visit to Lowell, and neatly evokes the town as seen through Kerouac's eyes over the years, and by Ferlinghetti himself. The nostalgia and longing - for the past, for a different America, for love - so often found in Kerouac's books is also expressed in the poem, and it has its own heartache. It's almost a lament, too, for "an America now long gone / except in broken down dusty old / Greyhound Bus stations / in small lost towns," and is touching in its tenderness.

LOVE IN THE DAYS OF RAGE by Lawrence Ferlinghetti . The Bodley Head, London, 1988.

INSIDE THE TROJAN HORSE by Lawrence Ferlinghetti. Don't Call It Frisco Press. 1988

THE CANTICLE OF JACK KEROUAC by Lawrence Ferlinghetti. Spotlight Press Editions. 1988

BOB KAUFMAN 1925-1986

With the death of Bob Kaufman in San Francisco in January another link with the early days of the Beats has been severed. Kaufman often tended to be overlooked when accounts of the movement were written, and yet he was an integral part of the West Coast scene for a number of years.

He was born in New Orleans in 1925 and was of mixed stock, his father being German Jewish and his mother a black Roman Catholic. He grew up speaking Cajun as well as English, and his later interests and inclinations often reflected his multi-culturality. When he was thirteen he went to sea as a cabin boy, and it was during this period that he was introduced to the works of Shakespeare, Melville, Hart Crane, T.S. Eliot, and Lorca. It's said that Kaufman memorised much of what he read in those days and, in later years, would often recite long passages to his friends.

He stayed at sea for a number of years, got involved in union activity, and was, most probably, also a member of the American Communist Party. In the immediate post-war period he took classes at the New School for Social Research in New York, studying sociology and labour organisation, and was reputed to have helped unionise black miners in the Southern states. This activity sometimes brought him into violent contact with the police. Kaufman's political involvements led to him being blacklisted and he was eventually unable to obtain work at sea.

In the early 1950s he was working in the kitchens of a Beverly Hills hotel, but heard about the poetry resurgence in San Francisco so handed in his notice and moved to that area in 1954. I'm not sure how much writing he'd done prior to that, but his work began to flourish in the prevailing atmosphere, with its mixture of poetry, jazz, and protest.

Kaufman became well-known around the jazz clubs and coffee-bars of the city, giving impromptu poetry readings, helping start *Beatitude,* and engaging in what might best be described as street-theatre activities. He was also well-known to the police, who arrested him thirty-five times in one eighteen month period. One of the more celebrated arrests led to him writing his "Jail Poems," published in the collection *Solitudes Crowded with Loneliness*. The San Francisco police didn't look too kindly on the Beats, and Kaufman was singled out for their special attention because of his independent turn of mind, and the fact that he lived openly with a white woman. For the record, there is a famous photograph of Kaufman in a coffee-bar confrontation with two policemen in *Contact* 6 (San Francisco, 1960).

I think it does need to be said that, by 1960 or so, Kaufman had a severe alcohol problem and was becoming dependent on drugs. His behaviour was often erratic, and he was given forced shock treatment after being arrested for a minor offence while on a visit to New York. The chaotic nature of his personal life worked against him utilising possible advantages, such as an invitation to read at Harvard University, and the fact that a couple of songs he'd written were recorded by popular performers of the time.

Kaufman returned to San Francisco in 1963, but was clearly in poor shape. He made a vow of silence (brought on by the assassination of President Kennedy) and this, together with his increasingly odd habits, detached him from Eileen Kaufman and many of his old friends. Kaufman kept up the vow (which included writing as well as speech) for ten years, during which time he scuffled to stay alive, existing on handouts and sleeping in sleazy hotels or in the local parks. He finally began to speak (and write) again in the 1970s, and his last collection, *The Ancient Rain*, included work produced between 1973 and 1978. But he never recovered his old form, and his life was marked by poverty and neglect.

As a poet Kaufman mixed the language of social and political comment with surrealist influences. He also had a nice taste for satire, as witness his famous *Abomunist Manifesto* ("Abomunists join nothing but their hands or legs, or other same" and "In times of national peril, Abomunists, as reality Americans, stand ready to drink themselves to death for their country."). And you can easily get an idea of his interests by flicking through his books and noting the references: Charlie Parker, Lester Young, Baudelaire, Poe, Camus, Hart Crane, and the writers and painters of the Dada and Surrealist movements are among them. In the early poems, at least, a bitter social conscience is often in evidence. What happened to the American Left as it fell apart in the McCarthy era is a fascinating topic, and it strikes me as logical that Kaufman, perhaps unable or unwilling to align himself anymore with orthodox political activity, should have moved towards the Beats who were, in the 1950s, displaying some kind of social criticism both in their work and their life-style. The biting tone of poems like "Hollywood" and "Teevee People," and the idea behind the short, but sharp "Patriotic Ode on the Fourteenth Anniversary of the Persecution of Charlie Chaplin," indicate where Kaufman's roots lay. He was also capable of digging below the surface of the romantic image of the Beats, as in "Bagel Shop Jazz," with its ambiguous summing up of the scene.

My own feelings are that Kaufman was a variable poet at best, though his successful poems were frequently more readable than many Beat offerings. The curious thing is that he was rarely, if ever, included in the major Beat anthologies. Nor has he been much written about in the critical studies that are now appearing. To the credit of the French it's said that, when his first book was translated and published there in the 1960s, they took to it with enthusiasm, and that he's still read in France. I would hope that some of his work will continue to be read in this country.

BIBLIOGRAPHICAL NOTE

Kaufman's three books were *Solitudes Crowded with Loneliness* (New Directions, 1965), *Golden Sardine* (City Lights Books, 1967) and *The Ancient Rain* (New Directions, 1981). City Lights also published three broadsides, *Abomunist Manifesto* (1959), *Second April* (1959), and *Does the Secret Mind Whisper?* (1960). Eileen Kaufman's slightly starry-eyed memoir of the late-1950s can be found in *185* (Mongrel Frees, San Francisco, 1973), and in a somewhat different form in *Beat Angels* (tuvoti, 1982). Barbara Christian's "Whatever Happened to Bob Kaufman" is in *The Beats: Essays in Criticism* (McFarland, 1981) and Steve Abbott's "Hidden Master of the Beats" in *Little Caesar* 12 (Los Angeles, 1981).

KEROUAC AND THE BEATS

THE DEATH of Jack Kerouac on October 21 came as a surprise to those of us who found his lively books to our liking. One had grown used to having him around, not so much as a major novelist - and Kerouac himself never claimed to be trying to write fiction in the accepted sense of the word - but as a rare individual who, erratic and irritating though he could be at times, frequently produced books of great charm and vitality.

He was born in 1922 and grew up in the industrial town of Lowell, where he had a happy and typical childhood. His books - thinly disguised autobiography - document this period, his schooldays in Lowell and New York when he gained some repute as a footballer (American style), his service in the Merchant Navy, and - in the middle and late-1940s - his connection with the writers and characters who later formed the nucleus of the Beat Generation: Neal Cassady (the prototype for Dean Moriarty in *On The Road* and himself now dead), Carl Solomon, William Burroughs, Allen Ginsberg and John Clellon Holmes. There is an intriguing portrait of Kerouac in Clellon Holmes's *Go*, a portrait which shows a darker side to his character than many people suspected from his own books.

Kerouac's first book, *The Town and the City*, was published in 1950, and although it did bring him a certain amount of attention - he was mentioned as being in the tradition of Thomas Wolfe - he soon decided to move on. Between 1951 and 1957 he wandered around America, working at various jobs and writing a fair amount of his total output. Most of the books from this period - some are still unpublished - only went into print when *On The Road* catapulted Kerouac's name into the headlines.

With the advent of the Beat craze Kerouac's books appeared regularly. *Tristessa, The Subterraneans, Maggie Cassidy, Doctor Sax* and *The Dharma Bums* all came out between 1958 and 1960, as did such lesser known items as *Mexico City Blues, The Scriptures of the Golden Eternity* and *Visions of Cody*. For a time it seemed as if the Beats were taking over and material by and about Kerouac could be found in all kinds of magazines. *Lonesome Traveler* collects some of the short pieces Kerouac did, including the wonderful " The Railroad Earth," one of his most sustained prose poems.

I don't think he ever took to the idea of being lionised and as the Beat literary movement was swamped by mass-media created Beatniks, who soon changed into Hippies, he retired to Lowell. He seemed disinterested in what was happening in San Francisco and New York in the middle-1960s and summed up his attitude in the words: "The Beat group dispersed as you say in the early sixties, all went their own way, and this is my way; home life, as in the beginning, with a little toot once in a while in local bars." His critics, however, insisted on linking him with a social movement he most likely found baffling.

It was perhaps inevitable that his output should slacken off in recent years, but he continued to publish reasonably regularly and although *Satori in Paris* was a disappointment, such books as *Big Sur, Desolation Angels* and *Vanity of Dulouz* proved that he was still capable of writing passages of highly evocative prose. Like many effusive and open people he could be a little overbearing but this was a minor fault.

It is interesting to look back over the past 10 or 12 years to find out why Kerouac attracted so much hostile attention from some critics. I would hazard a guess that his independence annoyed a lot of people. After all, he didn't play the literary game. Nor had he grown up in the kind of environment familiar to many literary types. His 1930s, for example, were not those of the Left-wing intellectuals. Kerouac wrote about everyday experiences as known to ordinary Americans; small-town life, the dance-bands and films and radio shows of the day, sport, teenage love affairs. It wasn't the total experience but Kerouac saw its values and bothered to deal with them lyrically.

Likewise his 1940s - and *On The Road* is about the frame of mind of the hipsters of the bop era and not that of the Beatniks of the late-1950s – had their own special flavour. Kerouac, along with a handful of other American writers, deserves credit for sensing the beginnings of an "underground" way of life in the activities of the bop musicians and hipsters.

But although one side of his personality pulled him towards the jazz clubs, the Beats, the characters like Neal Cassady, he was probably happiest when rhapsodising about the forests of the American North West, frosty mornings recalled from his childhood, the pleasures of working on the railroad, the desert at night. His capacity for capturing in words the sights and sounds he'd experienced was tremendous and beneath it all was a sad lament for an older America, one that he liked to think was more honest and open-minded.

There was no one else quite like Jack Kerouac and he'll be missed.

CATCHING UP WITH KEROUAC

At first sight one or two of the essays in Joy Walsh's small collection seem to incline towards the pretentious. "Kerouac: A Reichian Interpretation" and "Ecclesiastes and the Duluoz Legend of Jack Kerouac" might have more to do with impressing junior academics than with encouraging the reader to carry on. But the reader should carry on, because once past those awful titles he or she will find that Joy Walsh knows the value of brevity and makes her points without too much fuss. She also knows the texts of Kerouac's books and whatever she says is usually of relevance to what he actually wrote.

Which isn't to suggest that all the essays are of equal importance. For example, "Literature of the Fifties: Jack Kerouac and the Delicate Balancing Point" largely takes a hackneyed view of the decade. And it makes statements which are questionable, to say the least: "The beats wanted their writing, which was writing done by working-class writers, to sound as if it was coming out of the mouths of the people in the streets." By no stretch of the facts or the imagination could you describe Allen Ginsberg or William Burroughs as working-class. Nor could you describe their writing as an attempt to sound working-class. Kerouac did have closer links with the working-class, and an argument might be made for some of his writing getting close to the idiom of the "people in the streets" (and they're not all working-class, anyway), but a good argument might also be made against such an idea. He was probably far too individual to be representative.

Of more interest is an essay comparing Kerouac to Jack London in terms of their background and activities. This rightly mentions politics as a major difference between them. Those familiar with London's life will know that, despite some complexities of character, he was strongly inclined towards socialism. He wrote books which reflected his views - *The Iron Heel* and *People of the Abyss*, to mention two - and produced a great deal of journalism which supported his political beliefs. He also participated in political campaigns. Kerouac, on the other hand, was naive when it came to politics. He was a conservative in many ways, and had a small-town suspicion of communism, socialism, and metropolitan intellectual theories. Why the difference between the two men? Well, they were just two different people, of course, and that must explain part of it. Kerouac's French-Canadian and Catholic upbringing no doubt helped shape his social and political attitudes. And, on a wider scale, changes in American society generally between 1905 and 1935 (not to mention further changes between 1935 and 1955) must have been highly relevant. I sometimes suspect that Kerouac's innate conservatism came to the fore in the 1950s as a defence against being tarred with the anti-Communist brush that tended to be used against anyone expressing a dissident opinion.

A further essay looks at Kerouac as an "American Alien in America" and is of relevance to the one discussed above. And there's a short piece by Joy Walsh in *Catching Up With Kerouac* which touches on his links with work and industry. She points out how Lowell, his birthplace, was also virtually the birthplace of the industrial revolution in the United States. Labour struggles and union activity were not unknown in the area in the 19th Century and the early part of the 20th, though Kerouac doesn't appear to have had much interest in that kind of history. In this respect it's worth noting that his awareness of the I.W.W. (Industrial Workers of the World) seems to have come from Gary Snyder and the Western radical tradition, and yet the Wobblies were active in the textile towns along the Merrimac River around the time that they were on the move in the Mid-West and on the Pacific coast. One of the classic strikes in American labour history - the 1912 walkout in Lawrence - was led by the I.W.W., and involved many French-Canadian workers, along with Poles, Italians, and others. Was Kerouac such an "alien" that he hadn't come across accounts of events like the Lawrence strike?

Catching Up With Kerouac takes a broad view of its subject in that a number of the pieces focus on other Beats. There are interesting and informative interviews with Michael McClure and Herbert Huneke, together with poems by John Clellon Holmes, items on Corso, Ginsberg, and Burroughs, and a portfolio of photographs of the now-ageing Beat survivors. There's also an article by Gerald Nicosia which worries me a little because he seems to want to make Kerouac respectable by referring to the number of colleges and universities running courses on the man and his work. I suppose it's inevitable that Kerouac will increasingly be subject to academic study, but where will it lead to?

Probably to articles such as Harold Goldman's "In the American Grain: The Beat Sensibility Defined", which is thoroughly academic in tone and ideas. It is almost all derived from other people's theories about the Beats and their world, and smacks of having been put together at a library desk. Let me concentrate on just one part of Goldman's survey, and this is where it touches on the subject of jazz. And bear in mind that Goldman makes the point that the Beat sensibility can be related more to the late-1940s than the late-1950s. He talks about bop and cool jazz as if they were two quite distinctive styles played by musicians who never mixed and held to near-rigid notions of suitable basic material, tempos, and means of expression. There were, it's true, some general rhythmic, harmonic, and melodic differences between bop and cool musicians. But I stress the "general" because anyone familiar with the modern-jazz of the late-1940s and early-1950s will know that the two styles mixed freely in the work of groups and in the solos of individual musicians. Goldman doesn't mention which musicians he thinks belong in which category, with the exception of Lester Young who he clearly sees as typifying the cool. It's a fact of jazz history that Young was a major influence on the young, primarily white musicians of the cool school (Stan Getz, Brew Moore, Allen Eager, Zoot Sims, Herbie Steward, and many more), but he was also a major influence on bop tenormen like Dexter Gordon, Sonny Stitt, and Gene Ammons.

Goldman also claims that the boppers used popular ballads a lot as a basis for their work, and that this indicates "engagement". But the cool stylists probably employed popular songs even more, as witness the work of Stan Getz around 1950/52. And what about Lester Young's extensive use of ballads? Even arch-cool musicians such as Lennie Tristano and Lee Konitz built around popular songs. The fact of the matter is that jazzmen of all persuasions looked to popular songs because they made ideal vehicles either for new tunes (constructed on the chord sequences of the originals) or improvisation.

And when we reach Goldman's statement that in cool jazz the tempos were "slowed way down" one begins to wonder if he's actually ever listened to any of the jazz of the 1940s and 1950s. Has he heard the recordings Stan Getz made at the Storyville Club in Boston in 1951, or the airshots of Lester Young blowing up-tempo in the 1940s? (He ought to listen to Lester and trumpeter Jesse Drakes playing a sprightly version of the corny but catchy pop-song "Lavender Blue" for a musical contradiction of his ideas about slow tempos and disengagement). But there are so many questions one would like to ask Goldman. When Brew Moore recorded with Howard McGhee and J.J. Johnson did he play cool - as defined by Goldman - and they play bop? Did Allen Eager sound cooler than the impeccably poised bop trumpeter Fats Navarro when they played together at the Royal Roost in 1948? Jazz writer Ira Gitler reckons that Eager was such a warm, swinging tenorman that he almost had people dancing along the bar. How would Goldman categorise the elegant bop pianist Al Haig who was in demand to play with groups led by leading bop musicians (Charlie Parker, Dizzy Gillespie, etc.) and major cool jazzmen (Stan Getz, Zoot Sims, etc.). And just what label would Goldman pin on the performances of Brew Moore (cool) and Howard McGhee (bop) when they played with Machito's Afro-Cuban orchestra?

The point I'm making - and I've used the bop and cool labels out of necessity - is that things were not as clearcut as Goldman makes out. Even if we shift the cool tag further into the 1950s, and say that it relates to Chet Baker, Gerry Mulligan, and many of the musicians of the West Coast school it still doesn't follow the pattern that Goldman tries to apply. So, if his jazz theories are hazy (to put it kindly) is his whole article based on false premises? If there was such a thing as a Beat sensibility is he trying to define it in too rigid a manner? An understanding of the jazz of the 1940s and 1950s is essential to an appreciation of Beat literature, but one shouldn't set up rigid lines of demarcation. I doubt that Kerouac and the other Beats ever tried to separate bop and cool in the way that Goldman does. And that might indicate a telling difference between creative writers and academics. The creative writer knows that things don't fall into neat categories, whereas the academic wants them to. I don't think Goldman has done this, but I suspect that he has got his jazz ideas from books rather than from the actual music.

Statement In Brown and *Catching Up With Kerouac* are both worth the attention of Beat enthusiasts, though I suppose that they are part of a growing trend towards more and more academically-inclined surveys of the subject. Given the fact that the Beats are now virtually exhausted as a literary movement, and that the files aren't likely to produce many, if any, overlooked gems from the past, an academic take-over is in order. Ah well, the original work might survive it all.

Jack Kerouac Statement in Brown by Joy Walsh, Textile Bridge Press, 1984

Catching Up With Kerouac edited by V.J. Eaton. The Literary Denim, 1450 W. 1st Pl., Mesa, AZ 85201, USA. 1984

WRITING BEAT

Books about the Beats continue to appear regularly, though many of them these days tend to come from university presses. And I have to admit that my spirits sag a little when I see another serious tome that aims to tell us how and why the Beats were born, blossomed, and didn't die, certainly not in terms of the amount of attention they attract from academics anxious to have a book, or an essay in a prestigious publication, to add to their CVs. It was inevitable that this would happen. But as someone who first read the Beats, rather than reading about them, in the late-1950s, I prefer to dig out the books and the old anthologies and magazines, and recall how exciting all the activity seemed to be. It wasn't that the work was necessarily all that good. A lot of it wasn't and many of the minor poets, in particular, soon slid from sight. Most poetry doesn't last very long. But when it was new it did appear to be interesting and it was often fun to read. Looking through those forgotten little magazines does sometimes bring back the sense of adventure I felt at the time. And that's not something I can say regarding quite a few of the books about the Beats that I've encountered in recent years.

If I seem suspicious about the motives and achievements of certain academics I will make an exception in the case of John Tytell. I read his *Naked Angels: the Lives and Literature of the Beat Generation* (McGraw-Hill, New York, 1976) when it was first published, and recognised that he seemed to have not only studied the literature but had also tried to get to know the people (those who were still around and approachable) and understand what had made them the writers they were. He focused on William Burroughs, Jack Kerouac, and Allen Ginsberg, and placed them in context, which tended to be New York. In this connection it might be worth referring to the anthology, *Reading New York* (Knopf, New York, 2003) which attractively combines his own experiences with excerpts from a variety of writers, including, of course, the Beats.

Tytell continued with his interest in the Beats alongside writing a book about Ezra Pound, developing a successful academic career during which he had to face some opposition to his advocacy of poets who weren't in the canon, and getting involved in other activities. The two books I'm reviewing are almost summaries of his Beat involvements. They combine critical assessments with personal experiences as he encountered Burroughs, Ginsberg, and some lesser-known figures like Carl Solomon and Herbert Huncke. I have the feeling that Tytell rather wishes he could have been around earlier, and one of the gang, instead of arriving a bit later and interviewing them. I wonder if he would have fitted in with their often chaotic lives? He has the honesty to admit that he sometimes felt intimidated in their presence. An interview with a minor poet, Ray Bremser, who had served time in prison for armed robbery, was hastily terminated when he produced a stick of dynamite and waved it around. And an attempt to talk to Lucien Carr left Tytell holding on to the rail of the bar they were in as the flow of drinks got the better of him. Allen Ginsberg seems to have been the most accommodating of the Beats, which may point to his friendlier character, but could also have something to do with the fact that he was well aware of needing to create a literary reputation.

I think what has distinguished Tytell from many other academics is that he's always been conscious of the requirement to hold the reader's attention. There's a quote in *Writing Beat* which neatly sums up his approach: "What is crucial is that one sentence should lead to another if you have a story to tell, and narrative is a key element no matter whether the genre you have chosen is fiction or non-fiction." For me, this has meant that his writing about the Beats has never seemed forced. He's telling their stories and does it in the way he describes, letting one sentence lead to another, one experience to another. It's what he seems to do well. Some sections of *Writing Beat* are not strictly about the Beats and he might not be as successful with them. In a piece called "How to Write an Essay," he unblushingly admits that it was rejected by thirty editors of magazines before it finally found a home thanks to "an angelic editor in South Carolina" who offered to publish it. On the other hand, when he's writing about academic life, experiences with editors, and problems getting published, he's usually able to throw in entertaining stories about encounters with Anais Nin, Olga Rudge, Leon Edel, Peter Orlovsky and some less-famous characters. In Holland, leaving a church in Antwerp (he was born there but left to move to America as a child), he was surprised to see two semi-naked women beckoning to him. He quickly left the area. At a party in New York he had to leave suddenly when Anais Nin, noted for her "sexual voracity," climbed into his lap at the end of the evening. Tytell is, as he makes clear quite a few times, a happily-married man and

65

obviously didn't think that it was necessary to extend these experiences in the interests of academic research.

One of the people Tytell interviewed and also wrote about was Herbert Huncke, a drug-addict, thief, occasional writer, and jailbird, who, according to Tytell, "introduced Burroughs, Kerouac, and Ginsberg to morphine" injected into their arms. That happened in 1944, so it was early in the Beat story, and only Burroughs went on to become seriously addicted. Tytell looks at the origin of the word "beat," as used by Kerouac and others, and locates it in Huncke's references to "exhaustion, being beaten down, burdened and crushed by the weight of the world." And in "that exposed, defeated, vagrant state, an individual could afford to be extremely open and candid because there was nothing to lose." According to Allen Ginsberg this state could lead to "a kind of religious illumination." Jack Kerouac later also suggested that there was a religious aspect to "beat," though he additionally brought in the beat in jazz and other factors. It's interesting to note that in the interview Huncke never refers to any of this and instead sticks to facts about when and how he got to know the core element of the early Beat movement. But when asked about a "Beat movement," he replies: "About movements, I don't know. What's a movement?" Tytell tells him: "A few people who say something in a similar way and live in a similar way?" A lot of people, myself included, would probably want to point out that, in fact, the Beats were quite different from each other in both their writings and their lives. I think Huncke cleverly avoids getting pinned down in a discussion about a movement when he replies: "You know all those people sort of jacked up an interest in literature and poetry, something that had been sorely lacking. I guess there's always been such a group. Bohemians, is that what they're called?"

Tytell's interview with William Burroughs, a man who "had little patience for small talk" and caused Tytell to get the impression of a "crusty brittleness," is informative, though Burroughs, like Huncke, clearly has little time for any sort of philosophising about the Beats and confines his responses to questions to purely factual matters. Tytell records: "To my consternation, Burroughs insisted that because of stylistic differences he should not be identified with the Beat movement." According to Tytell, Burroughs "was an iconoclastic, an extreme individualist who lacked the qualities of sympathy so prevalent in almost all the other Beats, but the evidence of his participation in Beat history was overwhelming." True enough, but I'm surprised that Tytell was surprised that Burroughs denied being part of the Beat movement. So did Gary Snyder and Lawrence Ferlinghetti, though both were admittedly never part of the New York 1940s activity and saw themselves as coming from different traditions. They had their own reasons for being reluctant to be too identified with the Beats, despite their close relationships with people like Ginsberg and Kerouac. Ferlinghetti had experience of European bohemian-anarchist traditions, which is not to deny his knowledge of American dissenters, and Snyder had some West Coast radical roots to draw on as well as his deep involvements with Buddhism.

The question of a movement crops up again in the interview with Carl Solomon which I recall reading with interest many years ago in *The Beat Book*, one of a series of brilliant anthologies edited by Arthur and Kit Knight. It's a pleasure to see it in print again. Solomon, whose literary achievements tended to be limited to short prose pieces and occasional reviews, always fascinated me with his often quirky views and reminiscences. When the question of feeling if he had belonged to a movement was raised in his interview, he replied: "As a matter of fact, I hadn't felt that. I had just been through with a movement and I had an aversion to movements – after all, I had finished with the Communists. I was living on 113th Street, and I knew this guy Don Cook, and he first mentioned the idea of a movement in reference to the Beats, and I was shocked – here I was trapped by something I had been trying to get away from!" Some earlier comments by Solomon show how closely he was involved with the Communist Party at one time. Later, he recounts how he "broke with my CP friends that I had made at CCNY and I moved down to the Village and became interested in avant-garde art and existentialism with a circle of people disillusioned with the left, ex-liberals and progressives, I should say." And he had briefly visited Paris and encountered the lettrists and Antonin Artaud. Solomon did feel that, by using his experiences in *Howl*, Ginsberg had exploited him, just as Neal Cassady felt that Kerouac had exploited him when he wrote *On the Road*.

Another writer who probably now doesn't get the attention he deserves is John Clellon Holmes and it's perhaps unfortunate that Tytell's interview (another that originally appeared in one of the

Knight's anthologies) mostly focused on his relationship with Kerouac, though what he has to say is of value. Holmes was always perceptive and generous in his comments on his fellow-Beat, despite the strains in their friendship. These often occurred because Kerouac resented the fact that Holmes seemed to be consulted as an authority on the Beat Generation after his novel *Go,* which documents life among the Beats in late-1940s New York, had been published. Kerouac was also suspicious when he heard that Holmes was working on a jazz novel, something that Kerouac himself was keen to produce. He never did, but Holmes later published *The Horn.* At one point in the interview, Tytell asks Holmes about the role that music played in their lives, and he replies: "Well, young people in America, at least in the last three generations, have felt music as a very important part of their lives: In the thirties it was swing, in the late forties it was bop, then rock." I wonder if bop was ever popular in the way that swing had been and rock music was later? I don't doubt that bop was known and liked by the kind of people Holmes mixed with – writers, artists, intellectuals in New York and a few other cities – but it never seemed to me to have a wide circulation outside those places. Most blacks preferred rhythm'n'blues, and most whites, depending on where they lived, probably went for country-and-western sounds or the kind of pop music that got into the charts. Adventurous individuals in both groups did search for more-demanding music and listened to bop, but "individuals" is the key word. I think we have to be careful about accepting the personal experiences of writers as typical of whole generations.

There is so much of interest in these two books, both in the interviews and Tytell's own words, that I could carry on quoting and excerpting much more than I have done. Tytell says that Burroughs' view of creative writing courses was that they were "just a faddish university scam." There is some irony to be registered here as Burroughs himself was then teaching a creative writing course at a college in New York. It's informative to note how quite a few of the Beats found themselves incorporated into the academy they'd set out to challenge. John Clellon Holmes went into teaching, as did Ginsberg in due course. I'm not condemning them. Very few writers ever make enough money to support themselves and their families, if they have them. Teaching, especially creative writing, is a way to bring in some sort of a steady income. Ginsberg, in particular, was able to command quite high payments, if an account I recently read is anything to go by. The poet Ron Loewinsohn, who had known him in the 1950s, in 1996 met up again with Ginsberg, who asked him how much he was paid at UC Berkeley, and then said, "Well, I'm teaching too. They pay me a hundred grand just come in and teach one course a year." Loewinsohn said that he was taken aback: "Here was Allen Ginsberg, iconic figure of the Beat Generation, champion of spirit and compassion, playing a game of 'Who's got the bigger paycheck stub.' I didn't want to believe that Allen had succumbed at last to Moloch, 'whose blood is running money.' Had Loewinsohn misread the situation? I've read elsewhere that Ginsberg was generous about supporting poets and others who were down on their luck. The Loewinsohn comments are in "This is Nothing but a Lot of Poetry: A Memoir of North Beach" in *Beat Scene 75* (Coventry, Winter, 2014).

One or two things bothered me. Tytell refers to "the Welsh novelist D.H.Lawrence," something that will puzzle the people of Eastwood, Nottinghamshire, where Lawrence was born. He also mentions "the quiet college town of Lawrence, Kansas, a place once pillaged and burned by the notorious James gang." It was actually Quantrill's band of guerrilla fighters for the Confederacy who raided Lawrence in 1863, well before the James gang existed. It's likely that Frank James was one of Quantrill's outfit, but just among the rank-and-file. Tytell describes Lester Young as Kerouac's "friend," but I wonder if that was really the case? Kerouac did meet him (it's mentioned in *Maggie Cassidy*, for example) but is there evidence of an actual friendship? Elsewhere, when talking about Young, Tytell describes his "seething restless experimentalism." I don't think any jazz critic of repute has ever thought of Young as "seething" or radically experimental. The noted British musician and writer, Benny Green, summed up Young's music: "Lester Young did not in fact bring about very many or far-reaching harmonic amendments in the art of improvisation." It was Young's relaxed style, his sound, and his melodic phrasing, that had an effect on other musicians. Another point in connection with Kerouac's jazz interests (and they were sincere) relates to the tune "Kerouac," which cropped up on LPs of material recorded at Minton's in 1941. Tytell claims that it was Dizzy Gillespie who named the track concerned, but that's unlikely. Jerry Newman, who recorded it, only released the Minton's items some years later, and he came up with titles for what were, in many cases, previously untitled tunes.

I don't want to end by giving the impression that Tytell's books are full of questionable statements like those I've listed. They're not, and I'd suggest that anyone with a serious interest in the Beats should read them. I didn't agree with everything he says, and I'm not sure that his enthusiasm is always well-placed. Not all Beat writing was good. Likewise, not all Beat behaviour was admirable. To be fair to Tytell, he does raise questions about what really did happen when William Burroughs killed his wife in Mexico. And he seems to have wisely steered clear of Gregory Corso much of the time. But he's an engaging writer and he tells his stories clearly and with a minimum of academic jargon.

WRITING BEAT AND OTHER OCCASIONS OF LITERARY MAYHEM By John Tytell. Vanderbilt University Press. 237 pages. £19.95. ISBN 978-0-8265-2015-9

THE BEAT INTERVIEWS By John Tytell. Beatdom Books. 174 pages. £10.00. ISBN 978-0-9569525-9-2

BRION GYSIN

Brion Gysin died in Paris during the summer of 1986. A writer with at least some claim to Beat connections he was also a link to an older, international Bohemia that took in, among other groups, the Surrealists and the expatriates based in North Africa in the early-1950s.

Born in 1916, Gysin was educated in England and Canada and, when he was eighteen, moved to Paris to study at the Sorbonne. He was artistically active even then and came into contact with Sylvia Beach, Max Ernst, Picasso, Salvador Dali, and many others. In 1935 he exhibited with the Surrealist Group, but his drawings were removed from the exhibition on the orders of André Breton, and he was expelled from the movement.

Gysin visited North Africa in 1939, had a one-man show at a Paris gallery, and in 1940 moved to New York, where he painted, worked on Broadway musicals, and did a stint as a welder in a shipyard. In 1943 he joined the armed forces. After the war he researched in the history of slavery and wrote a couple of books on the subject. In 1950 he again visited North Africa, this time in the company of Paul Bowles, and decided to settle there. He was still painting and exhibiting, and in 1953 aimed to expand his activities by opening a restaurant in Tangier. It was during this period that he first encountered William Burroughs. He left Tangier later in the 1950s, and in 1957 moved into what was soon to become famous as the Beat Hotel in the Rue Git-le-Coeur, Paris. Here he worked with Burroughs, Ian Sommerville, Sinclair Beiles, Gregory Corso, etc. Gysin helped develop the Cut-Up method, and collaborated with Sommerville on his Dream Machine. The "history" of this period can be followed in such publications as *Minutes To Go* (Two Cities Editions, 1960), *The Exterminator* (Auerhahn Press, 1960), *Let The Mice In* (Something Else Press, 1973), *Soft Need* 17 (Expanded Media Editions, 1977), and *The Third Mind* (John Calder, 1979). *Soft Need* 9 (1976), and Harold Chapman's *The Beat Hotel* (gris banal, 1984) also contain Gysin material of interest.

Throughout the 1960s and 1970s, and into the 1980s, he continued to write and paint. His novel, *The Process*, was published in 1969, and his paintings were exhibited in New York, London, Rome, and other major cities. He was also active as a performer, designer, and film-maker. A more-detailed account of his activities and involvements can be found in *Here To Go: Planet R-101* (Re/Search Publications, 1982), an excellent illustrated anthology of interviews with Gysin.

Gysin had worked on and off in the 60s and 70s on a book tentatively called *Beat Hotel*, and excerpts from it were published as *Beat Museum-Bardo Hotel* in the Gysin issue of *Soft Need* and elsewhere. But it was only in 1986 that the completed manuscript was finally scheduled for publication as *The Last Museum*, and the book appeared just a few weeks after his death.

It needs to be said that it is more an evocation of the spirit of the *Beat Hotel* than a factual account of events there. In this it somewhat resembles Harold Norse's *Beat Hotel* (Atticus Press, 1983), which is similarly racy and surreal if not quite as ambitious. Gysin's story imagines a "hero" attempting to move the hotel, which he's purchased, to California so he can place it in his Museum of Museums. There may well be, in this idea of the past being bought and shipped elsewhere, a link to other Gysin attitudes, as when he once commented, "Communication was destroying the world of value around us, has destroyed it in my time. Electric light chases the world of the Little Folk away. Radio has ruined music once made by every man, woman and child in the community. Tourism has attacked ancient cultures like syphilis. Cameras have soaked up the soul with their theft of images of the holy places."

The Last Museum, once entered by the "hero," and the reader, then uses the Tibetan Book of the Dead as a framework, and embarks on a journey along the corridors and into the rooms. William Burroughs makes an appearance, and so does Dr. Benway, one of the characters in *The Naked Lunch*. But the exploration is as much of Gysin's past as of the people who at one time or another inhabited the Beat Hotel, and if Gregory Corso is encountered then so are Natalie Barney, Gertrude Stein, Alice B.Toklas, and a variety of Paris residents of earlier eras. And the real-life people, or the book's versions of them, take second place to a cast of characters from Gysin's imagination as he concocts a series of mad escapades involving princesses and prostitutes, Dykes on Bykes, Hags and Nags, and others too numerous to mention.

It's all good, and often bawdy fun, though perhaps a bit overstretched at 186 pages. Gysin, at times, seems to be struggling to sustain the tone, which is more often than not cute and camp. It's occasionally mildly outrageous, but lacks the savagery of Burroughs who, one can't help thinking, threw a long shadow over Gysin, Norse, and anyone else who decided to work with the technique used so effectively in *The Naked Lunch, The Soft Machine*, etc. Gysin may well have helped Burroughs develop those techniques but he certainly never applied them himself in a similarly-devastating manner.

But this isn't to denigrate his achievements. He was involved with a wide range of artistic endeavours, and his influence did touch a number of younger artists, writers, and musicians. He was also significant as a personality whose connections with Bohemian society from the Surrealists through to the Beats and beyond gave it a welcome continuity. Gysin was too experienced a hand to have been persuaded that the Beats were all wonderful, and there are a couple of minor asides in *The Last Museum* that hint at a slight mockery of them, but he deserves to be remembered for his stay in the Beat Hotel, as well as for his colourful and productive life generally.

BRION GYSIN 1916-1986

THE LAST MUSEUM by Brion Gysin.
Faber & Faber, London, 1986. 186pp., paperback.

EXODUS
A MAGAZINE FROM A CURIOUS SOURCE

Little magazines often have fascinating publishing histories, their editors, financial backers (if they had them beyond the editors' bank accounts) and their circulations, varying wildly, and their readerships being sometimes impossible to ascertain accurately. Some probably only circulated on a limited basis and the length of time they survived depended very much on the interest and goodwill of both editors and readers. Others lasted longer for a variety of reasons often relating to the supply of time, energy, and money available. There have never been hard and fast rules that can be applied when writing about little magazines, which is precisely what makes them so interesting.

Exodus appeared for just three issues in 1959 and 1960 from the Judson Studio, an art gallery linked to Judson Memorial Church in Greenwich Village. Many churches and religious organisations have magazines of one sort or another, ranging from cheaply-produced local parish publications to glossier and wider-circulated journals. But *Exodus* was a little magazine in the true sense of that term, with poems, stories, essays, and art illustrations. Religion wasn't an obvious factor in its contents, though a spiritual aspect was present. And it wasn't afraid to be controversial.

It may be useful to outline some facts about Judson Memorial Church to provide a background to the story of the magazine. The Church was established on Washington Square around 1890 as a Protestant ministry that would draw its congregation from people living in Greenwich Village, which was then less of an artistic enclave in New York than it later became. This is not to say that the area was completely devoid of artists and writers, but it certainly had a larger population of working-class Italian-Americans and Irish-Americans. The church had its ups and downs in terms of attendances, and financial matters, but eventually settled on a firm footing. It's easy to access on-line information about the church, so I don't think I need to say more, other than to point out that as the number of bohemians in the area increased efforts were made to make contact with them.

I'm jumping to the 1950s when a young man named Bernard Scott came to Judson and was appointed as a kind of "missionary" to the bohemian community. The idea was "that if the natives would not come to church, the church would go to them." So Scott started to wander the streets of the Village and go into its bars, coffee-shops, galleries, and bookshops. As he said in an interesting on-line memoir of those days, he "soon became a native Villager" himself, growing a beard and picking up on the hip slang then in vogue. In 1957 he became an associate minister of the church.

A gallery was opened on the ground floor of Judson and artists like Jim Dine, Claes Oldenberg, and Tom Wesselman, all of them soon to be linked to the Pop Art movement of the 1960s, had their work displayed there. Scott had accommodation connected to the church and recalled that people like Jack Kerouac, Norman Mailer, De Hirsh Margules (an old bohemian artist known as the "unofficial mayor of Greenwich Village" or the "Baron of Greenwich Village") and Paddy Chayefsky, visited him.

In 1959 Scott decided to start *Exodus*, a little magazine that would publish Greenwich Village writers, though not just those with a Beat association. In time it would be described by one newspaper as "not beat but definitely far out." Daniel Wolf, one of the founders of the famous Village newspaper, *The Village Voice,* was Scott's co-editor, and money to get at least the first issue printed came from a wealthy benefactor who was sympathetic to what the magazine aimed for. Years later, Scott commented: "Today it would be surprising for a little magazine to have spiritual undertones, but in those days it seemed to fit in easily with the soul-searching tenor of things in places like Greenwich Village."

The first issue of *Exodus* appeared in Spring, 1959, and immediately gave a good indication of what the magazine intended to do. The lead item was Seymour Krim's "The Insanity Bit," his long, harrowing account of his breakdown in the early-1950s. Krim had started to write the kind of personal pieces that would shortly provide the basis for his brilliant first book, *Views of a Near-Sighted Cannoneer,* partly, he acknowledged, due to a sort of "liberation" inspired by the example of what the Beats were doing. And a sample of it was demonstrated by Ray Bremser's "Poems of Holy Madness" in the same issue. Bremser had a reputation as something of a "hard man," having served time in prison on charges of armed robbery, and his writing, though hardly memorable, seemed to suit the mood of the times. I think the same might be said of Howard Hart's poems, a couple of which seemed too personal to be truly meaningful to anyone else. But perhaps they fitted into that Beat-period confessional style of poetry? Hart, a one-time jazz drummer and associate of Jack Kerouac, Philip Lamantia, and David Amram, was listed as Poetry Editor of *Exodus* so may not have been the best judge of his own poems. It's often wiser to get someone else to select them. That may have happened, of course, and it's impossible to know if it did. I don't want to comment on every item (there was a story by Bernard Scott, so the editors seemed to have made sure they were in the first issue, and again it's difficult to decide if Scott alone made the decision to use his own story), but it is worth mentioning a brief memoir by De Hirsh Margules relating to his brother, a painter who achieved a certain amount of prominence early in the 20th Century. Margules himself was an artist with a reputation, at least in the bohemian circles in Greenwich Village. He had spent time in Paris in the 1920s. Reading him in *Exodus* provided a link between the Greenwich Village of the late-1950s and earlier bohemian activities. There is, incidentally, a photo of Howard Hart and Marc Ratliff (the Art editor of *Exodus*) at a party to launch the first issue of the magazine in Fred McDarrah's *Beat Generation: Glory Days in Greenwich Village.*

Exodus 2 followed in the Fall of 1959 and packed in quite a few poets who were around Greenwich Village and featured in *The Beat Scene,* the anthology which combined Fred McDarrah's photographs with poems by many of those pictured. Stephen Tropp and his wife Gloria were well-known in the Village and continued to write and appear in print after the heady days of Beat activity in the late-1950s and early-1960s. They both participated in the poetry readings at the Café Le Metro and poems by them can be found in *Wormwood Review* 17, a special issue devoted to poets from the readings. Stephen Tropp was also in *Six American Poets,* edited by Jack Micheline and published by the Harvard Book Company of New York in 1964. But who were James Grady and Robert Hanlon? Grady certainly wasn't the well-known novelist of the same name. And Hanlon, bearded and wearing a beret in McDarrah's photo, seems to have disappeared quickly. Robert Cordier, on the other hand, had a long and productive career in theatre, cinema, and TV, as well as writing. Ron Loewinsohn isn't in *The Beat Scene* but did have poems in Donald Allen's *The New American Poetry 1945-1960.* I've just pulled a few names out of this issue and focused on poetry, but there were prose contributions from Ivan C. Karp, and John Williams, among others. Karp became a well-known art dealer, and from the content of his story I assume John Williams was the black writer who published several novels, including *The Angry Ones* and *Night Song.* There was also Seymour Krim's "Ask for a White Cadillac," one of his essays in which he talked about his experiences as a white man in Harlem. It may be worth noting that the Essay Editor of *Exodus* was Edward Marshall, a poet who was, like Ron Loewinsohn, in the influential Donald Allen anthology.

I'm commenting on contributors in a little more detail than might be thought necessary in a survey of a magazine because the third issue of *Exodus,* published in the Spring/Summer of 1960, was the final one. Bernard Scott in his memoir of his years at Judson did say that there had been circulation problems, though they were overcome and the magazine sold well. The usual financial matters affected *Exodus,* but it seems that what really decided that it should close down was Scott's "sudden departure" from Judson, though he doesn't identify the reason for leaving. The magazine had seemed to be on the way to establishing itself as a significant vehicle for new poetry and prose which didn't necessarily adhere to any one school or group. I have to say that, looking at them now, many of the poems, particularly those by unknown writers, haven't stood the test of time. Who were John Menken, Mike Shapiro, Leonard Melfi, and Seth Wade? *Exodus*, unfortunately, didn't print notes on its contributors. Little magazines should, of course, encourage new and unknown poets, and no-one can easily tell whether or not a poet will develop his or her work into something lasting and substantial. Melfi assuming it's the same person, was a playwright with numerous off-Broadway productions to his credit, and Wade, again assuming a connection, did later publish poetry collections with small presses. Diane Wakoski, who was also in this issue, was a poet with a rising reputation and had already been published in a number of magazines, including *Beatitude* and *San Francisco Review.* In 1962 she was one of the *Four Young Lady Poets,* a collection published by Totem Press. With a curious prose piece by De Hirsh Margules, some adaptations of Max Jacob's writing by Howard Hart, and stories by Curtis Zahn and Herbert Shore, *Exodus* at least went down fighting. Zahn was a quirky writer whose work was usually labelled avant-garde because of its leanings towards fantasy or surrealism. He was widely published in magazines in the 1960s and his collection of stories,

American Contemporary came out in a Penguin edition in Britain in 1968. Shore, judging from the content of the story, was an academic who wrote several factual books about conditions in Africa. I should add that, as Judson had a gallery that exhibited art, the magazine played on the connection by including work by Red Grooms and Claes Oldenburg. Both can be seen in action in Fred McDarrah's superb *The Artist's World,* his photographic record of the New York art scene around 1960.

Did *Exodus* achieve a great deal? Obviously, three issues of a little magazine, no matter how good its circulation, are bound to have a limited impact. But in its short lifetime it did manage to sustain a reasonably high standard, even if much of the poetry lacked virility and colour. But most poetry in any period rarely survives its initial appearance in print. What *Exodus* did do, and I think it's to its credit, is show that Greenwich Village had more to offer than imitations of the leading Beats. There were only a few of them, in any case, and most of the writers and poets spotlighted in something like *The Beat Scene* were not Beats. Bohemians, perhaps, but definitely not Beats. The contributors to *Exodus* were varied in their approaches to writing. They had their own voices and used them to good effect.

NOTES

Fred W. McDarrah's various books provide excellent background material for the three issues of *Exodus*:

The Beat Scene, edited by Elias Wilentz, photographs by Fred W. McDarrah. Corinth Books, New York, 1960

The Artist's World by Fred W. McDarrah. E.P.Dutton, New York, 1961

Greenwich Village by Fred W. McDarrah. Corinth Books, New York, 1963

Kerouac & Friends: A Beat Generation Album by Fred W. McDarrah. William Morrow, New York, 1985

Beat Generation: Glory Days in Greenwich Village by Fred W. McDarrah & Gloria S. McDarrah. Schirmer Books, New York, 1996

JANET RICHARDS AND HER COMMON SOLDIERS

As far as I know little attention has been paid to *Common Soldiers*, a book by Janet Richards that Lawrence Ferlinghetti described as an "undiscovered classic." In it she writes about many of the people she encountered in New York and San Francisco in the 1940s and 1950s. Richards suffered from what Ferlinghetti referred to as "frail health" for most of her life, but still managed to get around enough to meet musicians, artists, and writers. My main concern is to look at her activities in San Francisco in the 1950s (she was, for example, in the audience at the famous 6 Gallery reading in 1955 when Ginsberg performed *Howl* in public for the first time), but it's relevant to sketch in some of her earlier experiences. Janet Richards lived a bohemian life wherever she was.

She was born in San Francisco in 1915 and as a child was diagnosed with Albers-Schoenberg disease, a metabolic problem which causes bones to be extremely hard and inflexible and so susceptible to being easily fractured. Richards describes how her condition affected her, but it's not necessary to go into detail here. Part of her story is how she never let medical issues hold her back from doing what she wanted to do.

Before she left San Francisco she had briefly attended the University of California and had also spent time at the California School of Fine Arts. She met Manny Farber who would later become well-known as an art critic and painter, as well as a lively film critic. It's possible to get an idea of the range of his writing about films from *Negative Space: Manny Farber at the Movies* (Da Capo Press, New York, 1998). But I'm jumping ahead a little because it was only when Farber and Richards moved to New York in 1941 that he began to establish a name for himself.

"It takes a lot of nerve to move to New York, because you can die there of a destroyed spirit, if you're an artist," Richards said when she looked back on her arrival in the city. With Farber she soon found accommodation in Greenwich Village, and thanks to his quickly getting a job writing for *New Republic* they got to know young writers and bohemians like Isaac Rosenfeld, Seymour Krim, and Saul Bellow. Richards says that she never could read any of Bellow's books when he became famous and highly-praised. Krim, after a bright start and a breakdown, allied himself with the Beats in the 1950s. As for Rosenfeld, he wrote a novel, *Passage from Home*, that was highly regarded in the 1940s, a number of first-rate short stories, and some astute criticism, but later drifted into a kind of willed failure and lived a shambling bohemian existence until his death at the early age of 38. When Richards knew him, though, he was working steadily at his writing and was looked on as someone likely to succeed.

I've just pulled a few names out of the New York section of her book and she also met people like Woody Guthrie and Jackson Pollock. She had ambitions to be a writer and achieved a degree of success among the bohemian community when she had a story published in *Partisan Review*, a key magazine in the intellectual life of New York. A publisher expressed interest in a novel she was working on but eventually rejected it. This setback seems to have persuaded Richards that she had little or no real talent for fiction.

The marriage to Manny Farber failed and in 1946 Richards moved back to San Francisco. She had known Robert Duncan in the 1930s and quickly re-established contact with him: "When he came for dinner with me on Clay Street in 1946, he had already written *Heavenly City*, his first book of poetry. He wasn't interested in much except poetry and poets, and after we had finished our dinner we went upstairs to my room where he read his poetry for such a long time that when I aroused myself from the semi-conscious state that had crept upon my lulled mind, which in responding with full understanding only to snatches of Robert's long poems, still had been soothed and reassured by his rising and falling voice, I found it was past midnight."

Richards also got involved with the San Francisco jazz scene, though it needs to be noted that, in the late-1940s and early-1950s, traditional jazz, as played by Lu Watters, Bob Scobey, Turk Murphy, and Bob Helm, was still very popular. Modern jazz, especially bebop, hadn't been a major factor in the musical life of San Francisco when compared to Los Angeles. Richards refers to tenorman Brew Moore and says that he did play in a band led by Bob Helm but was never really accepted by the "New Orleans diehards" because he wasn't "one of them" in the sense of being devoted to traditional jazz. Moore, as a professional musician, was presumably just taking whatever jobs came up, but his real interest was in the "cool" style that Lester Young had pioneered.

Kenneth Rexroth was someone else she had met in the 1930s and who she soon encountered again in San Francisco. She describes his home as "furnished with an austerity that extended even to the beds, which were like rocks." But she added: "like everything else about Kenneth, austerity had a rationale. But a rationale in the Rexrothian sense is not a readily accessible self-explanatory set of ideas. There are paradoxes, contradictions, puzzles." And she says that it often baffled people that Rexroth could live in a place that was "as depressing and ugly as a room at the Salvation Army," while at the same time buying bronze Shivas and silk kimonos for his young daughter. She was aware of his shortcomings, such as "his arrogant seizure of all conversations," but says that he was "everything: conscientious objector, classical scholar, versed in all sciences, political wiseacre, extreme radical, painter, musician, Orientalist, poet, essayist, and the friend of all artists. It was to him that Allen Ginsberg first came on his arrival in San Francisco; it was Kenneth who backed him and Jack Kerouac to the limits of his power, when they were still unpublished." What she said about his tending to dominate conversations was not always true. At the meetings of the Anarchist-Pacifist group that Rexroth organized, and which were attended by "ageing veterans of unionized struggles in Italy and Germany," he "very largely took a back seat and let these old working men of wide, bitter experience talk."

There are a lot of people that Richards mentions as present at various get-togethers at Rexroth's, among them Harry Roskolenko and Holly Beyes. Roskolenko was a poet, novelist, and travel writer, who had left home at 13 and spent seven years at sea. A political radical, he had been involved with the Trotskyist movement in the 1930s. His autobiography, *When I Was Last on Cherry Street* (Stein & Day, New York, 1965) is a colourful account of his early experiences. Holly Beye was in Greenwich Village in the 1940s and San Francisco between 1950 and 1955, and functioned as a poet, playwright, and journalist. Her book, *120 Charles Street, the Village: Journals & Writings, 1949-1950* (Bottom Dog Press, Huron, 2006) is informative about bohemian life in the period referred to. It's worth mentioning these people, and others like them, to indicate how, in the increasingly paranoid atmosphere of the late-1940s and early-1950s, gatherings like those at Rexroth's home provided a kind of refuge for political radicals, artistic dissenters, and those who just generally found the conformist atmosphere of the wider society not to their taste.

As the 1950s progressed, Richards met Allen Ginsberg at Rexroth's: "It is hard to remember Allen as he was that night, in his gray suit and businessman's tie — tense, restless, as if knotted around a hard kernel of anguish — and to know, as I do now, that here was the same person who had already at that time been for years in contact with William Burroughs and other sublime junkies who influenced him permanently." Later, she and her husband drove Ginsberg and Peter Orlovsky "to the Hotel Wentley, celebrated by John Wieners, lived in by so many artists that they would fill a special hall in heaven."

Janet Richards had been friendly with Weldon Kees in New York and when he turned up in San Francisco she renewed their acquaintanceship. Looking back when she wrote *Common Soldiers,* she thought that "Weldon had the peculiarity, and it was also his greatest gift as a poet, of having become the intellectual intimate of hopelessness before he was adolescent. Even before he had been in love he had learned to mourn." She talks about his involvements with jazz and the world of the San Francisco artists. It's often forgotten that the Bay Area painters were producing work which equalled in vitality and quality that of the Abstract Expressionists in New York. In San Francisco, Clyfford Still, David Park, and Richard Diebenkorn, were among the most active artists. But Kees had problems which were unlikely to be cured by immersing himself in poetry, painting, and music. Richards records that she may have been the last person to speak to him before he disappeared (almost certainly a suicide) in 1955. Kees phoned and said that he'd like to see Richards and her husband, but they were about to go to the airport to collect someone. Kees then said that things were pretty bad and no-one seemed to be doing anything and that he might go to Mexico. Richards asked him not to make any decision until they got back. She didn't hear from him again and the next day was told that he had disappeared.

Lawrence Ferlinghetti was a friend and Richards speaks highly of him, stressing that he was in San Francisco before the Beat idea caught on and Ginsberg and Kerouac came to town: "North Beach suited Lawrence absolutely. It is still his home ground, to which he always returns. He came on the scene, as did many others of us, long before Jack Kerouac and Neal Cassady began creating out of their own originality that aura of marvellous intent and hypnotic achievement that attracted swarms of turned-on iconoclasts, and before Allen Ginsberg spun the aura into still more celestial distances." She was of the opinion that by the time the Beats turned up, "Lawrence was already a self-realised poet. I do not think Beatness affected at all his poetic vision, of which he was already in control. Beatness affected him politically, philosophically, and from it he formed habits of living that became permanent."

Kerouac impressed Richards as a "great writer," and one of her anecdotes is that she recalls being with Rexroth when he received a phone call from Kerouac who wanted the older man's advice about whether he should change his name. He was worried that his former wife might make claims on his income from *On the Road* when it was published. Rexroth told him not to be crazy and that he should "thank fate instead for the marvellous good luck of possessing such a stunning name." She does make it clear that Kerouac, like other Beats, only passed through San Francisco: "The Beats, whether artists or drifting drop-outs, have had an inflated idea of their place in the long history of bohemianism in North Beach; they are but one group of many who have flourished and gone."

As regards the famous 6 Gallery event, she remembered it in these words: "On the night at the 6 Gallery when Allen read *Howl* for the first time and we were all delirious, the soul of the celebration was Jack, an electric chorus of one, sitting behind Charles and me, very drunk. While Allen with inspired abandon read, Jack uttered grunts and other rhapsodic cheers and banged with his wine bottle on the floor."

I've obviously focused on Janet Richards coming into contact with various writers, musicians, and artists, and by doing so I've neglected parts of her book which deal with her family life and other matters. Read in full *Common Soldiers* is a convincing picture of bohemian life from the 1930s to the 1960s, and also a moving account of someone never allowing her health problems to overcome her need to create (she painted as well as wrote) or her desire to mix with people she found interesting. She continued to live in San Francisco until her death in 1985.

Common Soldiers - The Archer Press, San Francisco, 1979.

DISCOVERY : THE STORY OF A 1950s MAGAZINE

The 1950s saw the appearance of a number of paperback pocket-book size magazines. *New World Writing* (1952-1964) was, perhaps, the best-known of these publications, and it does have a place in Beat history because of Kerouac's "Jazz of the Beat Generation," published in issue 7 (1955) and Kenneth Rexroth's "Disengagement: The Art of the Beat Generation" in issue 11 (1957). But *New World Writing* wasn't alone in giving space to writers who, in one way or another, could be said to have links to what was known as The New American Writing, if that term is interpreted fairly widely. The short-lived *Avon Book of Modern Writing* (1953-1955) which lasted three issues, with Berkley taking over from Avon for the final one, published Anatole Broyard, Milton Klonsky, and Herbert Gold. And *Discovery* (1953-55), backed by Pocket Books, featured Chandler Brossard, Norman Mailer, Gold, Broyard, John Clellon Holmes, Klonsky, Alan Harrington, Kenneth Koch, and Paul Goodman. I should point out that the names I've selected are those with a connection, however tenuous, to what might be called the Greenwich Village scene of the 1950s. All the magazines I've mentioned published a wide range of other poets, essayists, short-story writers, and novelists.

Before looking in a little more detail at *Discovery* it is worth referring to a talk given by the novelist and essayist Isaac Rosenfeld in 1956, in which he questioned whether or not publications like those mentioned above could be said to be true little magazines : "The little magazines at one time were part of the image of garret poverty and obscurity. Now they survive, but survive with a certain opulence that threatens to crush them. Surely the specific idea of a little magazine, just as the specific idea of the avant-garde, gets lost in such a translation. And that idea was that of a small but vigorous and very vital, active, and conscious group which knew fairly well the sort of thing it stood for even if it had no specific programme and whether or not it had any political allegiance." It's interesting to note that there was something of a revival among little magazines which fitted that description of "garret poverty and obscurity" later in the 1950s and in the early-1960s when the Beats brought in a resurgence of bohemianism.

Discovery was edited by Vance Bourjaily, himself a writer who, in

1947, had published *The End of My Life,* a well-received war novel. It should be noted that the first issue shows John W. Aldridge, an academic and critic, as joint editor with Bourjaily, but he seems to have severed his links with the magazine after that. In a preface to the contents, the editors stated that the aim was to have a publication which would attract a large audience, pay its writers a fair rate, and allow them to write freely. *Discovery* would appear twice a year, and it was hoped that "the same audience which buys serious, paper-bound reprint books" would want to purchase it. There were indications that the post-war years had seen an upsurge in the market for something beyond pulp fiction as more and more people took the opportunity to extend their education, and the numbers attending colleges and universities increased. But did that suggest that there was a related rise in the demand for new writing? Paperback reprints of classic texts might be popular, and useful for students, but what kind of market was there for new poetry and prose? *Discovery* was something of a gamble for its editors and publisher.

I don't intend to give a detailed analysis of each issue of *Discovery,* and will only pick out certain items, especially those with, as noted earlier, some sort of relevance to the Greenwich Village scene of the period concerned. But it will be pertinent to mention other writers, if only to show the kind of company they were in. Chandler Brossard's "The Only Time" in the first issue (February, 1953) was the opening chapter of his novel, *The Bold Saboteurs,* due to be published later that year. Brossard had already created something of a stir with *Who Walk in Darkness* (1952), largely because its account of a group of New York intellectuals and writers included an unflattering portrayal of a character based on Anatole Broyard, who himself would appear in the second issue of *Discovery*. Others in the first issue were Norman Mailer with a war story, Herbert Gold, with an essay about his home-town Cleveland, and Kenneth Fearing, a poet who is sometimes cited as an influence on Allen Ginsberg, though he appears here with a short-story. Mentioning Ginsberg reminds me that his father, Louis Ginsberg, contributed a short poem, "My Sons, Watch Out," to *Discovery*. He was only a minor poet, but in 1953 was probably then better-known than his son. A curious piece, "Confessions of an American Marijuana Smoker," was said to be by "U.S.D. Quincey," an obvious pseudonym for Vance Bourjaily. It would form part of his novel, *Confessions of a Spent Youth,* published in 1960.

I've already mentioned that Anatole Broyard was in the second issue. His "Ha! Ha!" was a lively and provocative essay about the uses and effects of laughter. And so was John Clellon Holmes with "The Horn," an excerpt from what would become his second book, published in 1958 with the same title, and one of the few novels to try to get to grips with the world of the modern jazz of the 40s and 50s. It's worth noting that among the other contributors were Gil Orlovitz, often in little magazines at the time, and, in the 1960s, editor of a key anthology, *The Award Avant-Garde Reader* (1965), Evan Hunter, later to become well-known for *The Blackboard Jungle* (1954) and his crime novels under the name of Ed McBain, Thomas McGrath, a left-wing poet who had been blacklisted from teaching, and Pietro di Donato, whose *Christ in Concrete* had attracted a great deal of attention in 1939. I mention these names to draw attention to the kind of context in which people like Broyard and Holmes were publishing.

Alan Harrington and Allan Temko were writers on the fringes of the early days of the Beat movement in New York and both appeared in the third *Discovery*. Harrington's story "The Revelations of Dr Modesto" (part of a novel published in 1955 with the same name) was, according to a later account by Vance Bourjaily, "probably thrust on my attention by John Clellon Holmes," which points to the interconnections between these writers in the early 1950s. Harrington is best-known in a Beat context for his novel, *The Secret Swinger* (1966), which is a fictionalised account of his encounters with the Beats, particularly Allen Ginsberg, but he did produce several other books, such as *Psychopaths* (1972), with its astute comments on Neal Cassady. Allan Temko was someone else known to Holmes and had "studied at Columbia University" and worked as a journalist. His curious story, "Elegy on the Passing of Shepheard's Hotel," had been sent from Paris, where Temko was then living. A third writer who was very much part of Greenwich Village in the 1950s was Milton Klonsky, celebrated by Seymour Krim in his *Views of a Nearsighted Cannoneer* (1961), and seemingly talented, but who never fulfilled his potential. His ""Selected Spooks, Stars, Gods and Celebrities – an Essay" was an attack on the cult of celebrity and the role of mass man, and can be read with relevance today.

Anatole Broyard's story, "What the Cystoscope Said" in the fourth issue (September, 1954) was stated to be an excerpt from his novel-in-progress, other parts of which would be published in *Modern Writing* and *New World Writing*. But Broyard never did finish his novel and although he continued writing it was mostly as a sometimes controversial critic and essayist. His *Kafka was the Rage* (1997), though unfinished and published after his death, is an engaging memoir of Greenwich Village in the late-1940s. Broyard had some strong company, particularly with Saul Bellow's "The Gonzaga Manuscripts" in the same issue. Bellow had attracted attention with novels like *Dangling Man* (1944) and *The Victim* (1947), and his stories had been published in *The New Yorker, Partisan Review,* and other prestigious publications. In 1954 he was being critically praised for his new novel, *The Adventures of Augie March* (1953). Bellow's presence shouldn't be allowed to hide the fact that another interesting novelist and essayist, Harvey Swados, was also there. Swados was a writer with a social conscience that often came through in his work, and his story in *Discovery* reflects that fact. His collection, *Nights in the Gardens of Brooklyn* (1960), has some of his best stories, and his novel, *Standing Fast* (1970), is a powerful account of what happens to a group of radicals as they grow older and circumstances alter.

Optimism about the future of *Discovery* was still in evidence when the fifth issue came out in March, 1955, with more poetry than usual, including a contribution from Kenneth Koch, a poet associated with the New York School, Frank O'Hara, and John Ashbery. He was later included in Donald Allen's anthology, *The New American Poetry, 1945-1960* (1960). Also worthy of attention was Norman Rosten's poem, "The Whaling Museum." Rosten is probably unknown in Britain, and I doubt that he was ever well-known in America, but his long poem, "The Fourth Decade," ought to be remembered for its evocation of the trials and tribulations of the 1930s. Bernard Malamud, who like Saul Bellow, was starting to build up a reputation as a novelist and short-story writer, was alongside Koch and Rosten, and there was a long piece by Paul Moor, "The Spooks and Passport No. 83711," which was about the problems experienced by a journalist who fell foul of the anti-communist hysteria that swept America in the 1950s. It was an intriguing account of how rumour, guilt-by-association, and loose information about books and magazines a person had read, could lead to being persecuted, having one's passport withdrawn, and generally treated with suspicion, even if one had done nothing wrong.

If Vance Bourjaily had been looking forward to editing *Discovery* for many more issues, his editorial in the sixth announced that it was the last one in the present series and that "a change of concept" was being considered. The suggestion appeared to be that the magazine would re-appear in some sort of new format, or perhaps with a different schedule and contents, but in fact the sixth issue proved to be the final one. There were stories by Harold Brodky, Paul Goodman, and R.V. Cassill, the latter a writer who sometimes is associated with the Beats on the basis of a single story, "Fracture," which was included in the *Protest: The Beat Generation and the Angry Young Men* anthology published in 1958. He was far from being a Beat, however, and had a successful career as an academic, editor, and novelist.

It's difficult to know exactly why Pocket Books decided to pull the plug on *Discovery*, though it's more than probable that money was the main cause. The magazine may have sold comparatively well, if compared to the general run of little magazines which struggled to attract readers and obtain some kind of circulation beyond a purely literary audience. But it probably didn't sell enough to satisfy a commercial publisher like Pocket Books. I think it's noticeable that other similar magazines which were backed by big publishers also usually closed down when sales didn't match up to expectations. *New World Writing,* supported by New American Library, closed after fifteen issues, though a few more were published by Lippincott. Later, Saul Bellow's *The Noble Savage* (1960-1962), with backing from Meridian Books, got through five issues before disappearing. And even later still, running from 1967 to 1977 under the brilliant editorship of Theodore Solataroff, *New American Review* (the "New" was eventually dropped from the title) survived for twenty-six issues, though during that time there were three different backers, New American Library, Simon & Schuster, and Bantam Books.

I suppose what the history of *Discovery* tells us is that accepting support from a commercial organisation may initially seem to be a good idea, but that financial help will eventually depend on commercial considerations. Little magazines often rely on the generosity of editors, writers, and readers to survive, and they sometimes surprisingly manage to do so for many years, though the casualty rate among most magazines is high. *Discovery* and the others like it performed a useful role while they existed, and they certainly helped to publicise the work of writers who might otherwise have been limited to publishing in small-circulation little magazines. In this respect it's worth pointing out that Vance Bourjaily didn't aim for popularity by just choosing work by a few relatively established writers like Saul Bellow, Norman Mailer, William Styron, and Richard Eberhart, all with books to their name. Each issue of *Discovery* also featured writers who had previously published very little and, in some cases, were making their first appearance in print. From this point of view the magazine was doing what a little magazine ought to do and not just aiming to appeal to an audience wanting to admire the already known. It's possible to see why Isaac Rosenfeld was suspicious of the role of a magazine like *Discovery*, and it's true that, unlike small avant-garde publications with their limited circulations, it didn't claim to represent a particular group, movement, or approach to writing. Vance Bourjaily had to offer a broad cross-section of new writing which would hopefully appeal to a wider audience than little magazines reached. But he did also try to give a platform to young writers who were beginning to hint at new concerns.

NOTES

Each issue contained between 270 and 290 pages. The sixth and final issue had a list of all the contributions to the magazine.

Near the beginning of this article I referred to Isaac Rosenfeld's views on publications such as those I've discussed. The full text of his talk, "On the Role of the Writer and the Little Magazine," can be found in *The Chicago Review Anthology,* edited by David Ray, published by The University of Chicago Press, 1959.

Norman Rosten's long poem, "The Fourth Decade," is in *The Fourth Decade and Other Poems,* published by Farrar & Rinehart, 1943.

The essay that Milton Klonsky contributed to *Discovery* wasn't included in his only book, the posthumously published, *A Discourse on Hip: Selected Writings of Milton Klonsky,* edited by Ted Solotaroff, published by Wayne State University Press, 1991, but I recommend this book to anyone interested in the Greenwich Village scene of the late-1940s and the 1950s. Klonsky seems to have suffered from a writer's block much of the time, but what he did produce was always worth reading. Several of his essays were published in *New American Review* or *American Review* as it was known after its fifteenth issue.

THE BEAT SCENE : HOW INFLUENTIAL WAS IT?

There are those who will deny that *The Beat Scene*, the book edited by Elias Wilentz, and illustrated with photographs by Fred McDarrah, was influential in literary terms, and it's certainly true that it did have limitations from that point of view. It came out around the same time as Donald Allen's *The New American Poetry, 1945-1960,* and suffered in comparison to that interesting and perhaps even ground-breaking collection of contemporary work.

But I don't think it's fair to make such a comparison. The purpose of *The Beat Scene* was not to attempt a broad survey of trends in American poetry over a lengthy period, but instead to focus on the activities of the "young bohemian writers of New York's Greenwich Village," and Elias Wilentz's introduction placed them in a history of American bohemianism stretching back to the mid-1800s. The Beats had revived a bohemian tradition that had, in some ways, receded into the background during the 1950s when anything that appeared to be "un-American," from left-wing political involvements to avant-garde art and poetry and forms of social deviancy, could be looked on with suspicion. Wilentz claimed that during that period "almost the only Bohemianism around was that still practised by the 'the old-timers' of the Twenties and Thirties who had never given it up." The baleful influence of the rabble-rousing Senator McCarthy had spread from concerns about national security to popular questioning of anything outside a narrow norm recognised by the majority.

Wilentz also admitted that choosing a title for the book had not been easy, bearing in mind what was said about it casting a wide net in terms of the writers it covered. He justified calling it *The Beat Scene* on the grounds that, by 1960, journalists and others were referring to anyone appearing to hold to any kind of bohemian ideas or life-style as "Beat." As he pointed out, the only real Beats were those identifying themselves with "the ideas of Allen Ginsberg, Jack Kerouac, Gregory Corso, and Peter Orlovsky." And there were other poets and writers who were inclined more to describing themselves, if they felt the need to do so, as "underground" or "Black Mountain." He also pointed to "the numerous amorphous cliques" that tended to form around various little magazines, such as *Chelsea, Birth, Yugen,* and *Big Table*, and small presses like Totem, Jargon, and Auerhahn. It's also a fact that many poets and writers don't like to be tied to a specific movement or group and prefer to be just considered as individuals.

Still, it does seem to me that *The Beat Scene* did have an influence in the way it suggested that there was a certain kind of social approach to writing, and that it involved people coming together to perform their work, talk, drink, and generally get involved in at least some sort of group activity. The poetry readings at Café Le Metro, The Gaslight Café, Les Deux Megots, and the Tenth Street Coffeehouse, might indicate that poets, in particular, need to share their work with fellow-poets and whatever audiences they can attract. There was a revival of interest in the idea of poetry being read aloud, rather than just looked at on the page. It's probably impossible to determine if *The Beat Scene* influenced poets and others in towns and cities outside New York and San Francisco to start poetry readings, but it could be the case.

That Wilentz and McDarrah did not limit their survey to a handful of well-known Beats is easily demonstrated by having a look at some of the poets and writers in *The Beat Scene*. It's certainly true that the Beats were featured, and Kerouac at a reading was the illustration on the front cover. Inside, Ginsberg was seen in a number of photos and his poem, "I Beg You to Come Back and be Cheerful" was spread over several pages. Elsewhere, Kerouac, Corso, Orlovsky, Ferlinghetti, McClure, Philip Lamantia, Lew Welch, and Philip Whalen put in appearances, the latter five only visiting from the West Coast rather than being Greenwich Villagers. I'm placing all of them in a Beat framework, though several would most likely have denied being Beat. Ferlinghetti, for example, largely saw his role as a publisher of the Beats and didn't consider his own poetry as similar to what Ginsberg and Corso were writing. Philip Lamantia had been around since the 1940s when, as a very young man, he'd appeared in surrealist publications. And Whalen and Welch were both far too individual in their respective approaches to writing to be easily classified as Beats. Welch was with Kerouac and Albert Saijo as they knocked together a group poem in Fred McDarrah's apartment while he moved around and photographed them.

There were several other poets who could be said to have had links to the Beats, either by choice or because the nature of their work and activities appeared to place them in the same group. I'm referring to Ray Bremser, Diane Di Prima, Ted Joans, Leroi Jones, and Jack

Micheline. But, again, it's possible to see that each had individual characteristics that could equally set them apart from the Beats. I suppose Bremser might never have been published and seen in *The Beat Scene* had he not come across the Beats while in prison, and Leroi Jones likewise may have had some of his first impulses to write after reading Beat poetry. But Di Prima, Joans, and Micheline had somewhat different backgrounds. Ted Joans was influenced by European surrealist poetry and jazz, Jack Micheline's work showed stylistic traces of 1930s radical writing, and Diane di Prima would probably have written anyway, but got involved with the Beats when they came along in the 1950s.

A quick summary of the writers who might be legitimately identified, in one way or another, with the Beats accounts for only a small portion of the poets pictured in *The Beat Scene*. So, who were the others? It's not possible to look in detail at all of them, and, in any case, information about them is often scarce to come by. But some of the writers were reasonably established. Robert Creeley, Paul Blackburn, Kenneth Koch, and Jonathan Williams were all heavily involved with the New American Poetry of the late-1950s and early-1960s. Williams was also publisher of Jargon Books. All four were represented in Donald Allen's anthology.

On the other hand, who was David Galler? His photograph suggests a bohemian setting, but his poem is more formally written than much of the work in *The Beat Scene*. His book, *Walls and Distances*, was published by Macmillan in 1959 and a quick glance at the list of magazines Galler had appeared in will show that they tended towards the established and academic rather than the sporadic little magazines produced during the bohemian resurgence of the late-1950s and early-1960s. I'm not suggesting any criticism of Galler by saying this. His poems were well-written and interesting, and he showed that he shared a common interest with the Beats through his poem "Ballade of the Session after Camarillo," which was about Charlie Parker playing a gig "at the Royal Mansions Ballroom in the East Bronx on a snowy winter's night."

If Galler, who later published more books and had a successful academic career, clearly had talent, what are we to make of Sally Stern, Brigid Murnaghan, and John Fles? Stern's poem was reprinted in one or two later anthologies of Beat writing, though I tend to suspect it was largely because the editors wanted to include as many women writers as possible rather than for its qualities as a poem. Murnaghan appears to have been something of a character around the Greenwich Village scene. She did publish a few minor poems in Tuli Kupferberg's magazine, *Yeah*, and in *Swank*, a slick men's magazine when Seymour Krim edited several sections of Beat-related writing for it. But little more was heard of her in general publishing terms, though she was still alive and outspoken in 2014 as an interview on the internet demonstrates. John Fles was a minor writer who edited a one-shot publication, *The Trembling Lamb*, which featured Carl Solomon among others. He moved on to different things (music and "underground" films), as did some of the other minor characters in *The Beat Scene*. Bob Lubin "gave up writing to follow his interest in carpentry and architectural design," William V. Ward. one-time editor of *The Provincetown Review*, found employment with the New York City Board of Education. As Kenneth Rexroth once remarked, "The world is full of sea captains who used to play trombone."

Kupferberg and Krim were in *The Beat Scene*, too, though neither was Beat. Kupferberg had been around the bohemian scene for quite a few years, as references in his poems will show, and he edited a lively issue of *Birth* which was essentially a potted history of American bohemianism. His small book, *Snow Job: Poems 1946-1959*, indicates that he was publishing long before the Beats came along. As for Krim, he had been publishing short stories, essays, and reviews in a variety of publications, including *New Directions* and *The Hudson Review* since the 1940s, though a breakdown and the appearance of the Beats helped him revitalise his writing. He then began to publish in *Exodus, The Village Voice*, and other magazines. His book, *Views of a Nearsighted Cannoneer,* is a key document of the period. And he edited *The Beats*, a paperback collection that had quite a wide circulation, thanks to it being published by Gold Medal Books in 1960.

As I mentioned earlier, it's not my intention to look at everyone in the book. Some, like William Morris, had little to recommend them beyond the fact that they were around Greenwich Village when Fred McDarrah was prowling through poetry readings, bars, cafes, and other places with his camera. The photos of Morris are more interesting than the poem by him in *The Beat Scene*, or one or two other bits and pieces he published in *The Jazz Word, Gaslight Poetry*

Review, and *Gemini.* There were far more talented writers who McDarrah photographed, such as Edward Field, Thomas McGrath, and Kenneth Patchen. And what about Bill Berkson, Daisy Aldan, Jean Garrigue, and Paul Goodman? None of them could be called Beat, though they might be categorised as bohemians, and some probably wouldn't even welcome that. Thomas McGrath had a long history of left-wing activism and had been blacklisted from teaching jobs because of his membership of the Communist Party. Kenneth Patchen was far too independent to like any attempt to label him. And Paul Goodman wrote a book, *Growing Up Absurd,* that had some harsh things to say about the Beats.

Barbara Moraff, Lenore Jaffee, Martin Last, William Millet. It's fun to google their names and, in some cases, find out what they did after their days in Greenwich Village. Barbara Moraff, who also wrote under the name of Barbara Ellen, and had a good publishing record in magazines, left New York and moved to the country where she took up pottery and other activities. She self-published several collections of her poems in later years. There were many others who were pictured in *The Beat Scene* and additionally also had their poems in its pages. My main concern has been to point out that it was a much-more varied collection than its title implies and many reviewers at the time suggested. If someone was curious enough to track down a few of the names (not as easy in those pre-internet days) they would have discovered many fascinating facts about, for example, Willard Maas and Edward Dahlberg, neither of who could be said to be "young bohemian writers." Maas was born in 1906 and was involved with experimental film-making in the 1940s. And Dahlberg's first novel, the tough, proletarian *Bottom Dogs,* was published in 1929.

Some of the people portrayed by McDarrah did lend themselves to being lampooned, their determination to appear bohemian being obvious. Ambrose Hollingworth is an example, though not the only one. But if it's taken in the right way the book can be a useful guide to what was happening in Greenwich Village around 1960. Was it influential? I think so, though perhaps in ways that can be faulted as well as respected. It could be that too many people just glanced at the beards and curious clothing that could be seen in some of the photos and took them as a guide to what the Beats and many of the writers were getting up to. But there was more to *The Beat Scene* if you took the trouble to look for it.

The Beat Scene, edited by Elias Wilentz with photographs by Fred McDarrah. Corinth Books, New York, 1960.

There are several other publications which may be of interest:

"A History of New York coffee-house readings" by Carol Berge, in *Magazine* 2, edited by Kirby Congdon, New York, 1965.

The East Side Scene, edited by Allen De Loach, University Press, State University of New York at Buffalo, 1968.

Seventh Street: An Anthology of Poems from Les Deux Megots, edited by Don Katzman, Hesperidian Press, New York, 1961.

The Wormwood Review 17: *the Le Metro issue,* guest- edited by Allen De Loach, 1965. (No information about an editorial address is shown in the magazine).

All Poets Welcome: The Lower East Side Poetry Scene in the 1960s, by Daniel Kane, University of California Press, Berkeley, 2003.

A Secret Location on the Lower East Side: Adventures in Writing, 1960-1980, by Steven Clay and Rodney Phillips, The New York Public Library and Granary Books, New York, 1998.

Beat Coast East: An Anthology of Rebellion, edited by Stanley Fisher, Excelsior Press, New York, 1960. In some ways this complements *The Beat Scene* by using work by many of the poets photographed by McDarrah. Fisher himself appears in *The Beat Scene.*

Obviously, as the titles indicate, some of these publications cover a wider period than *The Beat Scene* related to, but they all contain information about how the poetry scene in New York developed in Greenwich Village and other locations in the city.

Fred McDarrah published several later books about the Greenwich Village literary and art scenes in the late-1950s and early-1960s, and they all contain photos of quite a few of the poets in *The Beat Scene,* along with notes about them.

I ought to also mention *The Gaslight Poetry Review*, a curious publication obviously linked to the readings at the Gaslight Café on MacDougall Street in Greenwich Village. It's undated (I would hazard a guess that publication was around 1959), and has no information other than that the publisher was John Mitchell. Most of the poets in it are also in *The Beat Scene* and some of Fred McDarrah's photos were clearly taken at Gaslight readings.

BETWEEN WORLDS
A SIXTIES MAGAZINE

The late-1950s and early-1960s were exciting years as the Beat movement seemed to spur people into producing publications aiming to print work by many of the new writers, and some older ones. The resurgence of interest in little magazines and small press publications saw writers and editors who had been around the bohemian scene for some time being noticed once more. Jon Edgar Webb and his wife, Louise "Gypsy Lou" Webb, had their roots in the 1930s and 1940s, and when they started the fine magazine, *The Outsider*, in New Orleans in 1961, they not only featured the Beats but also used work by Henry Miller, Kenneth Patchen, and Millen Brand, all of them from earlier non-establishment scenes. Others like Walter Lowenfels, one-time associate of Henry Miller in 30s Paris and later blacklisted because of his membership of the Communist Party, began to appear in print again. Sherry Mangan, active in the American Trotskyist movement for many years, was published in the final issue of *The Black Mountain Review* in 1957 which also featured Kerouac, Ginsberg, McClure and Snyder. And Harold Briggs, who opened a bookshop in New York in the 1940s which specialised in little magazines and offbeat literature, had work in *Sidewalk* and *White Dove Review* alongside newer American writers. A small book by Briggs, *Though Man Fly Angel High,* was published by Hors Commerce Press in California in 1964. When Briggs died *Wormwood Review* 40 (1970) ran a sixteen-page section devoted to his work as a tribute to him.

And then there was Gilbert Neiman who, for a time in the early 1960s, edited *Between Worlds*, a magazine published by Alan Swallow for the Inter American University in Puerto Rico. Neiman was born in 1912, and in the late-1930s he was one of a group of young, bohemian writers, including Weldon Kees, who were active in Denver. Neiman wrote poetry and short stories and was published in magazines such as *Accent* and *Poetry*, and he also did a translation of Lorca's *Blood Wedding* which was published by New Directions in 1939. His novel, *There is a Tyrant in Every Country,* was published in 1947. He was a friend of Henry Miller and, in fact, Miller's *The Air-Conditioned Nightmare* was dedicated to Neiman and his wife, Margaret. Miller's own work and books about him mention Neiman, sometimes commenting on his heavy drinking. There isn't a lot of information available about his activities after the late-1940s, but in 1960 he turned up as editor of *Between Worlds* and held that position until 1962 when the third issue appeared. Later in the 1960s Neiman became a professor of English at Clarion University in Pennsylvania. There was still a drinking problem if accounts on the internet by one-time students of his are anything to go by. He was warned that he would lose his job if he continued to turn up for classes while obviously drunk, and it would seem that he was eventually forced out of the university. He died in 1977.

I've sketched out some details of Neiman's life, insofar as I've been able to ascertain them, but it's primarily his role as editor of the three issues of *Between Worlds* that interests me. As I mentioned earlier, the first one appeared in 1960 and it was at once evident that Neiman, like Jon Edgar Webb, was keen to establish a connection between the Beats and earlier bohemians. There were four poems by Gregory Corso, including "For Hope Savage", and contributions from Gary Snyder, Phillp Whalen, William Burroughs, Ed Dorn, Harold Norse, and Lawrence Ferlinghetti. A minor Beat, Clint Nichols, who was in *The Beat Scene* anthology and one or two other publications around that time, was also featured with what might now be seen as a typical bit of Beat ephemera, with its almost-routine reference to Charlie Parker. What happened to Clint Nichols?

Alongside these newer writers Neiman placed Henry Miller, Alfred Perles, Marcel Duchamp, Man Ray, Malcolm Cowley, Herbert Read, George Dillon, and translations of various Spanish-speaking authors. It's impossible to know exactly how Neiman obtained work from people like Miller, Cowley, and Read. Did he contact them and, in a sense, play on his past associations? It's sometimes necessary to do that when starting a magazine. And it could be that the material Neiman used had already been in print elsewhere and he simply asked for permission to use it again in *Between Worlds*. It's perhaps not important to ascertain exactly how he went about assembling all the contents of his first issue, and sufficient just to point to his mixture of old and new writers.

Between Worlds was a bulky magazine (189 pages in the first issue) and presumably aimed to be an annual publication. The second issue came out in 1961, with the page numbers following on from the first and going up to page 349. Again, there was the mixture of older avant-garde writers with those from the contemporary areas of the New American Writing. It is possible in at least one case to determine how Neiman obtained some poems. Mina Loy was born in 1892 in London, though she moved to the United States around 1916. In the 1920s she was in Paris with expatriates like Ernest Hemingway, Robert McAlmon, and the surrealist Man Ray. Her poems were published in Dadaist magazines and her book, *Lunar Baedeker,* came out from McAlmon's Contact Press in 1923. She was seen as one of the finest avant-garde poets of the 1920s, but after 1925 or so she published very little and was forgotten by most people. Neiman had been introduced to her in the 1940s by Henry Miller, and decided to write to her when he became editor of *Between Worlds* to ask if she would contribute to the magazine. She responded with the five poems that he printed.

Alfred Perles cropped up again in issue 2 and there were poems from William Carlos Wlliams, Alan Ansen, Louis Ginsberg (Allen's father) Harold Briggs, and Walter Lowenfels. Representing newer writers were Robert Creeley, Kenneth Koch, Jack Hirschman, Larry Eigner, Barbara Guest, and Robert Kelly. I'm only listing a few of the poets and others in *Between Worlds* to give an idea of the contents, but in doing so it does raise the question of whether or not the magazine had any sort of editorial policy. Some magazines in the Sixties aimed to print material by a particular group of poets, but *Between Worlds*, like *The Outsider,* had a more open approach and spread its interests widely, as can be seen from the names I've referred to. The network of little magazines at that time is illustrated by the fact that *Between Worlds* carried advertisements for *Big Table, Chelsea, The Outsider*, and several other publications.

Neiman was still editing *Between Worlds* when the third issue appeared in 1962, this time with 126 pages of poetry and prose. Some of Neiman's old friends, such as Henry Miller and Anais Nin, were there, as was Mina Loy and Harry Roskolenko, another veteran of the 1920s and 1930s. Born in 1907 Roskolenko ran away to sea when he was thirteen and spent seven years in the merchant navy. In the 1930s he hoboed around, got mixed up with radical politics, became a Trotskyist, and wrote and published poetry in magazines like *Blues* and *Pagany* alongside Kenneth Rexroth and Louis Zukofsky. There were further experiences, including being a sailor during the Second World War, and travelling extensively after it.

Roskolenko's memoir, *When I Was Last On Cherry Street,* is a wonderfully vibrant book full of stories about his adventures.

Allen Ginsberg was in this issue and so was the ill-fated Gil Orlovitz. He was a poet and novelist who, in the 1960s, had a reputation as an experimental writer and appeared in various magazines and anthologies. His novels, with titles such as *Milkbottle H* and *Ice Never F,* were not likely to be widely popular, but he did have a minor reputation in Europe. In the mid-Sixties he edited *The Award Avant-Garde Reader* which included work by William Burroughs, among others. But Orlovitz had a drinking problem and there's a stark portrait of him in Donald Newlove's *My Drinking Days,* a book which looks at the way in which Newlove and many other American writers have battled with the bottle. Orlovitz eventually collapsed and died in the street and was given a pauper's funeral by the New York City authorities. Bearing in mind Gilbert Neiman's alcoholism it's curious that he used work by more than one writer with a similar addiction. The novelist and short-story writer, Robert Lowry, who had known Neiman since the late-1930s, was in the first and third issues of *Between Worlds* and also had a life scarred by booze, as well as mental problems. Perhaps it was just a coincidence that Neiman, Orlovitz, and Lowry were drinkers? After all, as Jimmy Charters, a legendary bartender in Paris in the 1920s, said when he wrote his memoirs: "Most writers are drinkers." He was probably right.

What happened to *Between Worlds* after the third one? Had Neiman moved on from the Inter American University in Puerto Rico? Did the University pull the plug on the magazine because of the cost of producing it? Was Neiman's drinking a factor in what happened? It's only possible to speculate about these matters in the absence of facts, and that takes us nowhere. Were there more issues of the magazine? I never came across them, if there were, and hunting around the internet hasn't turned up any information relating to issues beyond the third.

Three issues of a magazine which probably had a relatively limited circulation may not have been a major contribution to the literature of the 1960s, but the mixture of old and new writers, together with translations from Spanish and French authors, seems to me to have served a useful purpose. The way in which Gilbert Neiman, like the Webbs with *The Outsider*, pointed to the connection between the

Beats and other new writers, and their predecessors from earlier bohemian and non-establishment scenes, was important. Literature and art and music have lines of development and it's essential that we know about them.

NOTES:

It may be useful to give details of some of the books I mentioned in this article:

There is a Tyrant in Every Country by Gilbert Neiman. Harcourt Brace & Co., New York, 1947

When I Was Last on Cherry Street by Harry Roskolenko. Stein and Day, New York, 1965

Those Drinking Days: Myself and Other Writers by Donald Newlove. Junction Books, London, 1981

The Award Avant-Garde Reader edited by Gil Orlovitz. Award Books, New York, 1965

Milkbottle H by Gil Orlovitz. Calder & Boyars, London, 1967

Ice Never F by Gil Orlovitz. Calder & Boyars, London, 1970

FIELDING DAWSON : LIFE WITH FIELDING

Do you have a favourite writer? No, I don't mean your idea of the best writer, or the most promising writer. I mean, is there a writer you just like to read, and who, even if he isn't always perfect, at least keeps you interested and entertained. And whose books you buy as soon as they're out? Well, here's a chunk from one of my favourites:

> "I woke suddenly, and intuitively glanced at the time, got out of bed fast, talking to myself while I shaved and dressed automatically sorting through the papers on my desk in my office in the job in my head, and as I put on my tie I finished the letter to the fellow in Suffolk County reminding him of the COD fee the dispatcher Cerar at Sternberger Trucking had quoted me, and in back of that in my mind I began the claim against the New England Trucking firm St. Johnsbury about the Fitzgerald delivery, and I also completed the preparation of two refunds which would keep my company out of small-claims court, and as I stopped at my studio/loft door, as I always do - for a last look around - I saw my typewriter in a flash of wish and anger at the stack of blank white paper ready beside it, and the sheet in the machine half-filled with words..."

That's from *A Great Day For A Ballgame*, to my mind one of Fielding Dawson's best books, certainly his best novel. It's full of those crisp summaries of life as it is. It's the way it does go, up in the morning and, whether you like it or not, thinking about the job ahead of you. And what you could be doing.

> I got up this morning and made the coffee and toast and looking at the paper, another bomb blast and Stonehouse out on bail and politicians talking. I had to finish this boring job as soon as I got to work, and didn't want to do it, but it had to be done, and I figured if I got straight into it when I arrived I'd finish it by 11 or so. And just before I left the postman handed me a parcel, two LPs from Japan, and I wanted to play them right then, wondering what Stan Getz sounded like with Randy Brooks all those years ago -1945 - and whether the Hawkins disc had any alternate takes. And this review to write.

Of course, it perhaps isn't the greatest thing in the world to write about getting up in the morning, but it's real, and if the writer makes me think that what he's doing is believable - that it has a life of its own -then I'll carry on reading him. I get that feeling from Raymond Chandler and Ross Macdonald (and don't tell me their books aren't real, that is "true to life," because it's what they *make* believable that counts), and it's maybe no co-incidence that Dawson rates Chandler highly. It isn't only a question of what you do, it's the way that you do it. What distinguishes Dawson from other writers who try to plough the same furrow is the way in which he handles the language, and especially when he's dealing with dialogue. His ear for it is superb:

> "She sipped her drink and sighed. I relit my cigarette and my hand shook. I puffed. I was just a little startled, as she said, 'As rationalisations go, it's not bad. At least you've got one.' And she added, 'Do you do this often?'

> 'Do what often. No. And as I see you, never. It happened only once'. She smiled and I had a regressive twinge; the cue? Had I missed another one? Damn! cried the baby. 'No,'

> I laughed, "Do you?'

> 'No,' she said. 'But I'm not surprised. You're a known writer, no?'

> 'No,' I laughed and laughed to her, 'that is except -'

> Luckily I let it hang, because I didn't like the way her head had turned away, and then she looked fully at me. 'Sure you are. And you're the most self-conscious person I've ever met'.

> So I went to work and finished the boring job just after 11, and then I spent the next hour looking through a catalogue that came with the records, and writing a couple of letters. And at lunchtime I decided to go home instead of into town. I had a full hour, more or less, and managed to get through both sides of the Hawkins LP and although it didn't have any alternate takes it did have a couple of tracks I'd never heard before. I also read a couple of Dawson's short stories, "Captain America" and "Bonaparte's Retreat" - terrific.

It's the handling of the language that helps make Dawson's books real, and the people in them, too. And although the words may sometimes seem to cover banal situations they hide a wealth of meaning that bursts through when you get into the rhythm. The chunk I quoted above - again from *A Great Day For A Ballgame* - is taken from a section of the novel where the narrator (and it's Dawson, he uses his own name, so why bother to pretend otherwise) and the girl he's recently met are slowly sounding out each other, probing, they know they have something in common, but both have broken marriages behind them and they're careful, the dialogue skates over the surface, revolving around writers, mutual acquaintances, and so on, but breaking through every now and then and beautifully building up the tension. The kind of tension that you get when you meet someone you know is right for you, but you don't want to push it too fast in case it goes wrong, you want it to come in its own time. It's a form of suppressed excitement, and that's what Dawson manages to put into all of his writing. So that when the opening does come you laugh with the narrator. You feel good with him. Again, I'm reminded of Raymond Chandler, because in his books you feel the tension as the narrator exchanges words with a suspect and it builds up and breaks and you laugh out loud at it. Good jazz soloists used to do it, too.

> Back at work the afternoon went fast enough for me not to bother about it, and I strolled home in the hot afternoon sun. The house was empty and quiet, my son somewhere in the Lakes with a couple of friends, and as I usually do when I'm alone I put off making a proper meal and instead grilled a few sausages and tomatoes and watched the news on TV as I ate them. Then I read more Dawson, chunks of *The Black Mountain Book* and *An Emotional Memoir Of Franz Kline*, and listened to Lucky Millinder's band.

If Dawson is a master of language, he's also a master with fragments. And fragments are what his books are constructed from. This is not said in a derogatory way. My own idea is that most, if not all of us, live our lives in interlocked fragments. The basic continuity is ageing, and a pattern evolves through chance. In Dawson's books, by design or not, the chapters are usually short, the thread of the story isn't detailed in the sense of one chapter leading closely and logically into the next. The action jumps, and the thread is in the subject, so that you don't get a feeling of the characters suddenly appearing out of nowhere at the beginning of the book and disappearing into nowhere at the end of it. They live outside the confines of the pages, both during the action and before and after it. Which is possibly why Dawson doesn't have to write in everything about them. We *know* what they do in between the times he tells us about.

I suppose I essentially think of Dawson as a short-story writer even when the work I'm reading is described as a novel. As I've already pointed out, the brevity of the chapters, and the selective nature of the writing, directs the narrative into a short-story form. It's possible to pick up a Dawson book and begin reading it, for pleasure, at almost any point:

> "Ben Royal was off from Headquarters and blowing the most miserable trumpet anyone ever blew, and beside him, a tall thin Negro named Sanford, also from Headquarters, was playing a terrible tenor and in the back of that a German fellow was playing drums with a beat like how grandmother gave you silver dollars one at a time. His name was -son something. Erickson, Karlson, maybe. Karlson. Karlson was sitting in because Abe was on leave, Ben Royal said. Abe was blowing with a group in Paris, 'I got a card from Abe'. Nobody had seen Sam Funny so there was no bass. A very white guy named Leo was playing piano. He was new, had just arrived from the States with fresh stories about Bird at the Open Door, Miles sounded weak (Bozo winced), and he had a pal he knew once who had seen Tristano; new stuff with flutes and all that crap was going on on the West Coast, Leo said, out of his pale face...but as he played now, J.M.Davies laughed because Leo had to wait for Ben Royal and Sanford to blow all their notes away so he could play something."

There was probably a degree of selectivity in the way I chose that passage, because it obviously relates to a subject I'm interested in and my eyes would naturally fasten on to the names when I flicked through the pages of *The Dream/Thunder Road*, one of Dawson's three collections of stories. Still, it's a good passage and in its conciseness it catches the mood with a minimum of fuss.

> Well, around 8.30 I was thirsty and the record-player had been going continuously since 5.30 and Red Norvo and Tal Farlow were intertwining, and I thought I'll let this side finish and then get some beer. A few minutes later I walked to the shop and bought four cans of Long Life and as I came out of the shop she was walking towards me. The girl from the corner house. Blonde, and she's always busy in the garden and wears very short skirts and her thighs are firm and her whole body seems to

ripple. But tonight she was dressed to go out, in a long white dress, and her blonde hair piled up and she looked cool and fresh and lovely. I was conscious of my dirty jeans and torn shirt and for a moment wished I was neat and tidy and with her instead of walking home with four cans of beer to an empty house.

"Facts can make you weary," Dawson once remarked when introducing a collection of his stories (*The Sun Rises Into The Sky*), and it's primarily because he steers clear of unnecessary facts that his "factual" books - *The Black Mountain Book* and *An Emotional Memoir Of Franz Kline* - succeed so well. *Black Mountain* doesn't attempt to chronicle the complete history of that institution (it's maybe significant that Martin Duberman's vastly-detailed *Black Mountain: An Exploration In Community* draws only sketchily from Dawson) but is, instead, a *personal* history, with the special insights and gaps that the approach implies. Dawson is honest about what he doesn't know, i.e. he says he isn't sure of something if his experience and memory don't cover the subject in detail, But I get the *feel* of Black Mountain, of what it was like as an *atmosphere*, from the book, whereas a work like Duberman's (useful as it is) fills in the facts but usually doesn't get far beyond them. Likewise, the Kline memoir tells me about the painter as a man, and also creates the atmosphere of the world he moved in:

> "That night Jackson and Franz and de Kooning and Guston and I talked about comic strips. Guston talked about crosshatch, I about wash, and we agreed the line in *Grin and Bear It* was good, and *Napoleon, and Uncle Elby*, I thought George Price's line too static and Franz shut us all up with Krazy Kat. The bar closed and we stood on the sidewalk until dawn drinking from Jackson's fifth of Scotch, and yet I see Philip leaning against the building, face contorted, swallowing, gnashing his teeth and handing the bottle to me."

Maybe that quote - the whole book, in fact - tells us a great deal about Dawson too? You get the idea he was excited about being in such strong company. Excited almost to the point of occasionally making a fool of himself, and when he puts it into writing it can spoil a whole passage of otherwise good prose and even embarrass the reader:

> "The fellow was short, about Franz's size, and around his age, and also like Franz, stocky, with white hair and freckled

handsome face, strong deep crystal blue eyes that were, at that moment, brilliant in friendship.

'Franz!' the fellow cried, in an accent. He looked at me with a smile welcoming me. Franz said,

'Bill, this is the other guy from Black Mountain I told you about - Fee Dawson. Fee, this is Bill de Kooning.'

I was shattered in happiness - de Kooning raised his eyebrows as we shook hands, saying with amazing kindness,

'Well - would you like to come in?'

Now why anyone should get that excited about being asked into someone's home is a little difficult to understand. After all, de Kooning would hardly have turned Dawson away when he was with Kline, who was obviously welcome. And why say "amazing kindness" when it's so unnecessary? Gilbert Sorrentino once said of Dawson, "No critical eye for his work. Drenched with adjectives." And it's true of a fair amount of the early work, and a little of the recent material, though not to the extent of making it unreadable.

But I can find a few faults in Dawson's writing and it still doesn't lessen his appeal in my eyes. He's a writer of (and for) our time, alert to the movement and rhythm of the streets and the bars. He is, in fact, one of the best writers on the bar scene that I can think of, and much more alive to the fact that other people are in the place besides himself than, say, Charles Bukowski, whose bar-room encounters (entertaining as they are) are really only about him. Dawson gets the feel of the places in his stories, and the only other writer I can think of as having the capacity to do this - and it's in a different environment and from a different era - is Patrick Hamilton (try *Hangover Square* if you don't believe me).

I make no apologies for the fact that my appreciation of Fielding Dawson is highly subjective. I *feel* his writing emotionally rather than *analyse* it intellectually. But it should never be forgotten that he's a very intelligent writer, and that if the reader is prepared to extend himself and a good writer *makes* his readers work - the deceptively simple statements can open up his/her eyes to the world around them. I mean the *real* world. Because that's what Dawson, at his best, is writing about. A real world. A world he makes real.

So the four cans of beer are finished and the *California Boppin'*

LP has just ended and it's 11.30 and time for me to iron a shirt for tomorrow. Friday and the weekend ahead. A few drinks and Manchester on Saturday to see what the new records are, and what better for that relaxed Sunday than a Dawson book because writing this article has turned me onto reading them all again.

NOTES

Dawson's main books are the following:

An Emotional Memoir Of Franz Kline (Random House, New York, 1967)

Krazy Kat/The Unveiling & Other Stories (Black Sparrow Press, Los Angeles, 1969)

Open Road (Black Sparrow Press, 1970)

The Black Mountain Book (Croton Press, New York 1970)

The Mandalay Dream (Bobbs Merrill Co., New York, 1971)

The Dream/Thunder Road: Stories & Dreams (Black Sparrow Press, 1972)

The Greatest Story Ever Told: A Transformation (Black Sparrow Press, 1973)

The Sun Rises Into The Sky & Other Stories (Black Sparrow Press, 1973)

A Great Day For A Ballgame (Bobbs Merrill Co. 1973)

There are, in addition, a number of pamphlets, but potential readers should find the publications listed of sufficient interest. It will be seen that Dawson has had nothing published in this country in the way of books, and it strikes me that this is a sad comment on the average British publisher. It should be pointed out that Andrew Crozier's Ferry Press published Dawson's *Thread* some years ago, and a few little magazine editors have been interested enough to make his work available to English readers. I'm happy to be able to say that I used a Dawson story in one issue of my own short-lived magazine, *Move*, in 1965.

Should anyone be interested in reading Dawson's views on writing there is an interview with him in *Falcon 9*, Mansfield State College, Mansfield, USA., Fall 1974. And a major part of *Vort 4* (Silver

Spring, USA., Fall 1973) is given over to an interview with Dawson, plus various articles about him, including one excellent piece by Eric Mottram. I especially recommend this latter item because it frankly offers a deeper, more thoughtful analysis than my own impressionistic response to Dawson's work.

Finally, the Sorrentino comment on Dawson's writing is taken from a brief critical survey of contemporary prose stylists which was published in *The Floating Bear 30*, New York, 1964.

DESTRUCTION WAS MY BEATRICE

"For some, Dada was a mission; for others, it was no more than a convenient tool or weapon for advancing their own artistic ends."

I've quoted those words from Jed Rasula's introduction to his engaging book about the lives and times of the Dadaists because it seems to me essential to bear them in mind when considering what Dada was and how it developed. Any movement, artistic, literary, political, involves people who are attracted to it for a variety of reasons. They come and go, perhaps add something, perhaps take something away. And at some point, the movement shifts and shades into something else. That's what happened with Dada when it met Surrealism in Paris. Of course, some would argue that Dada never was a movement, as such. It might all depend on how you define a movement. Manifestos abounded among the Dadaists, but there wasn't a clearcut programme in terms of what they stood for. What they stood against might be easier to locate. But they were far too independently-minded as individuals to ever fully agree on a set of principles, and even if they had they would most likely have immediately disowned them.

Dada was born in Zurich in 1916. I suppose that's true enough, though qualifiers might need to be added in terms of earlier influences that affected the men and women who gathered at the Cabaret Voltaire in the Swiss capital. Did the Rumanians Tristan Tzara and Marcel Janco, for example, bring with them ideas that originated in the Jewish cafés of Bucharest? What was the effect of encountering Italian Futurism before the First World War? And what was known about Alfred Jarry's work? His play, *Ubu Roi*, which is generally acknowledged as establishing the Theatre of the Absurd, surely provided a basis for at least some of the Dadaist activities. Rasula records that Hans Arp, one of the originators of Dada, was familiar with Jarry and performed scenes from *Ubu Roi* at the Cabaret Voltaire.

The initial driving forces behind the founding of the cabaret were Hugo Ball and Emmy Hennings. They had both left Germany on forged passports after taking part in anti-war protests. Hennings had, in fact been imprisoned for a time. Ball was said to have "a scholastic temperament," but Rasula sums up Hennings in this way:

"The world of the demimonde was more familiar to Hennings, who'd been a chanteuse on every kind of stage, from fashionable showcases to dives – with more of the latter. She'd taken lots of drugs and lived the kind of bohemian life that made her an easy target for charges of prostitution, and she had been arrested several times for petty crimes."

For some months the pair had worked with a travelling variety show (see Ball's entertaining novel, *Flametti, or the Dandyism of the Poor)* with Ball, a competent pianist, providing musical accompaniment ranging from Chopin to popular songs. Back in Zurich, they contacted a retired Dutch sailor who owned a café in the bohemian district of the city. According to Rasula, "Ball pitched his notion of turning the place into an artists' cabaret, and the intrigued owner consented."

It's impossible not to wonder what the sailor thought once the cabaret got into full swing, but initially there didn't seem to be a specified attempt to aim for anything outrageous or likely to offend. Ball's advertisement in a local newspaper simply said: "Young artists of Zurich, whatever their orientation, are invited to come along with suggestions and contributions of all kinds." On opening night, according to Rasula, "a contingent of Russian balalaika players" turned up, as did some locals who wanted to read their poems – "it was like an open mic today" – and more importantly, Tristan Tzara, Marcel Janco, and Hans Arp put in an appearance. They would soon establish a rapport with Ball and Hennings and push the material performed at Cabaret Voltaire towards what we now identify as Dada.

It needs to be stressed that all the major protagonists of the early days of Dada were exiles of one sort or another from the war that was engulfing Europe in 1916. As such, they saw their activities at the cabaret as a form of protest against the madness surrounding them. In particular they pointed to the corruption inherent in the way language was used to promote patriotism. Ball felt that "language itself was being poisoned," and Rasula says that there "would be an aura of ghost dance religion in the nightly goings-on at the cabaret, as an air of exorcism, a ritual cleansing to purify a world mired in senseless slaughter."

Rasula is good at describing what actually took place on cabaret nights. This isn't easy, because unlike present-day performances filmed or recorded evidence doesn't exist. Some photographs were taken and these, together with memoirs by people who were present, have to suffice when it comes to trying to recreate the poetry readings, dances, and other aspects of a Dada evening. Rasula describes Richard Huelsenbeck as reading his poems with "snarling aggression," while "pounding on a drum and brandishing a riding whip or a cane."

What we really don't know is how the majority of the audience reacted to such behaviour. Were they truly shocked? Or did they expect provocation and revel in it when it came? As Rasula says, "The performances ran the gauntlet, from tender ballads to raucous stomping," and as there was an open-stage policy in operation all sorts of performers had an opportunity to show what they could do. Rasula refers to a Russian who read humorous pieces by Chekhov and sang folk tunes, and some students from Holland who pranced round with banjos and mandolins. Emmy Hennings, a key figure in the functioning of the evenings in Rasula's view, was described by a Zurich paper as "the star of the cabaret." There were other singers and some dancers from a nearby dance-school. I think the point to be taken from the range of material on offer is that it was a mixture and not just a sequence of Dada–inspired nonsense or sound poems and absurd sketches.

Ball and Hennings left Zurich after a time and Tristan Tzara soon began to dominate the proceedings. A cabaret was all very well, but if it was to widen its influence Dada needed a magazine and other publications and, if possible, exhibition space. There's an interesting comparison made by Rasula of the differences in character and temperament between Ball and Tzara. Ball was not a careerist, and "he had many interests ranging from politics to mysticism, with Dada tantalisingly dangling midway between the two." Tzara, on the other hand, "felt there was nothing magical about Dada; it was simply a vocational opportunity, one that he tackled with the diligence of an aspiring law clerk." That might seem a somewhat harsh summing up of Tzara, but it is probably a fact that without him and his talent for promotion, both of himself and Dada so that the two often appeared inseparable, the movement might never have become as notorious as it did.

By 1917 the idea of Dada had spread to Berlin, largely thanks to Richard Huelsenbeck, who returned to the city early in 1917. War weariness was beginning to set in as casualty rates mounted, victory seemed far away, and food shortages hit the general public. Huelsenbeck's view of his friends in the arts was that "None of us had much appreciation for the kind of courage it takes to get shot for the idea of a nation which is at best a cartel of pelt merchants and profiteers in leather, at worst a cultural association of psychopaths." Huelsenbeck began to push the notion of the new man, "who transforms the polyhysteria of the age into a genuine understanding of all things and a healthy sensuality." The snag was, as Rasula points out, that the idea of a "new man" could also be taken up by those on the right who saw him as "the pioneer of the storm" and a willing recruit into the ranks of the Freikorp when they smashed left-wing uprisings in the immediate post-war period.

In Berlin some of those associated with Dada, like the artists John Heartfield and George Grosz, were soon also members of the German Communist Party. But others, such as Huelsenbeck and Raoul Hausmann, kept closer to the kind of attitudes evident in Zurich. A manifesto they distributed with the magazine, *Der Dada*, demanded that a Dadaist "simultaneous poem" should be the Communist state prayer, and all clergy and teachers should abide by the Dadaist articles of faith, though what those were wasn't made clear, like so much else about Dada. Rasula tells us that the manifesto was reproduced in newspapers around Germany. Did anyone take it seriously? I somehow doubt it, though the thought of a few solid middle-class citizens huffing and puffing in indignation no doubt amused its authors. But in a country beset with hunger, massive inflation, violence on the streets, and other problems, it probably didn't mean a thing to most people. Dada did, however, attract the attention of those who saw it as being as much of a threat as communism. In time, it would not be safe to have been associated with Dada. So-called Degenerate Art was a favourite target of the Nazis. Grosz and Heartfield eventually had to flee from Germany.

Before moving on from Dada in Germany, where it didn't last long, it's interesting to mention the activities of Kurt Schwitters, a "natural born Dadaist," according to Rasula, in relation to Dada. Based in Hanover, he seems to have run up against a certain amount of snobbish reactions from the Berlin Dadaists who looked on him as provincial and petit-bourgeois. Schwitters ploughed his own furrow, called his work Merz, and had little or no interest in politics, though he too had to leave Germany when Hitler came to power.

While Tzara was still planning to move to Paris, and the Berlin Dadaists were reacting to the harsh social conditions in Germany, there had been some evidence of Dada activity in New York. In fact, it could be argued that there had been things happening in the city which may well have preceded the high jinks in Zurich. Marcel Duchamp had caused a fuss as early as 1913 when his *Nude Descending a Staircase* was included in the famous Armory Show and aroused responses that ranged from the outraged to the satirical. Later, Duchamp made the famous gesture of signing a urinal he bought from a shop and attempting to exhibit it as a ready-made or found object. Arguments are still heard about this, with some claiming that it led to the whole field of conceptual art and a consequent decline in drawing and painting skills.

Picabia also spent time in New York, and Man Ray was there, along with characters like the eccentric Baroness Elsa von Freytag-Loringhoven, the provocative poet Mina Loy, and Arthur Cravan, whose "speciality was insulting artists." Was there a New York Dada? Picabia was of the opinion that "New York is the Cubist, Futurist city; with its architecture, its life, its spirit, it expresses modern thought. You have skipped all the old schools and are Futurists in word, action and thought." The Dadaists might have approved of skipping "all the old schools," their manifestos often demanding the overthrow of the old, but there is something positive about Picabia's comments that they probably wouldn't have approved of, their own approach being essentially based on negativity. Destruction was "the characteristic expression of Dada." It might also be worth referring to Man Ray's reflections on whether or not there was Dada in New York: "There was no such thing. You can put me down as having said that. I don't think the Americans could appreciate or enter into the spirit of Dada."

Tzara did eventually make his way to Paris where his arrival was eagerly anticipated by Breton, Soupault, Aragon, and other young writers and activists. Their initial reaction on meeting him was one of slight dismay. The "diminutive and unprepossessing figure" they encountered didn't seem to go along with the man they'd imagined from his publications and letters. But, according to Rasula, Tzara soon convinced them of his talents as a public performer and publicist for Dada. The problem was that there was bound to be an eventual clash between Tzara and Breton, both men nursing a desire to be leader. There is an argument suggesting that Surrealism pre-dates or parallels Dadaism in some ways. The term was coined by Apollinaire in 1917, and Rasula says that "Surrealism was in the air long before it became formalised." Tzara's urge to be seen as head of the Dada movement led to him falling out with Picabia, with who he'd initially established friendly relations, Breton, and several more. Hans Arp called him Tzar Tristan, and another old companion from Zurich, Hans Richter, described him as "sensitive and aggressive, a magician with the alacrity of a weasel, arousing trust and suspicion" at one and the same time.

There were Dada demonstrations and performances in Paris, some of which were greeted with the usual rowdy responses, much to the delight of the Dadaists, and others which fell flat. Also, "The Dadaists were getting restless, a bit bored with Dada." Matters between Tzara and Breton came to a head when Tzara issued a statement saying, "Modernism is of no interest to me, and I think that it would be a mistake to say that Dadaism, cubism, and futurism rest on a common foundation. These latter two tendencies were based on the idea of intellectual or technical perfection above all, whereas Dada has never rested on any theory and has never been anything but a protest." Breton reacted angrily, and put out his own press release which insultingly referred to Tzara as promoter of a "movement" from Zurich which "no longer corresponds to any reality."

Rasula rightly points out that "The Dadaists themselves were inconsistent practitioners of their own ism," so they never really amounted to a movement. Dada did spread to individuals and small groups in other countries, though it made little headway in Russia and Poland, partly because Futurism had preceded it and "presaged many of the characteristics associated with Dada," but also because politics got in the way of attempts to advance Dada ideas. It's difficult to imagine Dada antics getting much of a friendly reaction in Russia once the Bolsheviks were in power. There were far more important things to attend to than listening to poets chanting meaningless phrases and insulting the audience. Avant-garde art and literature appeared to be a part of the process in the early days of the revolution, but it soon became obvious that artists and writers were expected to use their work to further the interests of the Party.

Interestingly, Tzara did join the Communist Party in the 1930s, causing Hans Arp to comment: "Some old friends from the days of the Dada campaign, who always fought for dreams and freedom are now disgustingly preoccupied with class-aims and busy making over the Hegelian dialectic into a hurdy-gurdy tune." Later, the old acquaintances of the Dada days in Zurich would bicker about who first came up with Dada as a name for their group. When the American artist, Robert Motherwell compiled his large book, *The Dada Painters and Poets,* in 1950, he had to contend with Tzara and Huelsenbeck each threatening to withdraw their contribution if the other was involved. What Hugo Ball, who had died many years earlier, would have made of such childish behaviour can only be imagined.

Jed Rasula has written a lively, detailed history of Dada which also includes much useful information about other movements, such as Futurism, Surrealism, and Constructivism. He refer to numerous individuals and publications, and generally succeeds in re-creating some of the sense of excitement, and fun, that the Dadaists experienced during their brief moment in the limelight. Did they have a long-lasting effect? Rasula thinks they did and refers to various artists, pop musicians, and others who he suggests display elements of Dadaism in their work. It's worth quoting some of what he says:

"Dada's recognition of the inherent artistic potential of rubbish and clutter, wreckage and chaos has had an enduring impact on subsequent artwork in every medium. As the twentieth century wore on, the iconoclastic animation of Dada would make it a vital source of inspiration for artists of all stripes. Far from being strictly a medium of destruction, Dada proved itself capable of being an inspiration, a progressive force."

Some critics will inevitably disagree vehemently with Rasula's opinions, and there's no doubt that an awful lot of mediocre and frankly bad work has been created by those who are believed to have taken Dada as their guiding light. Rasula isn't blind to this fact, and commenting on a claim by Greil Marcus that punk rock had a "Dada paternity," he asks, "but is every seething, indignant amateur a latent Dadaist? Can any sort of dissidence be tallied up on the balance sheet of Dada?" These are relevant questions and Rasula is right to ask them.

DESTRUCTION WAS MY BEATRICE: DADA AND THE
UNMAKING OF THE TWENTIETH CENTURY By Jed Rasula Basic
Books. 365 pages. £19.99/$29.99. ISBN 978-0-465-08996-3

TRISTAN TZARA

It's probably true to say that if the name of Tristan Tzara is known to British readers it will be most probably be because of his links to the Dadaist activity in Zurich and Paris between 1916 and 1923. He played a key part in events in both cities, but after 1923, when Dada more or less disappeared from view, and its role as an influential and controversial movement was taken over by the surrealists, Tzara tended to be pushed into a less-prominent position in the international avant-garde. He certainly didn't completely slide into obscurity and he continued to write. But I doubt that even the most enthusiastic of his advocates would want to claim any sort of fame, or notoriety, for him following the heady days of Dadaist provocation.

Tzara was born Samuel Rosenstock in Romania 1896. There appears to have been some confusion over the years regarding both his name and date of birth, a confusion that was never clarified by Tzara himself who, in Marius Hentea's words, "kept a mysterious aura about his origins." Hentea goes on to say: "If one fact is central to Tzara's childhood, it is being born Jewish." Very few Jews in Romania were classed as citizens, a fact which may have influenced his later feelings about taking pride in being stateless. Anti-Semitism was rife in Romania among both peasants and intellectuals, and after boarding school Tzara moved to Bucharest, a city that had some of the trappings of modernity alongside traditional habits and customs. It was in Bucharest that he came into contact with various young poets and artists, including Marcel Janco who later accompanied him when he arrived in Zurich. Tzara began to publish poems in some of the little magazines of the day. And he sampled the vibrant café life of Bucharest.

What was significant about Bucharest was that the French influence in cultural matters was strong. Hentea quotes one Romanian philosopher and literary critic as saying that Romania was "intellectually nothing but a province of French geography." Not everyone was happy about this state of affairs, though, and there were riots resulting from the staging of three French plays at the Romanian National Theatre. Tzara was firmly in the camp that welcomed French ideas and his poems showed that he had read Rimbaud and others. But it wasn't easy being a Jewish poet, with a liking for things French, at a time when certain critics talked about "today's Parisian insanities," and the word "foreigner" was a coded way of referring to a Jew.

When Romania seemed likely to be drawn into the First World War in

1915 Tzara was sent to Zurich to avoid being conscripted and so he could re-start his university studies, his student career at Bucharest having been disrupted by disputes with the academic authorities. The Swiss city was "an intellectual and cosmopolitan hotbed," largely thanks to the war having forced many artists and writers into exile there. James Joyce had arrived in 1915 and was busy with *Ulysses* and Lenin was busy plotting the overthrow of the Russian government. But neither Joyce nor Lenin appeared to have attracted much attention, certainly not as much as the Dadaists at the Cabaret Voltaire once they got up to their tricks.

Tzara's friend, Marcel Janco, was already in Zurich and introduced him to various artists who he met in cafes and a second-hand bookshop they frequented. But he later recalled that his first few months in Zurich were difficult and that "Boredom, with its painful varieties of melancholy, invaded." His academic record in Bucharest wasn't good enough for him to be able to enrol at the university in Zurich. He was, therefore, at something of a loose end until Janco, in February, 1916, took him to the Cabaret Voltaire. An advertisement had appeared in a local paper a few days previously saying that it was to be "a centre for artistic entertainment and intellectual exchange," and that young artists in Zurich were "invited to bring along their ideas and contributions." Tzara took some of his poems with him which were later described by Hugo Ball as "traditional-style," though they perhaps didn't seem all that out-of-place in a programme that included music by Saint-Saens and Rachmaninov. The "great matadors of the Dada movement," as Hans Arp described them, hadn't yet started to pool their talents to turn the Cabaret Voltaire into a location for artistic mayhem.

Hentea's book is a biography of Tristan Tzara, but he includes biographical sketches of many of the people that Tzara encountered, and Hugo Ball had as varied, and some would say chaotic life, as any in the ranks of the Dadaists and surrealists. He started as an apprentice in the shoe trade, had a breakdown when he was eighteen, studied philosophy and art in Munich and Heidelberg, joined Max Reinhardt's drama school in Berlin, worked in theatres in Munich and Plauen, launched a little magazine which the police confiscated as being subversive (according to Hentea the judge at Ball's trial said that the poems didn't make sense so couldn't be subversive), and promoted Futurist, Expressionist, and Cubist art. When the war started he moved to Switzerland with his companion, Emmy Hennings, "a cabaret performer, convicted thief, published poet, morphine addict, and registered prostitute." Ball eventually parted company with Dada. I recently read a translation of his

1918 novel *Flametti or the Dandyism of the Poor,* an account of the ups and downs of a travelling theatrical outfit. It isn't Dada, but it is thoroughly entertaining.

Once Tzara got involved with events at the Cabaret Voltaire he "did everything possible to make himself indispensable. He performed on stage, recited poetry, selected material for the evening programmes, and also displayed a reservoir of organisational skills." It may seem that every night was built around the kind of chaos associated with Dada, but Hentea points out that Tzara read poems by Verlaine, Mallarme, and Apollinaire, and that the star of the show was often Emmy Hennings who sang songs that the audience liked. It's true that some performances did involve nonsense poetry and members of the group in outlandish costumes, but I have the feeling that there may be a difference between what happened and what we like to think happened. The Cabaret Voltaire "became a meeting place of the arts. Painters, students, revolutionaries, tourists, international crooks, psychiatrists, the demimonde, sculptors, and police spies on the lookout for information." But Hentea adds that on some nights there were only a handful of people in the audience, and the Zurich police imposed a strict curfew which meant that bars had to be closed by ten o'clock. Performances had to start early. The local press doesn't seem to have taken a great deal of notice of what was happening at the Cabaret Voltaire. Its impact was to be felt later when reports of what had taken place in Zurich began to reach France, Italy, and other countries. And a kind of mythologizing about the Cabaret Voltaire started to develop.

It's stressed that "the desire to make overt political statements" was always affected by the police keeping a close watch on what happened among the Dadaists. And the fact that all the Dadaists were foreigners, and so liable to be deported if they broke local laws, helped to keep the lid on their activities. Hugo Ball was in Switzerland on false papers, and Tzara was ostensibly there as a student but wasn't actually a citizen of any country. It could be argued that the real political activity was, in any case, taking place not far from the Cabaret Voltaire where Lenin sat formulating plans for the Bolshevik take-over of Russia.

It would seem that the word "Dada" first appeared in print in Hugo Ball's editorial in *Cabaret Voltaire*, a publication designed to promote the movement. Hentea says that no-one has yet managed to come up with a convincing explanation of its origin. Arguments started as early as 1920 when Kurt Schwitters said that Richard Huelsenbeck was not a true Dadaist and that the description belonged really to Tzara and Hans Arp. Not much later, Christian Schad stated: "I was in Zurich at the time of Dada. Tzara has usurped his title of founder of Dada. He is not the inventor of the word." Tzara then asked Hans Arp to testify that he (Tzara) had first used the word. Arp duly came up with what Hentea rightly refers to as a "mock deposition" to that effect. And so it went on, with claims and counter-claims. In 1936 Richard Huelsenbeck stated that he got "dada" from a German-French dictionary, "dada" being the French for rocking-horse. Hentea points out that there was a hair elixir marketed in Switzerland under the name of Dada. He also stresses that the question of "use" of Dada as a name for the movement was more important than who hit on it. Huelsenbeck took it back to Berlin with him, but Tzara's "postal internationalisation" of it was probably more important in terms of reaching out to a wider audience and allowing individuals to "do with Dada whatever they wished, which was the modus operandi of the original Dada participants."

The Cabaret Voltaire eventually closed, but Tzara, still based in Zurich, was in touch with André Breton and others in Paris and would soon move there as the city, following the end of the First World War, began to regain its place as the centre of artistic avant-garde activity. Most of the original Dadaists had left Zurich for various reasons, and Tzara realised that if the movement was to continue it needed a new impetus. As Hentea puts it: "Tzara also knew that to truly internationalise Dada, Paris had to be conquered; its judgement was, as it had ever been, final."

What happened in Paris once Tzara arrived and met with Breton, Aragon, Eluard, and Soupault is documented by Hentea, and anyone wanting even more information can be usefully referred to Michel Sanouillet's *Dada in Paris* (MIT Press, 2009. See my review in *Northern Review of Books,* October, 2012). There were readings which turned into near-riots, publications, and the inevitable arguments among the participants, with Breton seemingly determined to take over Dada and shape it to his own tastes, which were what came to be known as surrealism. Tzara was increasingly pushed to the sidelines of most of the activity that took place in Paris. There were differences of temperament, as well as of policy. Hentea quotes a significant statement by Picabia when he announced his decision to break from Dada: "Dada, you see, was not serious, and it is for that reason that, like a trail of gunpowder, it reached the world; if some people now do take it seriously, it is because it is dead!" Picabia and Tzara had fallen out, but the latter must have realised that Picabia perhaps had a point and the influence of Dada in artistic circles was fading. Tzara himself continued to attract publicity for his personal behaviour, but it's doubtful if he had much influence on many other writers and artists. Some commentators might point to the article, "Some Memoirs of Dadaism," which he wrote for the fashionable magazine, *Vanity Fair,* as evidence that he was aware that Dada's role as a functioning movement was coming to an end. When, a little later, Tzara published *Sept Manifestes Dada,* critics indicated that the most recent manifesto was four years old. And they declared that the fact of the book being a de-luxe limited edition was even more evidence that Dada "had become a collectible museum piece."

By 1927 Tzara was conscious of his "increasing literary isolation," and he was critical of the way in which the surrealists were identifying with communism, "a bourgeois form of revolution" which would lead to "bureaucracy, hierarchy," and ultimately respectability. Tzara said that "Right now I continue to write for myself and unable to find other men, I keep searching for myself." I suppose there may be some ironies involved in the fact that Tzara was eventually accepted back into the surrealist group and later (post-1945) joined the French Communist Party. Breton was of the opinion that Tzara's desire to be part of the surrealists again was "strategically motivated." And other people referred tellingly to his *Manifeste Dada 1918* to point out that there was "an irresolvable contradiction between his former positions and his current fidelity to surrealism." Tzara's uneasy relationship to surrealism came to a head in 1935 when he was again expelled from the movement. Hentea provides a full account of what led up to Tzara's expulsion and it makes for fascinating reading even if, at times, one tends to despair at the way in which intellectuals and writers preen and posture while in the wider world major events are taking place.

Tzara became increasingly involved with the Communist Party and was in Spain for a time when the Civil War started in 1936. In 1937 he was one of the organisers of the Second International Congress of Writers in the Defence of Culture. There's no doubt that the Communist Party played a major part in what could be said by speakers at the Congress and Hentea quotes a *Pravda* editor who gave a speech in which he justified the purges being carried out in Russia. Hentea says that Tzara didn't go that far but "nonetheless agreed that liberty of expression could no longer be absolute given the greater goals of revolutionising society and sweeping away `centuries of oppression.' " To be fair to him he was not alone in the 1930s in moving away from a previous position of pacifism, liberal ideas of personal freedom, and detachment from extreme politics, to one of commitment. Hentea sums up his situation in this way: "In a world where saving one's skin no longer made sense because the problems of the times spared no one, the need for communal action was, in his view, indisputable. Tzara had the honesty to admit the individual cost that this would entail, yet a horrible moral algebra infuses his address."

When the Second World War started in 1939 and France fell to the Germans, Tzara as a Jew was clearly at risk. He moved to the south of country, which was initially controlled by Vichy, and managed to survive one way or another, even though he was at one point identified in a collaborationist publication edited by Robert Brassillach. He returned to Paris in 1945, associated with French communists like Louis Aragon and Paul Eluard, and attacked surrealism on the grounds that many of its leading lights had escaped abroad during the war, and the movement had consequently lost any kind of moral authority it might have gained had it played a part in the Resistance. Hentea ascribes his disillusionment with surrealism to his close ties with the Communist Party and his disappointment with André Breton.

When Robert Motherwell was preparing his ground-breaking anthology, *The Dada Painters and Poets*, published in 1951, he found that Tzara, along with other Dadaists, was keen to make sure they had a place in the history of the movement. Tzara initially wrote an introduction for the book which, according to Hentea, managed to avoid mentioning the Cabaret Voltaire, Hugo Ball, Richard Huelsenbeck, and several more who had been an integral part of Dada's early days. Huelsenbeck, for his part, wrote a manifesto which contained a note saying that, "for reasons of historical accuracy," it was necessary to point out that Tzara had not founded Dadaism. Tzara threatened to withdraw his introduction if Huelsenbeck's piece was in the anthology, and Huelsenbeck said he'd refuse to let other work by him be used if the manifesto wasn't included. In the end both pieces were dropped by Motherwell. It's intriguing to see how old friendships broke down as people competed for their places in history.

Tzara had continued to write poems whatever else had happened to him, and Hentea offers some useful analyses of them, especially as they were only published in small print runs and aroused no more than minor interest. I have to admit to having read little of Tzara's poetry, other than a few things in anthologies, though I recall that the English poet Lee Harwood published some translations in small presses many years ago and I must have seen those at the time. Tzara fell out with the French Communist Party over its interpretation of events surrounding the Budapest uprising in 1956 and this led to old friends refusing to speak to him and his being blacklisted by certain publications.

In his later years Tzara lived a quiet life away from any sort of spotlight. Hentea says that "he began an exhaustive study of anagrams in literature, starting with Francois Villon and then moving on to other writers of the twelfth to the sixteenth centuries, such as Dante and Rabelais." He didn't completely withdraw from other activities and Hentea mentions a ten-day conference, The First International Congress of African Culture, in Salisbury, Rhodesia. Tzara was there because he was an acknowledged expert "on the relationship between traditional African art and contemporary practice." When he returned to Paris he spent his days researching in the Bibliotheque Nationale, and his evenings at the Café de Flore with old friends. He was diagnosed with advanced-stage lung cancer, and died on the 24th December, 1963. He was buried at Père Lachaise. Hentea notes that the funeral was a "simple affair, but it could not escape the controversy that distinguished his life. Isidore Isou and his Lettrist friends planned a celebration of Tzara's work against the communist faithful who were now claiming his memory." The two sides exchanged insults over the grave.

How important was Tristan Tzara? He clearly played a key role in the birth of Dada in Zurich and for a time he was involved in events in Paris, though he was pushed into a minor position as André Breton and the surrealists came to the fore. Marius Hentea works hard to make a case for Tzara as a major player in avant-garde circles, and his account is convincing, at least to the point in the mid-1920s when he broke with the surrealists. After that he perhaps didn't appear to be relevant as he had once been, even though he lived through events such as the Spanish Civil War, the collapse of France, the years of occupation, the post-war years and the 1950s and communist activities. The story of how he escaped being rounded up with other Jews and sent to a concentration camp is fascinating in itself, and certainly needs to be documented as part of his life. And the post-war years are of interest for their portrayal of the twists and turns of French communism, and for Breton's attempts to revive the fortunes of the flagging surrealist group. But it's hard to get rid of the thought that had it not been for Dada we would know little or nothing about Tristan Tzara.

Marius Hentea has gone into a great deal of detail to tell Tzara's story and his book is well-researched (there are fifty pages of notes) and is a mine of information about Dada and surrealist events, little magazines, small-presses, and a variety of ephemeral publications It's always readable, too, and avoids academic jargon.

TA TA DADA : THE REAL LIFE AND CELESTIAL ADVENTURES OF TRISTAN TZARA

By Marius Hentea The MIT Press. 356 pages. £24.95. ISBN 978-0-262-02754-0

The Breaking of the Apron Strings

they cannot see you
as you are
how you've become
as you would wish
for them to see

a young lady
of eighteen, tall
and pretty and
very much a person
on her own

try as you will
she will not hear
does not want to
hear you
she is still your mother
you are
her baby

what is worse
is little sister
standing in the middle

watching all that's happening
not knowing
where her heart lies

that is the saddest part
of the scene
I play tonight.

That poem was not one of Joan Gilbert's best - as far as I know it did not appear in a magazine during the brief period when her work was being published - but it does neatly sum up one of the basic conflicts which preoccupied her. She was, at one and the same time, anxious to make her own way in the world and still maintain a close relationship with her family. I don't want to discuss her personal life in any great detail, but with poetry such as she wrote it is impossible to separate her actions and intentions from her writing; the latter was often an attempt to work out the reasons for the former, or at least to express them in a way which, I think, she thought would help her to clarify them. This could have resulted in a mere therapeutic exercise, of course, but in her case a genuine love of poetry, and a flair (it's necessary to be perfectly objective about this - her talents unfortunately never had a chance to develop fully) for its craft, ensured that what she put on paper came out as tiny fragments of art.

My own initial contact with Joan Gilbert was in late 1964, or early 1965, when I was gathering material for a little magazine which I was then publishing. She wrote from Buffalo in the U.S.A., and we started a regular correspondence (I never did actually meet her) which continued until shortly before her death. A few of her poems arrived, and the best of them had a freshness, and a lyricism, which I found attractive. She was very much of her generation, in many ways, and I don't think she ever denied this fact. Her taste for pop-music interested me, because it was perfectly natural and not an intellectual pose; she had grown up with the music, and enjoyed it, and she saw no reason why she should pretend different. The poems would sometimes quote from pop-songs (the title of one was "Eight Days A Week", the same as the Beatles recording), and she frequently referred to pop-music, and groups, in her letters. What is more important, though, is that she had taken something from pop-music in terms of its occasional (at its best) laconic manner of stating a situation. Her poem "What To Do" is a good example:

> what to do
> when he calls
>
> the feeling you once had
> is gone
> and there is nothing to say
> anymore

you wish there were
words, but what use
would they be

he is lying there
waiting, you know

the phone rings, you answer,
he says, "hello"

the silence is un
                    easy

It always seemed to me that if poets had to turn to pop-music for their inspiration then the kind of poetry Joan Gilbert wrote, as opposed to that we get from English 'pop-poets', was to be encouraged.

I don't want to give the impression that she was a 'pop-poet'; her interest in pop-music was just a part of her life, which is why it was so easy to understand. In some of her poems she attempted to say something about her reactions to her environment in a broad sense. She wanted to get at this, as her letters attest, but most of her early work is in a personal vein and deals with her love-affair with a young English poet, her family, and her friends. And she could deal with these subjects in a good-humoured, and astute, manner:

place two poets
under the same roof

let them share the
 same bed

listen to the same
sounds
the house makes

see the snow fall
from the same window,
> how it falls! all winter
> and disappears with spring

eat their food
in the same stuffy kitchen
and complain
of too much spaghetti
and meatballs
39¢ a lb. chopped meat

daffodils bloom
on their table

and don't get too much upset
if what they choose to write
sounds strangely
> similar.

The humour in that appears to me to be ironic, rather than bitter. There was, however, a note of sadness—I would say despair, but it sounds a little too dramatic, and the poems were usually too tightly controlled to give rein to histrionics—in some of her work, almost as if she knew that things wouldn't work out. She once remarked, in a letter, 'American kids have the tendency to mess themselves up very young', and I thought it a precocious statement, but also a surprising one because of the knowing tone (I'm judging from the whole of the letter) in which she said it. She had an honest appreciation of her own position.

The poems which dealt with her environment were invariably good ones. They referred to the physical, but implied deeper things:

From my window
I can see
houses

and beyond that

houses
juxtaposed

then cut off by sky
which is more often
grey
than any other colour

But in New York
I see people
upon others

against a land
more vertical than Buffalo's

and there are
people
lending colour
to the city.

When she spent some time in England she was often involved with
the differences - in the physical sense, and from the point of view of
the way of life and attitudes - between this country and America. She
once asked me if the North had plenty of 'wide open spaces', and
when I wrote back to say that I wasn't quite sure what she meant by
that term she clarified it with a poem:

No room to grow
nor can my mind
move beyond its
limitations

crowding every mile
leaving me alone, here

where it dips
and mountains inland
hills into plain

from Bristol catching
a lorry to London (another land

before me,
        laps of road
fenced on either side
thinking about that "long

tall Texan"
        "Marlboro-Country",
Gary Cooper's
West, I never saw

Sometimes, too, that ironic sense of humour would come through, as in the poem, 'Homage To Gilbert & Sullivan':

He is an Englishman
though that be
part Norse
his forehead and
nose

part French (from his mother's lineage)
even Scot
tartan of the Morrisons
and god-knows-what else!
(the pedigree of the mongrel, this one
he should arf
        arf
with a London accent
to be sure

When she returned to the U.S.A. she got more involved with the 'scene' and its attendant attractions. Our correspondence became spasmodic, and I don't think she wrote very much poetry in this period. I could be wrong about this, but as late as January, 1967, she published a poem in the Detroit paper *Guerilla*, which dated back to 1965, and her stay in England. The poem was called 'J.S. Bach', and is one of her best. The last few lines are particularly moving:

>   this is
> such an old country,
> listening to the Atlantic
> how well the sound travels
> from the west
> between us.

There is a beautifully lyrical poem (untitled, but published in *Move/3* and *Work/1*) which self-mockingly deals with the loss of virtue, and another one which makes a good comparison to it in that it refers to a far more disturbing - and eventually disastrous - loss of innocence. This latter poem - 'Heroin' - ends on a note of despair, and in its own small way is the tragic description of what Joan Gilbert's search for independence and experience had led her to. It's easy to be angry about this - my own feelings (both about Joan Gilbert and the way of life with which the poem deals) are strong enough to destroy my sense of objectivity—but the poem speaks for itself in a moving manner:

> some Spanish song
> sounds thru Huncke's window
>
> opposite the window
> I watch
>
> it does not matter
> where I am
> only that she sings
>
> a television set plays
> across the way
>
> children play games
> cursing loudly in Spanish
>
> keep singing sweet mother

It sounds so good
and I wish I could sing

at least cry
or leave this city
before I am slave to it

Joan Gilbert's poems were not perfect, but they had warmth and sometimes humour, and the best of them stay in one's mind. For someone so young she had a remarkable grasp of her own position in the world, and I occasionally wonder if this self-knowledge had its destructive aspect; it seemed to spur her on in the search for 'experience' (as if it was something which can be divorced from everyday life). It's possible to talk about her potential, and what might have been, but that doesn't help us to appreciate what she actually produced. Better to read the handful of poems she wrote, and understand what a sensitive young girl felt and thought.

TWO AMERICAN POETS

There is, in Edward Field's engaging memoir of New York literary life, *The Man Who Would Marry Susan Sontag*, an affectionate portrait of Richard Howard. Field describes visiting Howard's apartment where, he notes, "only the ceiling and the floor were not covered with books." And he says of Howard's poetry that its demands, "with its elaborate structure and language are relieved by his use of narrative and his dramatic sense somewhat in the High Victorian, Robert Browning mode."

Field neatly captures at least some of Howard's qualities and adds that he's "literary to the core." And reading through this splendid selected poems it struck me that some people could find the experience a little taxing. It assumes a knowledge of literary, artistic, and social history. There is, for example, a poem called 'Decades,' dedicated to Hart Crane, in which the following lines (referring to Crane's suicide) occur:

that April something, nineteen thirty-two,
when Wheelwright said you turned to Fish Food (he
turned it to advantage in the very first
of all your elegies, asking final questions:
what did you see as you fell, what did you hear
as you sank?)

Now how many readers, some academics apart, will recognise the reference to a 1930's poem by an almost-forgotten poet, John Wheelwright, who often mixed modernist techniques and Trotskyist politics? Very few, I'd guess. Howard even uses a line from Wheelwright's poem. I'm sometimes a little sceptical of poets who load their work with such references, but Howard has an appealing way of doing it, perhaps because his poems roll along easily so that the general meaning is obvious even if some of the specifics require more attention.

Elsewhere, Howard constructs a wonderful sequence based on the portraits taken by the famous 19th Century French photographer, Nadar, of celebrities like Wagner, Baudelaire, George Sand, and Victor Hugo. Is it necessary to have seen the photos to appreciate the poems? It helps, of course, but I don't think it's essential, and in any case if the poems push the reader into seeking out the portraits then

Howard has done what Harold Bloom suggests he does: "instructs by delighting, and delights by instructing."

I could carry on mentioning the many fine things to be found in this book (not all of them necessarily requiring an awareness of the writers and others Howard frequently names) and I'd still only touch on a small portion of it. But I'd like to mention one poem, a relatively short one, which particularly delighted me. I recently had a trip to York to see a small, but first-rate exhibition of paintings by the 19th Century artist, Henri Fantin-Latour. He's now mostly remembered for his brilliant paintings of flowers, though at the time he produced them he saw them mostly as a means of supporting his family. He had aspirations to produce more "significant" work, but the examples I saw seemed quite dull and mediocre. So, it amused me that Richard Howard appears to come to the same conclusion in his poem. The flower paintings, he says, were "wholly unjustified/ by any important theme or scheme," but they've lasted.

Inner Voices covers forty years of Richard Howard's intelligent, well-constructed poetry and is recommended to anyone with a liking for work that invites the reader to share in the pleasure that the poet clearly took in writing it.

A selection of Philip Levine's poems was published in this country in the early 1980s, but I recall that it didn't attract many reviews. And my own experiences over the years of mentioning his name to people who supposedly keep up with contemporary poetry have been that very few of them know his work. For myself, I have to say that I've been reading him since the 1960s and I've bought his books as they've appeared in American editions. If asked to name one poet whose work I admire his would immediately come to mind.

I have to admit, too, that my liking for Levine's poetry is based very much on an emotional response before an intellectual one. I admire his style and technique but it is often the subject-matter of the poems that initially attracts me. I'd like to quote the opening lines of 'To Cipriano, in the Wind,' a poem that, as with others by Levine, looks back to an America (and the world generally) of the Thirties and Forties when there was, despite all the problems that existed, perhaps a little more optimism around:

Where did your words go,
Cipriano, spoken to me 38 years

ago in the back of Peerless Cleaners,
where raised on a little wooden platform
you bowed to the hissing press
and under the flaring bulb the scars
across your- shoulders - "a gift
of my country"-gleamed like old wood.
"Dignidad," you said into my boy's
wide eyes, "without is no riches."

What Levine does as the poem progresses is build up the intensity, mixing in personal memories and larger issues (the Second World War), and though he doesn't specifically refer to politics, working around the theme of 'dignity' and remembering his boyhood dreams that 'someday this will all be ours.' The poem ends when he begs Cipriano to come back to tell him again that 'this world will all be ours.' Levine's political leanings will be obvious from what is said, though he nowhere waves a flag to indicate them. It's the anguish of both political and personal loss. But the anguish at lost hopes is pitched at a passionate level.

Perhaps not surprisingly the Spanish Civil War seems to have had a major impact on Levine, despite the fact that he was only eight when it started in 1936. One of his books, *7 Years from Somewhere*, has a front-cover photo of the grave of a Spanish anarchist, and another, *The Names of the Lost*, a photo of the remnants of the Spanish Republican Army marching into exile in France. Levine begins 'Francisco, I'll bring you Red Carnations' with the following lines:

Here in the great cemetery
behind the fortress of Barcelona
I have come once more to see
the graves of my fallen.
Two ancient picnicers direct
us down the hill. "Durruti,"
says the man, "I was on
his side." The woman hushes
him.

The poem continues, effortlessly but powerfully, each line breaking naturally, with the final word pushing the impetus forward onto the first word of the next line. There are few adjectives but the picture is vivid: 'The poor packed in tenenments/ a dozen high; the rich/ in splendid homes or temples.' Levine doesn't pretend to be a detached observer carefully keeping his distance from the people and events he writes about. He's there, with them and in them, so the reader isn't offered the clever ambiguities of the smart literary writer, though the poems never provide glib solutions to complex problems. Levine is a man puzzled yet fascinated by life.

One of the criticisms I've seen of his work is that each poem tends to be built around an anecdote followed by a rush of emotion. And it may be that there is some truth in that suggestion. But the quality of the anecdotes (the interest they arouse) and the level of the emotions are surely what enable the poems to succeed. Levine does what any writer, poet or whatever, does. He involves the reader right from the start, telling a story and, finally, bringing it to a conclusion with what is, in effect, a kind of summing up. A rush of emotion? Why not when the story has created a powerful effect?

I have a feeling that Philip Levine's poems may never become well known in Britain, and that their emotional intensity may almost embarrass some readers, while the free-flowing technique may make them uneasy. It appears that the poems are loosely structured, though in fact they're carefully constructed for maximum effect. It may look easy to write like Levine -letting it all hang out, it seems - but try it and you'll find that it isn't. But I urge you to look at his work. There are not all that many poets around who can touch the heart in a way that makes you think that Auden was wrong and that poetry can change things.

Stranger to Nothing Philip Levine (Bloodaxe 2006)

Inner Voices Richard Howard (Carcanet 2007)

EDDIE LINDEN

I once saw Eddie Linden plain, I've also seen him blurred, our paths usually crossing at various poetry readings, conferences, and festivals, where the booze flows freely, and the bar is always full of agitated poets, academics, critics, editors, and their assorted friends, lovers, wives, husbands, and what have you. Such events usually produce at least one Eddie Linden story, even if it does only filter through months later and probably isn't quite accurate. I mean, was he really in danger of falling from the balcony at the Cambridge Poetry Festival a couple of years ago? Well, I was there myself, and didn't see it, but someone did say that so-and-so had told him that...

And although I've often met Linden I've always been aware that the real man behind the literary personality didn't easily come through. I can recall conversations during which he mentioned (no doubt because of some common characteristics in our backgrounds) his working-class upbringing, time spent in factories, lack of university experience, and such matters. But I've never had a clear picture of the man in the sense of understanding what took him to London, and eventually into the world of poetry and little magazines. *Who is Eddie Linden* helps clarify things.

It is written in a curious style because what Sebastian Barker has done is talk to Linden and his friends, and then re-create his life in an autobiographical manner, despite the book being called a biography. But it isn't a "ghosted" autobiography, but rather an attempt by one man to get inside the mind of another and think his way. One problem that does occur with this approach is that of how close to Linden's actual speech patterns the book is. It doesn't sound to me like the man talking — though Barker will clearly have more experience of him than I have — and, in fact, the book occasionally veers dangerously close to reading (sounding) like a slightly-dated novel. This is especially true of some of the dialogue passages.

That may be a minor quibble, I agree, and the main interest obviously lies in what it tells us about Linden. And insofar as the early years of his life are concerned it tells us quite a lot. Born in Scotland out of a quick union between an Irish couple he was adopted and grew up as a member of a Scottish miner's family. Experiences with an unsympathetic stepmother followed, then a

Sisters of Charity Orphanage, lousy jobs at the pithead, in a lamp shop, a steelworks, and on the railways, and eventually a move to London, where he discovered homosexuality, Soho, and the New Left.

But whatever his larger involvements his personal hang-ups — those resulting from being a working-class, Catholic homosexual — always got in the way. He struggled to resolve the clash caused by being both a Catholic and a Communist, and also being a homosexual whose whole social background condemned such activities. In many ways, his journey through the New Left, C.N.D., occasional journalism, a scholarship to Plater Hall, and the rest, was a personal exploration for meaning and purpose, which isn't to say that Linden didn't work sincerely for the causes he was involved with. But it took an introduction to the society of poets and poetry in the early Sixties to seemingly focus his thoughts. He ran readings, mixed with various poets — John Heath-Stubbs is particularly mentioned — and launched *Aquarius*, the magazine he's amazingly kept alive despite what Peter Porter calls 'indifference and starvation by the world and its authorities.' I would guess it's the Linden poetry years that most of the people likely to read this review, and the book it deals with, will be familiar with. Unfortunately, *Who is Eddie Linden* doesn't delve very far into those years, or Linden's view of them.

Still, it's a lively and informative book, and it does help fill in some details of the life of a man who, whatever his faults, at least tries to operate outside the area occupied by those whose sole purpose in life seems to be to make poetry safe for schoolteachers. There's an independent, and sometimes irreverent air about both Linden and his magazine, and it helps provide a counter-balance to the increasing hordes of play-it-safe types. Keep at it, Eddie, and never let the bastards grind you down.

WHO IS EDDIE LINDEN? Sebastian Barker. Jay Landesman Ltd.

MALCOLM COWLEY

Malcolm Cowley (1898-1989), poet, editor, essayist, reviewer, made one great mistake in his lifetime, and that was in the 1930s when he continued to support Stalin and asserted his belief that the Moscow Trials provided evidence of the guilt of those charged with conspiracy and other alleged crimes. At a time when many writers and intellectuals were backing away from support for the Communist Party, Cowley, though never a member, was a faithful fellow-traveller. He later came to the conclusion that he had been wrong, but by then the damage had been done and his reputation in certain quarters was to suffer for many years. And Cowley himself continued to agonise over his actions (or lack of them) and attempted to explain why he had consistently refused to face up to the fact that the Soviet Union had declined into a dictatorship and that innocent people were being sent to their deaths.

There was, however, far more to Cowley than this failure to face reality which can, perhaps, be explained by looking at the social, economic and political circumstances of the time, and the fact that Cowley, as a literary intellectual, may have had a naïve faith in the intentions of politicians. He had a long and distinguished career as a writer and editor and, despite that early error, deserves to be remembered for it.

Educated at Harvard, Cowley went to France in 1917 and, as a member of the American Field Service (a voluntary organisation), he drove a truck transporting supplies to the front line. Later, he returned to France and was there between 1921 and 1923, so mixed with Hemingway, Robert McAlmon, Mina Loy, Harold Stearns, and others of the expatriate community in Paris. But Cowley didn't just limit his activities to what was, after all, a fairly narrow, though productive, community of largely American writers. He spoke French and got to know Louis Aragon, Tristan Tzara, and the Dadaists, who he admired for their energy and enthusiasm, if not always for their almost-wilful determination to be obscure and contemptuous of any audience they might attract.

This was a period when little magazines flourished, and Cowley was connected, in one way or another, with *Broom* and *Secession. Broom* was edited by Harold Loeb (the basis for the character of Robert Cohn in Hemingway's novel of the Paris expatriates, *The Sun Also*

Rises) and *Secession* by Gorham Munson, and though Cowley was involved with both magazines he seemingly preferred Loeb's approach to editing to that of Munson. Reading the letters in which he writes about Loeb and Munson, it's easy to see how Cowley was acting like many young writers in any period with his mixture of self-interest in wanting to be published and noticed and genuine concern for advancing the cause of new writing generally. Hans Bak says that Cowley's letters (not necessarily all included in the book) show that he was "embroiled in unsavoury and unproductive literary politics," which is true enough, but often fairly typical of what happens among writers. Cowley's *Exile's Return* is a classic account of his years in France, but it can be useful to read Gorham Munson's *The Awakening Twenties* for an alternative view of events surrounding *Broom* and *Secession.*

When Cowley returned to New York he worked briefly for a catalogue service, but then began to freelance full-time as a writer. His poems appeared in magazines like *Poetry* and *The Dial* and his articles and reviews in *The Saturday Review of Literature* and *The New Republic,* among others. His letters refer to not having been so poor since he left college and life being a succession of "financial scrapes." In one letter he tells William Carlos Williams that he has "just borrowed money to pay the rent, after worrying about the subject for two weeks." And he adds that he envies Williams because he has a regular income from his job as a doctor. The letters, and others like them where Cowley is attempting to drum up writing assignments, and sometimes lamenting that he's having to take on hack work that he thinks will stop him writing poems or "essays of any value," will seem familiar to anyone who has wanted to be a freelance writer. It wasn't likely that Cowley would ever make enough money from poetry to survive on that, nor was he cut out to be a successful novelist. The academic world wasn't then as widespread as it later became, so a career there, assuming Cowley wanted one, wasn't on the cards. What he needed was some sort of position which would involve writing, and also enable him to still freelance when he wanted to, and in 1929 he accepted a job as a junior editor at *The New Republic,* This ended his financial worries, and as Hans Bak puts it, would eventually provide him with "an influential platform from which to speak out on the intellectual, literary, and political crosscurrents of the turbulent 1930s." Speaking out wasn't necessarily a total blessing, as noted earlier, but in 1929 it probably seemed a golden opportunity to make a mark in the intellectual world of New York. Cowley's book of poems, *Blue Juniata,* was published in 1929 and was positively reviewed, so he appeared to be at least part way up the ladder of success.

The financial crash of 1929 radicalised many writers, Cowley among them, and by 1932 he was sufficiently close to the Communist Party to support its candidates in the presidential elections, march in the May Day Parade, and visit Kentucky to support striking miners. Cowley had by this time more or less assumed the role of literary editor at *The New Republic,* and was able to recruit contributors who shared his literary and political interests, though he was not dogmatic to the point of excluding writers who had what Bak calls "independent minds." One of these was Nathan Asch, son of the famous Jewish writer, Sholem Asch. Nathan Asch was himself a novelist (*Pay Day*, published in 1930, is a typical novel of the period) and Cowley had known him in Paris. Asch's career didn't prosper and it's to Cowley's credit that he kept in touch with him over the years and encouraged him to write his memoirs. It was Cowley who persuaded the editors of *The Paris Review* to publish Asch's "The Nineteen-Twenties: An Interior," an evocative account of expatriate Paris, in their summer, 1954 issue.

Cowley's *Exile's Return,* his book about the literary generation of the 1920s, was published in 1934 and immediately attracted hostile attention from critics who thought that the activities of writers who had abandoned America to pursue their dreams and write their books abroad were irrelevant. They had none of the special characteristics Cowley claimed for them. In his later memoir, *The Dream of the Golden Mountain: Remembering the 1930s,* he recalled that the reception given his book by the majority of reviewers was a "shattering experience while it lasted." When it was re-issued in 1951 it received much better reviews.

In 1935 Cowley delivered a paper at the First American Writers' Congress, an event largely dominated by the Communist Party. He also involved himself with the League of American Writers, an organisation which included communists and fellow-travellers. He sometimes had his doubts about the extent of communist influence, but thought that all the different parties on the Left ought to act together in opposition to Fascism. The Popular Front line was then in its ascendancy. His activities didn't endear him to everyone, and in

1936 Felix Morrow wrote an article in *New Militant,* a Trotskyite publication, under the heading, "Malcolm Cowley: Portrait of a Stalinist Intellectual." And John Dewey accused Cowley of an obvious anti-Trotskyite policy in the way he ran the literary section of *The New Republic.*

Cowley's political involvements did not stop him publishing new writers in the magazine. John Berryman, Tillie Olson, Josephine Miles, Richard Wright were among them, along with more-established poets like Marianne Moore and Wallace Stevens. He also continued to support, in various ways, writers he admired, such as F. Scott Fitzgerald, whose reputation in the 1930s had slumped, partly because his books no longer appeared regularly, but also because the politics of the time did not consider his subject-matter as relating to problems such as unemployment and the rise of Fascism. Socially-conscious literature was in demand. In a letter written in 1934 he says that he intends to review *Tender is the Night* himself, even though Fitzgerald had asked that it be given to a younger reviewer. Cowley's response was that a younger critic would probably want to know why Fitzgerald wasn't a proletarian novelist, and he preferred to avoid that situation. I think in some ways this shows that, despite Cowley's own political leanings, he was capable of judging books for their own achievements and not because they did (or didn't) meet some radical requirements. It's easy to see how he differed from someone like Mike Gold, the Communist Party's chief literary critic, who tended to value books for the level of their commitment to the Party line.

Doubts about his own support for Stalin and Russia continued to grow in Cowley's mind, though he defended his position in long letter to friends and associates. The Spanish Civil War, and the fact that Russia was the only country prepared to support the beleaguered Republic, persuaded him to overcome suspicions about what was happening in the Soviet Union. Long letters to Edmund Wilson and Hamilton Basso attempted to explain why he had not broken with the communists, and what had inclined him to sign a letter which accepted the legitimacy of the trials in Moscow. But the 1939 Nazi-Soviet Pact, the Russian invasion of Finland, the start of the Second World War, and the fall of France, were the final straws as far as Cowley was concerned. He resigned from the League of American Writers and withdrew from other commitments which might link him to the Communist Party. The result was that, although he continued to be attacked by the right and the non-communist left, he soon began to also fall foul of the communists.

Cowley had lost his editorial position at *The New Republic*, though he continued to contribute articles and reviews to it, and in November, 1941, he was asked to go to Washington to work for the Office of Facts and Figures. It was something that wasn't to last long as his radical involvements in the 1930s caught up with him. The FBI had been keeping a file on him, and his government job came to the attention of Martin Dies of the House Un-American Activities Committee who called Cowley "one of the chief Communist intellectuals." He was forced to resign and revert to his situation as a freelance writer and editor. But in 1944 he was granted a five-year stipend by the Bollingdon Foundation which meant that he could concentrate on several long-term projects, such as a one-volume history of American literature that he been commissioned to write. And he took on other tasks. He was responsible for assembling *The Portable Hemingway,* and later, *The Portable Faulkner,* and *The Portable Hawthorn.*

The post-1945 years found Cowley busy as writer and editor, though he continued to worry about his earlier defence of Stalin. And he viewed with dismay the rise of anti-communism and the way in which the innocent were condemned along with the guilty. To give Cowley his due he never became one of those one-time radicals who turned informer or wrote books outlining his activities and asking for forgiveness. He accepted that he'd been mistaken in the 1930s, and sometimes attempted to explain why, but in a letter to Dwight Macdonald in 1947, he stated that rank-and-file American communists, none of them spies or saboteurs, were now "a dissident and persecuted minority," and the country would be lessened if there wasn't a place for political minorities. His own past came to haunt him when he was summoned as a witness in the Alger Hiss/Whittaker Chambers confrontations, got involved in a notorious affair at Yaddo, and was attacked by right-wingers when he was invited to be a guest-lecturer at the University of Washington. The Yaddo incident was chiefly caused by a manic Robert Lowell who somehow managed to persuade other residents at the retreat that the director, Elizabeth Ames, had been involved in subversive activities. The FBI were contacted (Ames's secretary had been passing information to them about guests at Yaddo who made what she considered questionable political comments), and Cowley, a member of the Yaddo board of directors, was also drawn in. It was a shabby episode and, as Cowley said in a letter to Granville Hicks, it seemed as if the "whole world is in a paranoiac phase and sensitive individuals become victims and representatives of a general condition."

Cowley continued to function as a reviewer and essayist, and in 1950 he wrote to Kenneth Burke (a friend for many years) about Ernest Hemingway's *Across the River and Into the Trees.* He hadn't liked the book and told Burke that the problem was that Hemingway "has been living for ten years in an alcoholic haze and can't write any longer except an occasional paragraph." He compared him to Scott Fitzgerald who, after his breakdown, "could at least do the early chapters of *The Last Tycoon.*" Cowley was in touch with Fitzgerald's daughter in 1950 regarding a new edition of *Tender is the Night* which would incorporate changes that Fitzgerald had planned but never made. Cowley did have some misgivings about tampering with the novel's basic structure, but eventually decided to follow the instructions found among the writer's papers.

Among the newer writers that Cowley spoke up for in the 1950s was Jack Kerouac, and he was responsible for placing excerpts from *On the Road* in *The Paris Review* and *New World Writing* and for shepherding the book towards publication in 1957. Cowley worked closely with Kerouac on editing it, and there's a letter in which he tells him of an encounter with Allen Ginsberg who Cowley thought was wrong to encourage Kerouac to "do nothing but automatic writing." As Cowley pointed out: "Automatic writing is fine for a start, but it has to be revised and put into shape or people will quite properly refuse to read it – and what you need now is to be read, not to be exhibited as a sort of natural phenomenon like Old Faithful geyser that sends up a jet of steam and mud every hour on the hour. You've got the speed, but you also need the control." Wise words.

There is much more in the letters from the 1950s on about writers that Cowley encouraged or tried to revive interest in. He helped Ken Kesey obtain a contract for *One Flew Over the Cuckoo's Nest* and encouraged Tillie Olson. And the letters are scattered with references to Dawn Powell, Otis Ferguson, Nelson Algren, Elizabeth Madox Roberts, and many others. He remembered the old bohemian, Joe

Gould, and the expatriate writer and publisher, Robert McAlmon. And, of course, he commented on what he was doing in terms of writing, editing, and lecturing. It's useful to read the letters with copies of some of Cowley's books handy. *Think Back On Us, The Flower and the Leaf, And I Worked at the Writer's Trade,* are just some of them, along with others I've already mentioned, and there is *The Portable Malcolm Cowley,* which would make a useful introduction to his work for anyone not familiar with it.

I always considered Malcolm Cowley one of the most readable of critics. Perhaps he was that way because he wrote to be read by non-specialist readers and not to make an academic reputation or career. His letters show that he cared about books and writers, and that he stayed loyal to people he liked. His one big mistake, made in the 1930s, continued to dog him for many years and caused him much heartache. He was still being attacked for his support of Stalin when his memoirs of the 1930s were published in 1980. He had been wrong, and he knew it, but thought that his enemies like Sidney Hook and Joseph Epstein misrepresented him.

Hans Bak has done a wonderful job of editing the letters and there are ample notes to guide readers through the literary and political worlds that Malcolm Cowley lived in.

THE LONG VOYAGE: SELECTED LETTERS OF MALCOLM
COWLEY, 1915-1987
Edited by Hans Bak. Harvard University Press. 800 pages. £29.95. ISBN
978-0-674-05106-5

NEW FICTION, 1972

'Alienation,' Jimmy Reid said recently, 'expresses itself in different ways for different people,' and although he was using this phrase in the context of a speech which primarily dealt with the pressures exerted by distant economic forces and decision-making, he might almost have been talking about contemporary literature, so much of which is activated by a need to register a reaction to rapidly deteriorating situations. The characters fumble their way through the crumbling cities and wrecked marriages like newly-blind men stumbling around crowded rooms they once lived in with ease.

L. J. Davis's ironically titled *A Meaningful Life* is set in present-day New York, the place which, more than any other, offers a frightening panorama of both the fading promise and oncoming threat of life today. Its 'hero' (a word I always find unsatisfactory in a case like this - perhaps 'victim' would be better) is Lowell, a colourless failure, one-time aspiring novelist, now working on a third-rate trade journal, and married to Betty, a dull dependable woman who views every departure from routine with a worried frown. Lowell wants to be accepted as an individual, to make himself known to people, and to this end he buys a broken-down house in a broken-down part of the city, determined to resurrect it and so add something to his own life and that of the surrounding neighbourhood.

But events work against Lowell. The area is already too far gone to respond, and in any case Lowell has been conned and the house is due for demolition. He shambles on, trying to save something from the wreck of his life, but uncomfortably aware that it's too late, the ship is on its way down. And even in total defeat he still cannot claim any attention. He is involved in a horrific incident, in which a man is killed, and no one wants to know about it. After all, the dead man is as nondescript as Lowell so why should anyone care?

A Meaningful Life is a grim novel, in which Mr Davis goes a long way towards capturing the despair and black humour of our time, and yet it ultimately fails. Its author seems only aware of Lowell's feelings, perhaps because he sees his position as that of the artist in society. But isn't it true that we are all now suffering, all isolated, and shouldn't a novelist try to transcend the purely personal and demonstrate the wider breakdown? Lowell's wife, the easily ridiculed

147

father-in-law, the bitchy mother-in-law, even the people who mock and swindle him - are they not victims too? The vision here is limited and it indicates a too concentrated concern with self.

Paddy Kitchen is much better at constructing a novel in which the characters have depth and colour and often genuinely react to each other. Vanessa is an up-and-coming architect, Elinor a minor and maybe up-and-coming novelist, both struggling to assert themselves as women and as artists. Vanessa involves herself in an affair with a visiting African architect, aware that it cannot last but anxious to savour the moment's fulfilment. At the same time she works on the plans for a new art school and in this we see her need to construct something of substance in the larger society. Elinor is less confident, some of her energy sapped by a marriage which, if not unhappy, lacks spirit. And in her writing she finds herself searching for a style or theme that will allow her to deal with matters other than the momentary.

Miss Kitchen is, in her own way, dealing with aspects of alienation. Vanessa and Elinor want to make contact, on a personal level and through their work, but are often frustrated. Elinor, for example, betrays her essential lack of belief in an audience for her books by her actions at a weekend seminar when she can find nothing constructive to say and so retreats into abuse, both of herself and the audience. Eventually one can't help thinking that writing for her is not so much a desire to communicate with others, but a need to prove to herself that she exists. The impression is skilfully built up until her basic insecurity comes through as her dominant characteristic.

Paradise is a steady and truthful novel, and Miss Kitchen's concern for the detail of everyday life shows her to be a writer with an awareness of the fact that the seemingly ordinary can often conceal a mass of confused feelings and attitudes. It is no ordinary writer who, in a description of a simple domestic encounter between wife and husband, can subtly bring out the differences in temperament and background of the two.

We may all be alienated now, but the condition is not completely a product of post-1945 civilisation. The 19th-century French poet, Rimbaud, was a prophet of our great malaise, and hunted for meaning in poetry, in the heady days of the Commune and in Africa, a continent then full of promise and adventure. *A Season in Abyssinia* deals mainly with his sojourn in that country when, after abandoning poetry, he drifted there in the hope of making a fortune as a trader.

It is one of the great and unsolved literary mysteries that a writer of such genius should disappear into the unknown, but Mr Strathern does manage to suggest the confusion that existed in Rimbaud's mind, and he skilfully sketches in the chaotic uncertainties of a man who, disgusted with his own failings, tries to plan ahead, and a man who is too steeped in the sensations of the moment to ever discipline himself to succeed, at least in the business sense.

Literary historians may quarrel with Mr Strathern's portrait of Rimbaud, but insofar as his book is a novel he has created a very real character, whose personality etches itself on the reader's mind. And he backs it up with a gallery of minor types, ranging from a broken-down English eccentric, anxiously grubbing around the trading post and trying to keep up appearances, to a flamboyant Armenian, forever on the make. Like Rimbaud they are outcasts, unable to return to their own countries and merely tolerated by the natives. They rotate around each other, all the time sliding towards ruin, and it is in this disaster area that Rimbaud attempts to work out his salvation. *A Season in Abyssinia* has faults - including some occasionally clumsy writing — but it also has power.

After such books what are we to make of *The Wanted Man?* It is almost mythical England, with a quiet country village, amiable judge, retired naval officer, vicar, fussy ladies and, of course, a mysterious stranger.

I have to admit that, living my life in the industrial North, I find such places totally fascinating. The people there bumble along (few of them are required to work for a living), keeping themselves apart from the rest of the country and yet qualified to discuss it and suggest ways in which it can be improved. I take it that Mr Cecil is being satirical? Or is he? Whatever his purpose he can be quite enlightening. The vicar is quoted as commenting, in response to a criticism of banks:

> I have little doubt that most people in the country directly or indirectly owe their means of livelihood to the banks.

Which might be a neat way of explaining why they feel that their lives are controlled by distant decisions. In other words, why they are alienated. And that's where we came in.

A MEANINGFUL LIFE by L. J. Davis. Constable
PARADISE by Paddy Kitchen. Gollancz
A SEASON IN ABYSSINIA by Paul Strathern. Macmillan
THE WANTED MAN by Henry Cecil. Joseph

WALT WHITMAN

Many years ago I attended an event celebrating the links between Walt Whitman and some of his 19th Century admirers in Lancashire, England. During the discussions I happened to mention that Whitman had frequented Pfaff's saloon on Broadway in New York and mixed with the bohemian crowd gathered there. An academic from a local university immediately pounced on me and remarked that "if" Whitman had indeed been a regular in Pfaff's it obviously had little or no effect on his life or writing so wasn't a subject worth considering. I couldn't help having the feeling that this person thought that poets all led quiet lives devoted to producing poems for scholars to study, rather like the man himself (he was a minor poet as well as a lecturer) who wrote carefully and with an eye to attracting praise from his fellow-academics. He was a pleasant-enough man, and I rather liked him, so it didn't seem worthwhile arguing and I let the matter drop.

Of course, it may have been a fact that at the time I'm talking about (the mid-1970s) not too much was known in England about the bohemian side of Whitman's activities. But it was familiar territory for anyone interested in the history of American Bohemianism. Albert Parry's ground-breaking *Garrets and Pretenders: A History of Bohemianism in America*, originally published in 1933, and with an easily-available reprint from Dover Publications in 1960, had a chapter about Whitman at Pfaff's. And the fact that he had functioned as a journalist should, perhaps, have given a lead in terms of suggesting that Whitman would have known and mixed with many of the people who came together at Pfaff's. In any case, Henry Clapp, the instigator of the bohemian gatherings there, was one of the earliest advocates of Whitman as a poet.

Things have changed somewhat since the 1970s and there is now a fair amount of material around to locate Whitman among the bohemians. Recent publications include Mark A. Lause's *The Antebellum Crisis & America's First Bohemians* (Kent State University Press, 2009); Joanna Levin's *Bohemia in America, 1858-1920* (Stanford University Press, 2010); and *Whitman Among the Bohemians*, edited by Joanna Levin and Edward Whitley (University of Iowa Press, 2014). To which we can add Justin Martin's *Rebel*

Souls.

To understand the importance of Pfaff's as the focus of attention for what are referred to as "America's First Bohemians," it's necessary to look in a little detail at the life of Henry Clapp, the man who started it all. There had been individuals who could be described as bohemians, had the term been in use in America before 1850 (Edgar Allan Poe, for example), but it was Clapp who brought together writers, artists, actors, and others, to become identified as a group seemingly representing certain characteristics that outsiders would label, often dismissively, bohemian. Clapp, born in Nantucket in 1814, had something of a checkered career as, among other things, a journalist (he had even been imprisoned at one point for insulting a judge) before going to Paris in 1849 to attend a three-day world peace congress. Finding it so interesting and attractive he stayed on for another three years, and his experiences in the French capital were to change his life. The 1840s in France were years of turmoil in many ways, both politically and artistically, and Clapp appears to have been fascinated by the atmosphere of personal freedom when compared to what he had experienced in the United States. Clapp had been brought up in a fairly restrictive, almost puritanical way, but in Paris he soon learned to adapt to café life, and to drink and mix with friendly women.

While Clapp was in Paris Henry Murger's bohemian sketches that had been published in an obscure magazine, *Le Corsaire-Satan,* were transformed into a play with the help of Theodore Barriere. Few people, apart from fellow bohemians, had paid much attention to the sketches, but the play was an instant hit. It was followed by Murger's novel, *Scenes de la vie de Boheme,* which just collected the sketches and loosely linked them. It's impossible to know whether or not Clapp saw the play, but he certainly was aware of the bohemian life of the Latin Quarter. When he returned to America in 1853 he earned a living as a journalist and translator, and he began to think of finding a suitable location for like-minded people to socialise. Around 1856 he spotted a basement saloon called Pfaff's which was on Broadway, "a few doors north of Bleecker Street." Its owner, Charles Pfaff, was friendly, liked the idea of his saloon becoming a centre for writers, artists, and performers of various kinds, and agreed to Clapp and his friends having a corner which would be reserved for them. Clapp, of course, would preside at the head of the table. He would soon be called "The King of Bohemia."

Justin Martin says that Clapp's "first recruit was Fitz James O'Brien, a friend and fellow-journalist." O'Brien was a bohemian by nature. Born in Ireland he had moved to London and squandered a large inheritance. He left England suddenly when the husband of a woman he was having an affair with came back from India. When he arrived in New York he lived the high life at first, but soon switched to living in run-down rooming houses. A drinker, he often got involved in brawls and was thrown into jail. To raise money he churned out bits of fiction, poetry, criticism, and straightforward reporting for a range of publications. A friend said that "Haste is evident in all that he wrote," because he couldn't be bothered to work on things if he could sell them immediately. He wrote a play which ran successfully in New York for a time, and a number of short stories, some of which are still reprinted in fantasy and horror anthologies. Perhaps the most-famous one is "The Diamond Lens," in which a man looks through a microscopic lens and sees a beautiful woman in a droplet of water. He falls in love with her but knows she'll soon disappear.

More recruits to bohemia turned up at Pfaff's, including the journalist Charles Halpine, George Arnold, a poet who made a living of sorts "writing poems for newspapers, a career that's unimaginable today," and Thomas Nast who was later to become famous as "the preeminent political cartoonist of nineteenth-century America." Not all bohemians were fated to be failures or soon forgotten. But Martin, listing a cast of "poets, playwrights, painters, and sculptors," refers to the one thing they had in common – "crushing poverty." And he adds that New York was similar to Paris in that both cities "lured in far more artists and writers than could possibly be supported."

Walt Whitman discovered Pfaff's, or more likely heard about it from fellow-journalists, "sometime in 1858." He was 39 and struggling to establish a reputation as a poet, but mostly without success, though he did have some self-published work to his credit. Martin says that Clapp was "thrilled to have Whitman, even a reticent Whitman, at his table." The poet said very little and largely kept clear of the verbal competitiveness that the others indulged in. In later years he recollected: "My own greatest pleasure at Pfaff's was to look on – to see, talk little, absorb. I never was a great discourser, anyway – never." Clapp was keen to have him there, nonetheless, because he considered that he could see what others could not – that Whitman was a major poet and was controversial. As for Whitman himself, it's Martin's contention that, being among the bohemians "goaded him on. Soon he was writing fresh poems." It was true that, in time, Whitman often left the alcove where the bohemians sat and moved among the general clientele in Pfaff's. It fitted in with his celebrations of ordinary people, workingmen, who didn't expect him to compete against them with clever quips and repartee. And "Pfaff's was a place where gay men could meet, in an era when such matters were not so clearly defined and delineated." Whitman referred to a group of young men he mixed with as "my darlings and gossips," and "my darling, dearest boys."

Fitz Hugh Ludlow arrived at Pfaff's with some success behind him. His *The Hasheesh Eater* had been "a literary sensation" in 1857 as it charted his experiments with drugs "at a time when tired old rules and failed authority were being questioned." He was young, just twenty-one when he was welcomed by Clapp, and despite his book selling well he was "a dirt-poor celebrity – a not-so-unusual combination in nineteenth-century America." So, he tried to place criticism and stories in magazines and newspapers, but the "pressure of the New York literary game was immense." And Ludlow may have claimed that he'd given up using hashish but he'd started using something even more likely to make demands on his energies and general disposition – opium. He never did have any success as a writer after *The Hasheesh Eater*. His wife ran off with the painter Albert Bierstadt, with whom he was supposed to collaborate on a book about travelling across America, and he eventually succumbed to tuberculosis and died in 1870 in Geneva.

One thing about Pfaff's, or at least the group that clustered around Clapp, was that women were welcome if they had talent of one kind or another. Ada Clare turned up with aims to avoid a future of "a series of little acts, a dead level of vapid monotony," and ambitions to be an actress. She did get some roles but failed to make an impression due to being unable to project enough to engage the audience. But she did start to place essays and poems in a Sunday newspaper. At Pfaff's she soon achieved the title of "The Queen of Bohemia," partly because she could hold her own in conversation with the men, partly because she was pretty, and partly because she was not afraid to admit that she was an unmarried mother, thanks to an affair with the composer, Louis Moreau Gottschalk. She clearly had some skills as a writer and contributed well-written articles to magazines and newspapers, even if she was limited as an actress, and she should have had a novel, *Asphodel*, published in 1860. But the publisher went bankrupt and the "original handwritten manuscript, proofs, plates" somehow disappeared. A later Clare novel, *Only a Woman's Heart,* loosely based on her liaison with Gottschalk, did appear but largely raised a negative critical response. She became disillusioned with writing and tried to return to the stage, though again without achieving any prominent roles. Her ending was tragic. Visiting a friend she picked up a small dog and was bitten on the face. She soon started to show signs of insanity. The dog had rabies. Clare was thirty-nine when she died in 1874.

Martin names several other women who were seen in Pfaff's, among them the journalist Jenny Danforth, Dora Shaw, an actress and poet, and Marie Stevens Case, a novelist and translator from the French. But the most famous, and the one who is sometimes still written about today, was Adah Isaacs Menken. Her fame may rest on her performances in a play called *Mazeppa: or the Wild Horse of Tartary* where in one scene she wore a flesh-coloured body-stocking that accented her buxom shape, and was tied spread-eagled on the back of a horse while it galloped around the stage and, in some lavish productions, up what was supposed to be a mountain. All this was a travesty of a Cossack story, Byron's poem about it, and a stage adaptation by Henry Milner. The person on the horse had been a man in all these versions, but a woman, especially in a sheer body-stocking, pulled in audiences. Menken toured with *Mazeppa* across America and in Europe where she met Charles Dickens and tried to interest him in her poetry. He described her as "a sensitive poet who, unfortunately, cannot write." Menken wanted to act in other plays besides *Mazeppa*, but often had difficulties remembering her lines. When she starred in *Les pirates de la Savanne* in Paris the problem was accented by the fact that she couldn't speak French, so the playwrights re-wrote the script to make Menken's character into a mute whose tongue had been cut out by Indians. They also added a scene where Menken was stripped, or at least reduced to a body stocking, and strapped to the back of a horse. It was obvious that she never would get away from that part. The play ran for 150 sold-out performances, according to Martin. Menken cultivated a friendship with Alexandre Dumas and never denied rumours about a possible sexual aspect to it. But in 1868 she started to suffer from "a mysterious ailment" and withdrew from public performances of any kind. She passed away in that same year. Martin says: "In true Bohemian fashion, Menken died penniless in Paris. She was thirty-three years old, according to the best estimate." And, again in true Bohemian fashion, she was buried in Paris, in Montparnasse cemetery.

What of Henry Clapp? He never rated highly as a writer, but he did establish a magazine, *The Saturday Press,* which published many of the people who came to Pfaff's. And Clapp used his publication to promote the work of Walt Whitman. Also, because of the way that other magazines and newspapers across America often reprinted items from *The Saturday Press,* he did help to spread the word about Whitman and several more of his authors to wider audiences. Clapp additionally continued to push the idea of bohemianism, though in the post-Civil War period it was harder to convince readers that it was something that offered an alternative to conventional living. A more-serious mood had taken over and with westward expansion gathering speed, "Go west, young man" may have seemed a more-enticing prospect than joining the bohemians at Pfaff's. Clapp's publication had its ups and downs and eventually closed its pages for good. Clapp scuffled, scrounging money from old friends, drinking hard, and ending his days in poverty. He died in 1875 in an asylum, which is where alcoholics were often sent in those days. He was sixty.

There were others from the Pfaff's crowd who died young. George Arnold, known as the "Poet of Beer," died when he was thirty-one, though from unknown causes. Charles Halpine died from an overdose of chloroform, a "drug he was using recreationally." Fitz-James O'Brien had only just turned thirty when he died, but in his case that was due to complications resulting from a wound he received while fighting with the Union army. Actor Edwin Booth hung on until he was almost sixty, and became very successful, which is more than can be said for his younger brother, John Wilkes Booth, who was killed in a gunfight with police after he'd assassinated Abraham Lincoln. To counterbalance the early deaths it's necessary to mention William Winter, a one-time regular at Pfaff's, who became drama critic for *The New York Tribune* and held the job for forty-four years. He also wrote several books. Thomas Aldrich, who had assisted Clapp with *The Saturday Press,* published several volumes of poetry, and was appointed editor of the prestigious publication, *The Atlantic Monthly*, though Martin tells us that "he continued to smoke a little clay pipe, a vestige of his wild youth." Clapp had brought the clay pipe habit with him from Paris and Aldrich copied him.

I suppose it's only fair to ask what the bohemians left behind in terms of any successful, or long-lasting work? It never bothers me that a lot of writing doesn't stay the pace. Many novels, stories, and poems fall by the wayside, as does most criticism and commentary. Of Pfaff's bohemians it's obvious that Walt Whitman was the one major poet who could be found there, though there were quite a few minor ones. I've mentioned earlier that some of Fitz James O'Brien's stories are still in print and worth reading. Fitz Hugh Ludlow's *The Hasheesh Eater* is also available. I recall that it had some currency in the 1960s when there was an upsurge of interest in earlier accounts of experiences with drugs of various kinds. Ada Clare's novel, *Only a Woman's Heart,* can be found in reprint form, though reading it may be to satisfy one's curiosity rather than for its literary qualities. The same might be said for Adah Isaacs Menken's *Infelicia*, her posthumously-published collection of poems, though Martin does add that "her works are composed in free verse and contain assorted experimental touches." That's perhaps not too bad a list from any group, bearing in mind that a lot of the writers at Pfaff's were journalists, and/or contributors to often short-lived magazines and newspapers, and ephemera was their stock-in-trade. There may well be worthwhile things buried in long-forgotten publications. I'm also reminded of something that John Clellon Holmes said when considering the literary aspects of the Beat Generation, "probably all that will last out of our Beat years are a rash of vaporous anecdotes, and the few solid works that were produced."

REBEL SOULS: WALT WHITMAN AND AMERICA'S FIRST BOHEMIANS By Justin Martin. Da Capo Press. 339 pages. £18.99/$27.99. ISBN 978-0-306-82226-1

THE HOSANNA MAN

There is a story behind this book. It was originally published by Jonathan Cape in 1956, when Philip Callow was thirty-two, and was his first novel. It received several positive reviews, but was withdrawn and pulped when someone claimed that he could be recognised as one of the characters in the book and that he'd been libelled. John Lucas in his useful introduction to this new edition states that the person concerned was a Nottingham newsagent. The problem seemed to revolve around a second-hand bookseller in *The Hosanna Man* who, it is suggested, has a sideline in under-the-counter pornography. It's perhaps worth noting that, in the 1950s, censorship was much tighter than it is now and if anyone had a taste for pornography, then it could only be satisfied by finding a bookseller of one kind or another who would supply it secretly and for a price. Either that or by perhaps taking a trip to Paris, where it was easier to pick up such material. And when it came to a case involving libel, publishers were nearly always likely to take the easy way out and withdraw a book rather than risk going to court and facing heavy legal costs and possible damages. This would certainly have been the attitude they adopted when the author was unknown and unlikely to be of any great financial value to the publisher.

One can imagine what the effect must have been on Callow. Cape not only withdrew his book, they also cancelled the contract for a second one that had been accepted. On top of that he was advised to settle out-of-court and paid £300 to the complainant. That may seem a paltry sum by today's standards, but in 1956 it was fairly substantial and was certainly a blow for Callow who was then earning a living as a clerk. Luckily, the second novel that Cape now wouldn't handle was accepted by Bodley Head, and he went on to publish more novels, together with biographies of Whitman, Van Gogh, Chekhov, and others. But he would never allow *The Hosanna Man* to be reprinted, even when it would have been safe to do so. John Lucas says that Callow was always reluctant to talk about the book and its background.

Like many first novels *The Hosanna Man* is clearly autobiographical. The central character, Louis, is at a loose end in Coventry and decides to move to Nottingham in pursuit of Stella, a married woman with whom he has had an affair. He's young and shy, and she has obviously had other relationships and appears to thrive on the kind of edginess they bring. As she says at one point, "I love an intrigue," and blowing hot and then cold is a part of the game for her. Louis is confused and his situation isn't helped by the fact that he hasn't a job, and the accommodation he has found in Nottingham isn't likely to offer an opportunity for him to develop his talents for watercolours and writing poetry. He has taken lodgings with an elderly couple who are almost-Dickensian in their behaviour and odd relationship. Some of Callow's skills as a writer can be seen at work in his descriptions of these people.

Unable to establish any sort of satisfactory re-union with Stella, Louis is intrigued by an advertisement he comes across in a local paper. A small group is looking for financial backing for its members' artistic endeavours, and though Louis doesn't have any money he decides to contact them. I have to admit that it was at this point that I began to acknowledge a kind of affinity with Louis as he gingerly approaches Kelvin, who seems to be the leader of sorts of a band of provincial bohemians. My feeling of recognition stemmed from a somewhat similar experience in the 1950s when I returned to my home town from army service and began to associate with local jazz musicians, art students, and would-be writers. They often seemed to cluster around someone who appeared to have more energy and drive than most of the others, and who they looked up to and admired. Charismatic might be a useful term to use, though it didn't take much to appear colourful or seem charismatic in the drab world of 1950s Britain. Kelvin is a painter and occasionally writes poetry, though when he shows some of his poems to Louis they're virtually unreadable, having been scribbled down at great speed. When Louis asks why he doesn't copy them out clearly, Kelvin replies, "Who wants to copy things when you can be creating them?" There's a foretaste here of the loose ideas of spontaneity that were thrown around so much during the heyday of the Beats. And, in fact, the Beat movement, certainly in its early days in Britain, really just seemed to be an extension of a bohemian life-style that had been there for some years. It's perhaps significant that there are no references to politics in *The Hosanna Man*, and someone speaking to a crowd is only observed in passing and without any indication of what the speaker is talking about. When the group that Louis gets involved with have a film show in someone's house they watch *The Cabinet of Doctor Caligari*, and not *Battleship Potemkin*, as might have been the case in the 1930s or 1940s.

Through Kelvin, Louis encounters other members of what is a floating fraternity of painters, booksellers, drunks, and the general oddballs that could be found in any provincial town or city in the 1950s, and who perhaps attached themselves to its bohemian clique because it was, in some ways, more tolerant of eccentricities and misbehaviour. Callow's perceptions of this sort of society are quite acute and he's particularly good on the role that women played in it, ranging from the amateur painter Stella, to the bookseller's wife, and Catherine, a young widow who Louis, having given up any hopes of seeing Stella again, soon establishes a close relationship with. She, like Louis, is on the fringes of the group and conscious of the fact that at some point it will be necessary to move away from it. It's too incestuous and someone like Kelvin inclines towards wanting everyone to be like him, bitter and frustrated.

It may seem that I've focused too much on the sociological aspects of *The Hosanna Man*, but I'm not about to apologise for that. Some novels lend themselves to being studied in this way and provide fascinating pictures of life at certain time and in certain places. At their best, as with *The Hosanna Man*, they're often more accurate and informative than pure sociological studies. And they're easier to read if they're as well-written as Callow's book. His prose style is very direct and he can evoke a character or a scene in a few well-chosen words. It seems simple, but it isn't and a lesser writer would soon lose the reader's interest by either paring things down to a point where the narrative lacks drive and colour, or by trying to say too much and so overwhelming the story with unnecessary detail. Callow strikes a balance by just providing enough information, while at the same time letting his characters describe themselves by the way they speak and act in certain circumstances. There isn't a plot as such and the story simply follows a day-to-day outline. Some characters come and go with hardly any impact on Louis, just as people do in real life. It's the quality of the writing that keeps the reader interested and involved.

Some of the reviews of *The Hosanna Man* tried to locate it in a tradition of proletarian writing, perhaps because metropolitan critics needed to label a book they otherwise found difficult to categorise. But is has little or no relationship to the kind of novels of working-class life that came out of the 1930s and 1940s, and were still sometimes published in the 1950s. Does anyone now read Len Doherty? Louis may come from a working-class background, and he's worked at jobs that would be seen as working-class occupations, but his interests and ambitions are not those of most of the people he's worked with. And the people he takes up with when he arrives in Nottingham couldn't be described as working-class. Even George Meluish, a rough-spoken artist who probably does have good proletarian roots, seems set apart from the wider society and is contemptuous of the mass of people. Maybe Marxists would have described him as a rootless individual? The term bohemian might be better, though those with romantic notions of what bohemianism implies won't understand that.

It's good to see *The Hosanna Man* back in print. Had the critics who read it in the 1950s been really perceptive they would have seen that it was exploring something different, and doing it in a well-written way.

THE HOSANNA MAN – Philip Callow. Shoestring Press. 240 pages. £9.99. ISBN 978-1-907356-87-2

THE STREET OF WONDERFUL POSSIBILITIES

Tite Street in London's Chelsea is a relatively short thoroughfare between Queen's Road and the Embankment. It probably doesn't ring as many bells as Cheyne Walk or the King's Road if it's mentioned in conversation, and yet, for a period between roughly 1880 and 1914, it was home to a variety of artists, writers, and others, and constituted what might be seen as London's bohemia. It was, it needs to be said, a bohemia that mostly excluded the poverty-stricken artists and students often associated with notions of bohemian living, but I don't think there's any doubt that the life-styles of many of the inhabitants of the houses on Tite Street would have seemed to observers to fit into a context of bohemia. "Gentlemen bohemians" might be a handy way to describe them. I ought to mention at this point that in referring to the years 1880 to 1914 I'm not denying that artists continued to live in Tite Street in later years. They did, but I think it's probably true to say that the period concerned was Tite Street's heyday, no matter that Devon Cox records that, as late as 1994, Princess Diana came to Tite Street to sit for a portrait being painted by the American artist, Nelson Shanks. The real action in Tite Street had taken place around a century before.

Cox points out that much of the physical appeal of Tite Street resided in the fact that many of the houses had been built to specifications laid down by artists and their architects, in particular a noted one called E.W. Godwin. He gave them an individual appearance. He was also someone who understood what artists required, both in terms of studio space with adequate lighting and of residencies that would highlight their good taste and their material success. In an age when many artists depended on patrons and their commissions for a living it was considered essential to be able to present a confident front (house and person) to visitors.

One of the first artists to establish himself in Tite Street was the American, James Abbott McNeill Whistler. He had kicked off his career in Paris, mixing with painters, writers, and art students. Among the people he knew was George du Maurier who would satirise Whistler as Joe Sibley, the "idle apprentice, the king of bohemia," when he published his novel, *Trilby,* in serial form in *Harper's New Monthly Magazine* in 1894. Du Maurier never did have much patience with the kind of affectations that Whistler projected, and in true English fashion preferred artists who extolled common-sense and practicality, and were down-to-earth in their behaviour. By that time Whistler had established a reputation as an artist and he quickly threatened to sue unless the character was changed when *Trilby* appeared as a book. The required alteration was made and Sibley disappeared from the text. It's of interest to note that an edition of *Trilby* based on the version that appeared in *Harper's* was published by W.H.Allen in 1982. But all that came later, and in the early-1860s Whistler moved to London, where he found a different atmosphere: "There was no café culture, no artistic quarter, no friendly exchange of ideas. In Paris, studios had been open ateliers and salons where fellow artists were free to come and go at will, inspecting their work, and engaging in discussion." According to Cox, artists in London locked themselves away and the Royal Academy ruled the roost when it came to judgements on what was acceptable.

Whistler initially had some success with the British art establishment, and one of his paintings was accepted by the Royal Academy and praised by John Everett Millais. And there was something of a little bohemia in Britain centred on a house in Cheyne Walk where Dante Gabriel Rossetti, the leading Pre-Raphaelite painter, lived alongside the poet Algernon Swinburne, novelist George Meredith, and several others. Cox recounts how the habit of Swinburne and Simeon Solomon (an artist who would later die in St Giles's workhouse of chronic alcoholism) sliding naked down the banister handrails upset some of the more-straight-laced inhabitants of the property. When Whistler found accommodation in nearby Queen's Road he quickly established a routine of open house on Sundays and began to attract artists, writers, and intellectuals. Swinburne was among the guests and later published a poem, "Before the Mirror," inspired by a Whistler painting, *Symphony in White No.2: The Little White Girl,* that the Royal Academy had accepted. Poems by Swinburne, and paintings by Whistler and Rossetti, soon began to be lumped together as belonging to the "fleshly school." A better way of describing what was happening could be that it was the start of the "aesthetic adventure" that would culminate in the late-1890s when the sensational trial of Oscar Wilde brought not just the weight of the law down on so-called decadent behaviour, but also the weight of public opinion down on writers and artists who appeared to have any kind of connection to avant-garde, offbeat, or effete-seeming paintings and poems. William Gaunt once summed up the situation following the Wilde affair: "It had caused a wholesale literary and social fumigation. An exaggerated robustness was one of the consequences."

But that had yet to arrive, and by the late-1860s and early-1870s Whistler had established a reputation as a portrait artist and as something of a character, flamboyant in dress and behaviour. The flamboyancy may have been somewhat tame when compared to what went on in Paris, but it frequently shocked the respectable in London. As did Whistler's capacity for making enemies. Still, he was earning good money with his paintings and in 1877 he signed an agreement to have a house built in Tite Street. As Cox indicates, the location had several advantages from Whistler's point of view. The land was cheap to lease from the Metropolitan Board of Works, it was in Chelsea, and it gave the artist instant access to the Thames which had begun to provide subject-matter for him.

It may have been the case that artists, at least if they were successful, could be acceptable in polite society, but their mistresses weren't. Maud Franklin, Whistler's model and mistress, may have lived with him, and had his child, and she could be at home to the male visitors who came to his Sunday soirees, but she would never be invited to call at the houses of married fellow-artists or his rich patrons. Cox describes Franklin as "a typical Whistler girl – demure, Celtic-looking, pale-skinned and red-headed." But a friend of Whistler's had a more-downbeat opinion of her as "not pretty, with prominent teeth, a real British type."

If Whistler had openings to the upper reaches of London society he also knew some of its rogues and rascals. The agent and dealer, Charles Augustus Howell, had worked as Ruskin's secretary until he was fired, helped Rossetti retrieve his poems from Lizzie Siddall's grave, and had come to Whistler's assistance during a financial crisis by selling some of his sketches. The artist later saw one of them in a pawnbroker's window described as a first study for St Peter's by Michelangelo. Howell also paid Whistler to paint a portrait of his mistress, Rosa Corder, a talented artist who may not have been as disreputable as Howell, but fell under his influence, and cheerfully helped him to forge paintings and etchings by Millais, Rossetti, and others. There's a reproduction of Whistler's *Arrangement in Brown and Black:Portrait of Miss Rosa Corder* in the book, and a description by the actress, Ellen Terry, which points to her being the kind of person who would immediately attract attention when she walked into a room. Someone said of Corder, she "exuded sex appeal and knew it."

Whistler's fame, or notoriety, soon received something of a setback. As well as painting portraits that were looked on favourably, he had been producing pictures of scenes along the Thames and elsewhere which were more-experimental and influenced by what he had seen in Paris. His *Nocturne in Black and Gold: The Falling Rocket* had been exhibited at the Grosvenor Gallery in London and viewed there by the noted critic, John Ruskin. He was outraged by what he saw and in an article for the magazine, *Fors Clavigera,* he said, among other things, that he "never expected to hear a coxcomb ask two hundred guineas for flinging a pot of paint in the public's face." Whistler was equally outraged and sued Ruskin for libel. The trial that followed allowed Whistler to make some assertive statements regarding his skills as an artist, and the jury found in his favour. But he was awarded only a derisory one farthing in damages and had to pay costs, almost as a comment on his making such a ridiculous issue about Ruskin's remarks, and perhaps because a certain arrogance in Whistler's attitude was noted and it annoyed people. Whistler was bankrupted and had to sell his Tite Street house, along with many of his possessions, though Charles Augustus Howell seems to have turned up to help smuggle some paintings out, and help himself to a few of them. And then Whistler headed for Venice to fulfil a commission from the Fine Arts Society, leaving behind his pregnant mistress, Maud Franklin.

Oscar Wilde's wealthy friend, Frank Miles, asked E.W.Godwin to design a house for construction in Tite Street, and when it was completed the pair moved in together. Despite Wilde's later obvious leanings their relationship may not have had a sexual side to it (opinions vary about this), and Miles, an artist, seems to have shown a preference for young girls. One of his "discoveries" was Sally Higgs, "a pretty girl about sixteen years of age" who functioned as a maid and model. Previously a flower seller outside Victoria Station, she was described as "a born Bohemian" and was soon "one of the most sought-after models in London." She could be seen in Lord Leighton's *Day Dreams*, a painting exhibited at the Royal Academy in 1882. Cox doesn't relate what happened to Sally Higgs as she got older, though he does refer to an anecdote about her turning up at Miles's house some years after his death and requesting to be allowed to have a look around it to remind herself of "the scene of her triumphs and happiness." That might be taken to suggest that all had not gone well for her later in life. As for Frank Miles, his penchant for teenage girls brought on brushes with the law and attempts to blackmail him, according to Cox. He did have some success as an artist, but became almost a recluse in his Tite Street house and spent more time in his garden than his studio. He eventually committed himself to an asylum in Bristol suffering from syphilis and died there in 1891. Cox gives the date of his death as 1890, but most other sources say 1891.

Wilde and Miles had parted company years before the latter's death, and the poet and playwright had, of course, gone on to great success with plays such as *Lady Windermere's Fan* and *The Importance of Being Earnest*, his public appearances, and the novel *The Picture of Dorian Gray*. He had also come to represent the popular idea of an aesthete and was frequently lampooned in *Punch,* as well as in stage productions like Gilbert and Sullivan's *Patience*. But Wilde, married and with children, was leading a double-life, the dark side of which involved male prostitutes and a liaison with Lord Alfred Douglas. The story of his encounters with Douglas's father, Wilde suing for libel and losing, and then being prosecuted for indecency and sentenced to two years in prison, which effectively destroyed him and led to his early death, is too well-known for me to repeat here. He had bought a house in Tite Street when he became famous and affluent, and his public disgrace led to it being ransacked by hostile crowds. The sight of someone like Wilde crashing to earth brought on a backlash against the idea of aestheticism, French influences, and painting and writing that didn't adhere to a notion of healthy living and clean morals. There was probably a great deal of hypocrisy at work when such attitudes became paramount, but for the press and the powerful it was an opportunity to stoke up resentment against someone who had for years provoked comment because of his wit and success. While he could be satirised he was probably safe enough, but once he broke the rules about public displays of deviant practices he became the victim of what the anarchist Kropotkin liked to refer to as "organised vengeance called justice."

While the purpose of this book is to focus largely on Whistler, Wilde and Sargent, it does also bring in a cast of minor characters who add colour to the narrative. Examples would be Lord and Lady Meux. He was the son of a wealthy baronet who owned the Meux brewery. Harry Meux grew up mostly in boarding schools in Britain after his father became mentally ill and his mother deserted the family and moved to France. When Harry was twenty-one he inherited an allowance of £28,000 a year, an enormous sum at the time. He met Susan Valerie Langdon who was from a small fishing village in Devon and was working as a singer, dancer, and barmaid in casinos, dance halls, and similar places. Cox suggests that she may also have been a prostitute. She was said to be a "dazzling beauty," and she and Harry eloped and got married. She was several years older than Harry and had "knocked around London for ten years" before she met him. Obviously, his relatives weren't happy with the marriage and Lady Meux, as she became, was never going to be accepted in society. Whistler painted her twice and there would have been a third painting but he destroyed it after she'd argued with him about the time taken for the sittings. Whistler didn't like to be criticised, but she gave as good as she got when they fell out and told him to keep a civil tongue in his head. The paintings certainly do show her as a very striking woman, and Whistler probably had no need to flatter by making her seem more attractive than she was.

The more I read about Lady Meux the more I liked her. She was known to drive around London in a phaeton pulled by two zebras, collected artefacts from Egypt, owned racehorses, donated some guns to British forces during the Boer War, and finally left everything in her will, including her interests in the Meux brewery, to a naval officer she had met and admired for his services against the Boers. I rather think that she may have been getting a little of her own back for the way the Meux family had treated her. It's of interest to note that Devon Cox makes some plausible links, in terms of rich young men and ladies from another class, between the Meux relationship and that of Dorian Gray and Sibyl Vane in *The Picture of Dorian Gray*, though there are also significant differences. And Wilde could additionally have had in mind the case of the aristocrat artist Archibald Stuart-Wortley who married the actress Nelly Bromley after getting her pregnant. Cox also shows how Wilde drew on his Tite Street environment for descriptive material in his book. The artist's studio had links to Frank Miles's place of work, and the

Theatre Royal had some similarities to the actual Casino de Venise, where Harry Meux most likely first met Valerie Langdon or Val Reece, as she was known. Incidentally, I've referred to Sibyl Vane, which is how the name is shown in my old Penguin copy of the novel, but Cox has it as Sybil, as does another source I consulted. A minor point, but it aroused my curiosity. Was the Penguin version a misprint?

John Singer Sargent, like Whistler, was an American who arrived in London via Paris. He had trained "in the atelier of renowned French society portraitist Carolus Duran," and had exhibited successfully at several annual Paris Salons. But in 1884 he experienced something of a setback when his portrait, *Madame X,* caused a scandal. As it was shown at the Salon the painting was of a lady in a low-cut evening dress with straps, one of which had slipped off her shoulder. This was taken by many viewers and commentators to suggest a pre or post-sexual situation. Sargent later re-painted the strap in its correct position on the shoulder, as can be seen in the reproduction in the book. More information about this episode in Sargent's life can be found in Deborah Davis's entertaining *Strapless: John Singer Sargent and the Fall of Madame X* (Sutton Publishing, 2004).

Feeling that his reputation in Paris as a portrait painter had suffered a setback because of the scandal, Sargent moved to London in 1886 and a studio-flat in Tite Street. He was a far less outgoing character than Whistler. His life was said to be "as orderly as that of a bishop," and he dressed formally, even when working in his studio. But though reticent to talk too much about his work he didn't lack in confidence when it came to his skills. He was initially less successful in London than he was in Paris, but when his work was shown in America it was highly praised. Cox sums up his situation: "Since his arrival in London, Sargent had perplexed the Royal Academy. He was an outsider – an American trained in Paris, and painting in the French style, and a card-carrying member of the New English Art Club – yet he could no longer be ignored." He was elected as an Associate of the Royal Academy in 1894. After that, his career never looked back, though in time he tired of the endless commissions to paint portraits of the titled and wealthy. When Lady Radnor asked him for a portrait of one of her daughters his response was: "Ask me to paint your gates, your fences, your barns, which I should gladly do, but NOT THE HUMAN FACE."

There were tragedies among the Tite Street painters. Charles Wellington Furse had a fiancé, Eleanor Butcher, who died of tuberculosis, the scourge that had afflicted the bohemians in Henry Murger's novel of life in Paris in the 1840s. And Furse himself later succumbed to the same disease. Marian Collier, an artist herself and married to the successful John Collier, died young after suffering from acute post-natal depression. Roger Brough, who travelled to Paris with Samuel Peploe, had mixed with the Glasgow Boys in the 1890s. He had some success in Paris with his attractive painting, *Fantaisie en Folie,* which is in Cox's book, and on his return to Britain he moved into a property in Tite Street. His future looked promising, but he was involved in a railway accident in 1905, was badly burned, and died in hospital. Much later, Peter Warlock, a musician not a painter, was found dead in his flat in Tite Street. There were doubts about whether his death, caused by coal-gas poisoning, was an accident or suicide, and even a suggestion of murder by a rival composer who was the sole beneficiary of Warlock's will which was due to be changed.

As I mentioned earlier, the heyday of Tite Street was probably during the years covered by the activities of Whistler, Wilde, and Sargent. There were other talented arrivals, including the American Anna Lee Merritt, who established a reputation as a portrait artist despite a prejudice against women working in that field, and Romaine Brooks, another American, though she made a greater impact in Paris in the 1920s. Edith Elizabeth Downing, a noted suffragette activist as well as an artist, lived in Tite Street, as did Hannah Gluckstein and Glyn Philpot who, among other things, painted a portrait of Siegfried Sassoon. And Augustus John, the roaring boy of the British art scene, was there, too, and stuck it out during the Second World War. He painted a portrait of Field Marshall Lord Montgomery in 1944, though the famous soldier wasn't too impressed with the result. He wasn't over-keen on the artist, either, and said: "Who is this chap? He drinks, he's dirty, and I know there are women in the background." Bohemianism obviously wasn't to the priggish Montgomery's liking.

There is, I think, an interesting question that arises in relation to most of the artists clustered around Tite Street and Chelsea in general. Were they an avant-garde? Perhaps they sometimes were in relation to much of what was hung on the walls of the Royal Academy. But with the exception of Whistler, whose paintings of the Thames and similar subjects can still surprise as they approach the abstract, there was little that seemed truly innovative or experimental in any way. I'm not suggesting a qualitative judgement when I say that. Personally, I'm a great admirer of Sargent's portraits and of other works, such as Charles Wellington Furse's *Diana of the Uplands,* and Archibald Stuart-Wortley's *The Sleep of an Acorn,* both of which are attractive to look at. The Tite Street painters didn't lack in skills. But compared to what was happening among the more-adventurous artists in Paris around 1900 they usually appeared conventional. It's true that things were changing in London. The New English Art Club had been established as a kind of alternative to the restrictive opinions expressed at the Royal Academy, though in time some of the "old guard" in that organisation would be left behind by younger members. Walter Sickert, one of Whistler's former pupils, was reacting against what he termed "Sargentolatry," and would eventually be the leading light in what became known as the "Camden Town Group." And Roger Fry would soon bring Post-Impressionist paintings to London. Outside London, in Newlyn and St Ives, and in Scotland, artists, many with experience of working in Paris and other Continental cities, were incorporating new ideas into their paintings. But this is not to denigrate what had happened in Tite Street. Within its framework it had been a centre of artistic activity, with numerous talented painters living there or nearby, and there is nothing to be gained by comparing it unfavourably to other places.

The Street of Wonderful Possibilities is a splendid book, well written in a way that is entertaining and informative without lapsing into art jargon or academic theorising. And it is beautifully illustrated with many of the paintings referred to and also photographs and drawings of Tite Street and its houses. There are ample notes and a useful bibliography. I can't recommend it highly enough.

THE STREET OF WONDERFUL POSSIBILITIES: WHISTLER, WILDE & SARGENT IN TITE STREET By Devon Cox. Frances Lincoln Limited. 287 pages. £25/$40. ISBN 978-0-7112-3673-8

THE TASTE IN MY MIND

I have to admit to being partial to essays and reviews. Good ones, at least. Too many essayists and reviewers (especially) seem to think that writing about a particular poet or book is an excuse for them to demonstrate how clever they are. The idea that what they're supposed to be doing is informing the reader, and potential purchaser of the book(s) in question, of what a poet may have to offer in general, or in a specific volume, appears to be alien to them. They're out to establish a reputation for themselves, and if it's necessary to destroy someone else's in order to do it, then that's what they'll do.

So, it's a pleasure to come across a reviewer and essayist who takes the view that he has a responsibility to the subject of his criticism and to the reader. In his introduction Tony Roberts refers to "celebratory essays" and says that what he offers is "an informative, entertaining commentary on some of our best poets, an illustration of poetry's power – in the right hands – to enthral." Note that "entertaining," and consider how many writers, of all persuasions, fail to be entertaining in the best sense of the word. It doesn't imply a leaning towards quick and easy offerings. But it does suggest that it's necessary to keep the reader interested. And it's worth bearing in mind that Eliot was of the opinion that poetry is "a higher form of entertainment."

Keeping the reader interested is something that Tony Roberts does well, and it may be that his penchant for allowing the poet to speak wherever possible is the key to his success. His opening essay about Robert Lowell's *Life Studies*, "that ground-breaking National Book Award winner which helped launch the controversial 'confessional' school of poetry" is flecked with judicious quotations which help lead the reader through Lowell's work. I can't claim any expertise in relation to Robert Lowell's poetry, so the combination of positive critical commentary and the lines of verse gave me an insight into what the poet had been aiming for.

Roberts is knowledgeable about "Robert Lowell's Circle," as he calls it, and other pieces relate to John Berryman, Elizabeth Bishop, Theodore Roethke, and the almost-forgotten Randall Jarrell. Roberts suggests that it's his poetry that is now overlooked, in comparison to his criticism, though I wonder how many people, outside of the academic world, bother to read the criticism these days? Not many, I suspect. But it isn't the criticism, or Jarrell's curious campus novel (one of the first of the genre?), *Pictures From An Institution*, that Roberts is concerned with. His survey of Jarrell's poetry is meant to revive interest in it, and it does, again by following informative linking passages with apt lines of the actual poems. I was taken to my bookshelves to find the full texts, and that indicates how Roberts has succeeded in his aim of pointing to the value of Jarrell's work beyond those heavily anthologised poems like "The Death of the Ball Turret Gunner."

I don't think there's any point in denying that this group of poets had common problems in terms of mental instability. You can get a good idea of what their lives were like from Eileen Simpson's memoir, *Poets In Their Youth*, where the struggle to create in the face of (or because of?) their mishaps and misbehaviours is brilliantly narrated.

A range of other American poets, some probably known to British readers, some probably not, are dealt with by Roberts. I doubt that Michael Mott, Robert Hass, Dave Smith, Michael Waters, and George Goode have had much circulation here, even if a few of their books have been published in Britain, thanks to imaginative presses like Bloodaxe and Shoestring. They tend not to be reviewed widely. That Roberts takes the trouble to write about them is to his credit and our benefit. I'd be unaware of Dave Smith's work had it not been for Roberts, for example, and his relatively short piece about George Goode prompted me into wanting to read more. I did previously know about poets like Richard Hugo and James Wright, but in both cases reading what Roberts had to say about them took me to the bookshelves and Hugo's *Making Certain It Goes On* and Wright's *Above The River,* large collections of their work. Roberts isn't given to eye-catching phrases and works in a more-relaxed and subtler way when drawing the reader's attention to specific parts of a poem or to its overall effect. Sometimes it requires quiet prompting from an astute critic to remind me that I have books I've neglected for far too long.

There are individual poems, too, that reading Roberts takes me back to. He makes a passing reference to Donald Justice's wonderful "Dance Lessons of the Thirties," which I first read in *New Criterion* many years ago and made a point of copying. Its final line, "O little lost Bohemias of the Suburbs!" delighted me and still does. There are lines, too, from W.D. Snodgrass's often-anthologised "April

Inventory" that have stayed in my mind for years and came to the surface again when reading Roberts on his work. At the risk of repeating myself I want to say that it's a sign of a good writer if the reader is prompted into remembering poems he or she has read, and wants to refer back to them because the enthusiasm of the essayist or reviewer is evident.

Is it only Americans that Roberts writes about? The short answer is no, and there are excellent appraisals of Charles Tomlinson, Elaine Feinstein, David Harsent, and several other non-Americans. It's noticeable that Roberts likes to concentrate his attention on poets who, while hardly neglected, are perhaps never likely to be highly popular, if poets can ever be said to achieve that status. Some do seem to forever be doing the rounds of festivals and the like, and attract attention from the media in various ways, but none of those I've mentioned are in that category. This isn't a comment on the quality of their work, but rather a reference to the fact that it requires a greater level of appreciation than can always be guaranteed at readings attracting large audiences. Before leaving this section in Roberts's book let me say how pleased I was to see him writing about Ford Madox Ford's poetry. It isn't well-known, but deserves to be. Again, Roberts was responsible for bringing a favourite poem to mind, in this case Ford's lovely "Champetre."

The last part of *The Taste In My Mind* is devoted to "Poets in Prose," with essays about Shakespeare, "Edmund Wilson among the Poets," Louis MacNeice, Turgenev, and more. There is also a splendid piece about Hemingway's *The Sun Also Rises*. I was pulled towards this immediately because it's a book that I first read in the 1950s when I was in the army, and which started off a life-long fascination with the expatriate experience in Paris in the 1920s. And a collector's inclination to locate books by Robert McAlmon, John Herrmann, and others, and copies of magazines like *This Quarter, Transatlantic Review* and *transition*. Roberts provides a succinct summary of the story, with asides about Hemingway's character, including the anti-semitism which comes across in the novel. Robert Cohn, who the hero, Jake (Hemingway) doesn't like, was clearly based on Harold Loeb, who had annoyed Hemingway by bedding Lady Duff Twysden, the real-life person behind the fictional Brett Ashley. Hemingway had tried but failed. Roberts doesn't explain all this, and is probably not interested in the gossip behind the book. He rightly focuses on it as literature. I admit to a taste for knowing what may have given Hemingway the impulse to write the book, but I accept that the true test of it is as a novel. Hemingway wasn't obliged to tell it exactly as it was.

I hope I've managed to get across at least some of the range of Tony Roberts's essays and reviews. His skills are evident in every piece as he deftly moves in and out a poet's work and points to its qualities. Or he intelligently analyses Edmund Wilson's understanding of poetry, and his encounters with Isaiah Berlin. And considers Robert Browning, Louis MacNeice, and Marilynne Robinson's novels. There is much to be gained from *The Taste In My Mind*, and I recommend it to anyone who likes to read clear, well-written commentary and criticism.

THE TASTE IN MY MIND By Tony Roberts. Shoestring Press. 284 pages. £12. ISBN 978-1-910323-17-5

AN UNHOLY ROW

In 1950 I was fourteen and I heard a Dizzy Gillespie record that changed my life. Well, perhaps it didn't actually do that, because I still had to go out in the morning on my paper round and then dash off to school. But it certainly opened up a whole new world for me, one which revolved around the weekly *Melody Maker* and the occasional jazz record I could afford to buy. Jazz wasn't at all respectable in 1950 and bebop in particular was frowned on or laughed at, even by many jazz fans. I'd come to it straight from listening to big-bands on the radio and getting hold of a few Les Brown and Gene Krupa discs. Traditional jazz didn't mean much to me. Bebop was what I was interested in. The American poet, Gilbert Sorrentino, once said that bebop was for him an entry into a whole new world of culture and that prior to it culture had meant doing your homework every night and going to the opera. It was, perhaps, a slightly tongue-in-cheek statement, but I knew what he meant.

Those reminiscences were triggered by Dave Gelly's short but excellent survey of jazz developments in Britain and the way in which audiences responded to them. As he points out, when the war ended in 1945, the radio played "an immensely important part in everyday life." With regard to music, the influx of American troops into Britain had an effect in terms of altering the approach of British bands as close contacts with American musicians in the Glenn Miller and Sam Donahue orchestras introduced new ideas and sounds into their musical thinking. There were radio programmes, too, that brought British and American musicians together. And the radio stations set up by the American Forces Network (AFN) often featured the latest records by the best American bands and musicians. British jazz and big-band enthusiasts frequently listened to these stations rather than to the BBC.

It is true that a lot of the music heard over the radio wasn't necessarily pure jazz. But styles mixed easily and Gelly states that "some of the most popular records of the first few post-war years contained a strong element of one kind of jazz or another." He mentions records by Pee Wee Hunt, Nellie Lutcher, Frankie Laine, and Louis Jordan, as examples. There were others and though it might be moving the timescale slightly around Gelly's it sticks in my mind that plenty of swing records by the likes of Charlie Barnet and

Tommy Dorsey could be heard on the radio. Barnet's *Skyliner* was the signature tune for one popular AFN record show in the late-1940s. And around 1950 or so even Woody Herman's bop-flavoured *Lemon Drop* sometimes cropped up on the *Family Favourites* programme. Older listeners were perhaps less thrilled by it than I was. I recall seeing Gene Krupa's band playing *Lemon Drop* in a musical short that accompanied the Western I'd gone to see at a local cinema, and the baffled reaction of many in the audience, young and old, to the bop vocal and saxophone solo, and the sight of the band in berets and dark glasses. I'm not convinced that the handful of examples Gelly uses, or the few that I've added, indicate any important trend in popular music in the late-1940s and early-1950s. Most popular music was mediocre and had no jazz content.

There were, of course, many jazz fans who were not interested in big-bands, small groups playing swing, and later bop, or performances which might have a kind of jazz tinge. These were the dedicated revivalist purists, often referred to as "mouldy figs," who thought that the only true jazz came from New Orleans and Chicago and that anything else wasn't worth considering. They were fanatical in their devotion to documenting the music, tracking down recorded examples, and playing their version of it. As Gelly notes, "commercial" was, for them, a term of abuse, and he goes on to provide a quick summary of the kind of attitudes, including a suspicion of professional musical skills, that the more extreme revivalists might display at times. The problem was, of course, that those attitudes could lead to revivalist jazz often being "badly played, out of tune, and because the players could only manage to get around in a limited number of easy keys, monotonous." The hard-core fans of this kind of jazz were predominantly male, though the fact that, whatever its faults, the steady beat made it ideal music for dancing, or jiving as it was called, meant that couples did frequent the clubs where the bands played. As I recall it, there was often a link between local amateur jazz bands and the local art school, with the students being enthusiastic supporters of traditional jazz, if only because they associated it with having a good time. And it seemed slightly rebellious and colourful in the world of austerity Britain.

The post-war period also saw the birth of bop in Britain as the new sounds slowly trickled over from America. Bop required greater musical skills so appealed largely to professional and semi-professional musicians who were employed in dance-bands on a national or local level. Gelly neatly sums up the differences between the worlds of traditional and modern jazz: "The earliest stirrings of revivalist jazz in Britain took place in suburban front rooms and the back rooms of pubs. Those of British bebop are to be traced to the peripheries of the dance-band world and long-defunct musicians' hangouts." The history of British bop still hasn't been written in full and is mostly to be found in scattered articles in jazz magazines, sleeve notes for LPs and CDs, and passages in books by or about people like Ronnie Scott and Johnny Dankworth. But Gelly does provide a useful account of the major events, such as the determined efforts of Scott, Dankworth, Hank Shaw, Laurie Morgan, and a few others, to get to New York so they could hear Charlie Parker, and the founding of the Club Eleven in 1949. He also rightly points to the little bands organised by Tito Burns as among the first to try to incorporate bop into their repertoire. It may be that Burns aimed for what Gelly calls "pop-bebop," but he did employ forward-looking young musicians.

Bop mostly attracted a different kind of listener, though it's difficult to be too specific about this. He makes a passing reference to skilled working-class males as being among bop's audience, and I have a feeling he may be right. But I suspect that genuine bop was always a minority interest, attracting individuals rather than groups, and it might be almost impossible to pin down exactly who did listen to it. There were few clubs outside London and some other major cities where bop was played. My own experience as a young enthusiast in the early 1950s saw me grabbing at any chance I got to experience music that I thought had some relation to bop. As a sixteen-year old I scraped enough together in 1952 to spend a few days in London so I could get to the Studio '51 Club and hear British modernists like Johnny Rogers, Dizzy Reece, Kenny Graham, and Eddie Blair. I saw Sarah Vaughan at a Sunday afternoon concert in Preston in 1953 and recall that also on the bill was a British band that had won a *Melody Maker* competition. A small group within it played a version of Dizzy Gillespie's *The Champ*, a tune which most British bands, including those led by Ted Heath and Jack Parnell, recorded. Ronnie Scott's fine nine-piece band came to a local dance-hall one Friday night and I was one of those ignoring the dancers and crowding around the front of the stage. Many years later I had the opportunity to tell Benny Green that I remembered him and the other musicians chanting "Oo-shoo-bee-doo," though I doubt that he wanted to be reminded of this concession to popular taste. The big thrill was in September, 1953, when I was one of the five thousand fans who crossed the Irish Sea to hear Stan Kenton in concert in Dublin. Kenton wasn't bop, but the 1953 band had musicians like Conte Candoli, Lee Konitz, Zoot Sims, and Frank Rosolino (who had performed the bop vocal in that Gene Krupa film mentioned earlier), and Gerry Mulligan had provided some of the more-modern arrangements. We had to go to Dublin because there was a ban on American bands playing in Britain. And there were experiences which provided snippets of jazz within mostly commercial frameworks, such as the occasional instrumental numbers that leaders like Teddy Foster and Joe Loss had in their repertoire and which might feature a tenor-sax or trumpet solo by some young musicians paying their dues in touring dance-bands. Most of all there were bop records on labels like Vogue, Esquire, and Melodisc, and I collected those avidly.

Jazz generally increased in popularity in the 1950s. Gelly attributes this, in the revivalist and traditional jazz fields, at least, to leaders like Graeme Bell and Humphrey Lyttelton playing for dancing. The purists were not happy with the growing popularity, and their suspicions about "commercialism" were justified in some ways as entrepreneurs moved in and began to organise concerts at the Royal Albert Hall and similar locations. New names began to come to the fore, including Chris Barber and Acker Bilk. And Trad Jazz, a watered-down version of New Orleans, soon began to dominate the pop charts. It was music that had none of the raggedness of the revivalist bands, and certainly none of the complexities of modern-jazz, the term that had taken over as bebop spread out and changed in the 1950s. Gelly says that "trad was never the kind of music which set out seriously to alienate parents or the older generation." He's insightful and fair to Bilk in particular and stresses that he was an excellent musician who made some attractive records which appealed to a wide audience. There was nothing wrong with that, even if diehard supporters of traditional, as opposed to trad, jazz looked on popular success with suspicion.

The audience for modern jazz also grew as the 1950s saw the ban on American musicians finally lifted and the Count Basie band came to

Britain, as did package shows like Norman Granz's Jazz at the Philharmonic, and another one that went under the name of Jazz from Carnegie Hall. British audiences could see and hear Stan Getz, Dizzy Gillespie, J.J. Johnson, Coleman Hawkins, and others in these star line-ups. There also were tours by individual groups led by Dave Brubeck, Miles Davis, and Thelonious Monk, with British groups like the Jazz Couriers or Joe Harriott's often opening up the concert. And Ronnie Scott's Club in London brought in Zoot Sims, Dexter Gordon, and others as soloists backed by British musicians. It could have been that the audiences for the larger touring groups, and especially the package shows, were there because of a few names like Oscar Peterson and Ella Fitzgerald, and that the interest in most of the soloists was largely confined to a relatively small circle of dedicated jazz fans. London may have been able to provide a jazz audience of a reasonable size, but elsewhere it was often difficult to sustain enough interest to have a jazz venue open on a regular basis. There were always exceptions, of course, in places like Manchester and Birmingham, but they often had to bring in American jazzmen, or an established name from London, to get enough customers to keep going.

The big-band culture which had enabled many musicians to survive was steadily declining in the late-1950s and early-1960s. And the few bands that did manage to get enough bookings to pay their way had to compromise by featuring singers (Ted Heath had three, if memory serves me right, when I saw his band during a summer season in Blackpool in the 1950s) and including a lot of commercial material in their performances. That had always been true, of course, because a big-band playing modern jazz wasn't going to have widespread support. I went to a Sunday evening concert by the Johnny Dankworth Orchestra in 1954 while I was waiting to be sent to an army camp in Germany, and I remember being disappointed by the fact that so much of the programme was, to my mind, commercial. I'm thinking back sixty years so I can't be specific about what I heard. But it may be significant that a minor hit record, *Experiments with Mice,* that Dankworth had in the 1950s was, in Gelly's words, "a superior kind of novelty." I'm not in any way condemning Dankworth or any other bandleader for having to compromise in order to make a living, and just want to point out that the audience for a big-band playing only modern jazz was far too small to support it on a full-time basis.

179

Gelly says that the "audience for modern jazz in Britain not only grew substantially but matured" in the late-1950s, and he attributes this to many young people – "sixth formers, undergraduates and the like" – becoming bored with trad jazz. He also credits the rising interest in the Beats as having an effect because of their liking for jazz and their frequent references to it in their novels and poems. The jazz musician had become a kind of hero in the style of the bohemian, someone living the sort of life that separated him from the general population and often prepared to make sacrifices, perhaps even die, for the sake of his art. Along with this there was the way in which jazz, especially of the modern kind, had achieved acceptance among intellectuals and was written about in Sunday newspapers and weekly journals like the *New Statesman*. Before I went into the army in early 1954 I read about jazz in the *Melody Maker* and *Jazz Journal*, and none of the people I would have thought of as intellectuals took it seriously. When I came back to Britain in 1957 the intellectuals were telling me that jazz was art because they took it seriously. I admit to feeling resentful because I'd always known what Charlie Parker's true worth was and I didn't need someone writing for a posh paper or magazine to explain it to me. Curiously, I had much the same experience with the Beats and other writers, whose work I found for myself long before it became widely-known or popular, and when it was often sneered at and dismissed. Later, I was told that I ought to take those writers seriously by intellectuals and academics who had suddenly decided they were worthy of attention. I was more amused than resentful that time around.

It needs to be said that in the early-1960s modern jazz almost collapsed in terms of popularity. Trad jazz still continued to have an audience for some years, but the rise of rock'n'roll in the late-1950s had started to pull away young people who were looking for music that went along with dancing, having a good time, and perhaps provided a kind of revolt against older generations. When rock music began to broaden and take on intellectual pretensions, along with its relationship to forms of social and political protest in the 1960s, I think it appealed to those who may at one time have been inclined towards jazz. It may also be true to say that after 1960 or so developments in free jazz and other experiments took modern jazz even further away from any kind of popular appeal. I doubt that the audiences that went to hear Dave Brubeck, Ella Fitzgerald, Oscar Peterson, and the Modern Jazz Quartet, would have wanted to listen to Albert Ayler or Archie Shepp. Things did pick up in the 1970s and 1980s and I heard a lot of good jazz throughout both decades, though mostly in small clubs. And there were jazz festivals, though I never could really adapt to listening to jazz in the open air and with the musicians some distance away. And I wonder how many genuine jazz fans there are now. There are still a couple of nationally published jazz magazines, though I suspect that for one of them the circulation may be declining as old age creeps up on the readers. And coverage of jazz elsewhere tends to be sporadic and rarely in depth. It's not true to say that jazz is dead, and there is still plenty of activity of one kind or another around the country, but it certainly has much less of a broad appeal than it once had.

Gelly's survey only takes us up to 1960, though he does have something to say about jazz today. And the question arises of whether or not much of what now passes for jazz is truly jazz. As he says, it might all depend on how you define jazz. I've got to admit that the predominance of singers tends to incline me towards relying on my CD collection and old LPs for my jazz entertainment. I'm not suggesting that the singers are bad, nor that they often use good material, and that their accompaniment is provided by competent musicians with jazz inclinations. But the end product doesn't really get through to me as jazz. Nor does a lot of the purely instrumental music that now claims to be jazz. These doubts may well be due to my own blindspots, limitations, and prejudices. Perhaps I'm still hooked on the atmosphere of the days when bop was relatively new to me, jazz was where you found it, and it was exciting to discover new records and musicians? Nostalgia can become a problem. Still, I was talking to a friend recently and told him about hearing Dexter Gordon in Ronnie Scott's original club, the basic cellar with just plain chairs lined up in front of the musicians. In response, he told me about a recent visit to the current club with its high admission charge, expensive but average food, and overpriced drinks. And I thought, it's not a place for an old man who remembers what it was like fifty years ago. And could they now feature anyone of the musical stature of Dexter Gordon?

All that aside I want to say how much I enjoyed Dave Gelly's book. It's well-written, gives an intelligent and informative summary of the period concerned, and is short and to the point, something to be welcomed in an age when big books seem to be taking over. It has a number of entertaining anecdotes, and there are relevant notes, a short but sufficient for the purpose bibliography, and a useful guide to available CDs. I'd recommend *An Unholy Row* to anyone wanting a brisk account of jazz in Britain in the 1940s and 1950s.

AN UNHOLY ROW : JAZZ IN BRITAIN AND ITS AUDIENCE 1945-1960 By Dave Gelly. Equinox Publishing. 167 pages. £25. ISBN 978-1-84553-712-8

TUBBY HAYES

British modern jazz of the 1945-1960 period has never really been given the attention it deserves. One or two books have been published about someone like Ronnie Scott, and a scattering of articles in jazz magazines have tried to draw attention to certain of the musicians active in the years referred to. There have been CD re-issues of some of the sounds produced by those musicians, though much still remains in the vaults, if it has survived at all. And it's a fact that, when it was being played, most British jazz was looked on as an imitation of what was coming out of New York and Los Angeles. I have to be honest, and admit that in the 1950s I bought LPs by American jazzmen and rarely, if ever, thought of purchasing any by our home-grown players. Even when I heard them live it was, on a number of occasions, when they were on the same bill as visiting Americans. There were some practical reasons for this, the main one being that money was tight and I had to limit what I spent to cover a few essential records and tickets for concerts which featured Dizzy Gillespie and Stan Getz. An LP re-issue of some sides by Charlie Parker was always going to take precedence over one by, say, Johnny Dankworth. And the chance of seeing Gillespie and Getz on stage was, it seemed to me at the time, more important than visiting Manchester to listen to Jimmy Deuchar or Don Rendell in a little jazz club.

I did, however, see and hear quite a few British jazzmen over the years, among them the tenor-saxophonist Tubby Hayes. I saw the Jazz Couriers (the group he formed with Ronnie Scott) more than once, and I recall hearing Hayes in one of the London clubs, though the intervening years have pushed its name from my memory. But recollections of my encounters with Hayes and his music came flooding back as I read Simon Spillett's entertaining biography of him.

Hayes was born Edward Brian Hayes in 1935 and, by the age of sixteen was skilled enough as a saxophonist to be playing in a group led by Kenny Baker, a leading British trumpeter. Hayes wasn't among the first wave of British musicians to be influenced by the new sounds of bebop which were then filtering through from America. Ronnie Scott, Johnny Dankworth, and others, were keen enough to want to know more about the music being produced by

Dizzy Gillespie and Charlie Parker that they took jobs with the bands playing on cross-Atlantic liners so that they could get to New York and hear it live and not only on records. But Hayes was influenced by the music he heard on 78s. Spillett says that the first Charlie Parker record that Hayes owned was a 78 of "Stupendous." I can't resist mentioning here that it was the first Parker record I bought and was one side of a Parlophone disc, the other side being Howard McGhee's "High Wind in Hollywood." Both tracks appeared to me to be totally representative of the new.

If Hayes was quickly picking up on bebop when he was very young, he was hardly making a mark as a pupil at the school he attended. By the time he was fifteen he had left school and was working in a local band, though its musical range didn't encompass much more than "weddings, tea-dances and suburban youth clubs." When he did get the opportunity to perform in the West End he appears to have also embarked on a long career of heavy drinking. As Spillett puts it: "Having now entered a tough, adult profession wherein seasoned players would expect a newcomer to prove his mettle in all sorts of ways, Tubby Hayes was growing up as fast as a hothouse flower." Growing up fast was, as his later life would show, to have had a major effect on his health.

There's a chapter in Spillett's book where he talks about what life was like in the early 1950s for those musicians working with touring bands like Kenny Baker's. Distances between venues were affected by the fact that the motorway system hadn't then been developed. Accommodation was often fairly basic – Vic Ash recalled a boarding house in Manchester where the bandleader had his own room but the rest had to bunk down in a dormitory with eight beds in it: "You can imagine the grunts and groans and odours during the night." And "the lethal food served by the nation's transport cafes" added to the problems that youngsters like Ash and Hayes had to contend with as they attempted to carve out a career as professional musicians. Drinking and smoking were part of the routine of life on the road, and Spillett points to the opportunities for casual sex as some female fans "would make themselves readily available." It could be an exhausting life, in more ways than one, and there's an account of Hayes passing out when the Baker band was appearing at the Winter Gardens in Ventnor. Reports at the time said that it was due to "the effects of heat," which may have been a polite way of putting it.

Hayes worked his way through other bands, including those led by Roy Fox and Tito Burns, though neither offered wide opportunities for him to display his skills as a jazz soloist. Burns did have a track record as one of the first bandleaders to try to introduce bop to a wider public than that found in a few jazz clubs in London and one or two other major cities. But by 1952 or so he was struggling to stay solvent and so had to compromise with the music his group could play. As for Hayes, he was beginning to make something of a name for himself as a jazz soloist in clubs in the capital, and Spillett states that he was often working with leading British modernists. He mentions Ronnie Scott, Leon Calvert, Joe Harriott, Les Condon, Victor Feldman, and Dickie Devere, as among them. But it was a small world and the "now forgotten suburban venues" that Spillett refers to were often little more than a room in a pub, despite having names like the Robin's Nest, the Royal Roost, and the Lion's Den. It was probably around this time that Hayes began to dabble with "stimulants other than alcohol," according to one of his friends.

Still, Hayes was beginning to come to the attention of musicians and fans. He worked with leading orchestras like Ambrose and Vic Lewis, and it was with the latter that he was a featured soloist and first appeared on records. In 1954 he joined drummer Jack Parnell's lively band and it was while it was working at the Winter Gardens in Blackpool that Hayes and his wife were arrested for possession of cannabis. I can recall the reports in the press at the time and how unusual it all seemed, drug use not then being something that was known to be prevalent among British jazz musicians. Phil Seamen, also with Parnell, was a heroin addict, and there had been some notoriety surrounding the raid on the Club Eleven in 1949. I was later to get to know about casualties like Tommy Pollard and Dickie Devere, but as an eighteen year old provincial jazz fan in 1954 I thought of drug addiction as something mostly related to certain American musicians.

By the mid-1950s Hayes had formed a musical relationship with trumpeter Jimmy Deuchar and together they played jazz that was, in Spillett's words, "already firmly rooted in the hard bop vein." They were heavily influenced by the records that were beginning to be released by specialist labels like Esquire and Vogue, and it was occasionally said of Hayes that his playing too often tended to respond to the latest styles coming from America. He wasn't alone in this among British jazz musicians and throughout the 1940s and 1950s most British modern jazz, good as it sometimes was, inevitably sounded like a copy of American sounds. Hayes, earlier in the 1950s, had clearly listened to records by Stan Getz, Wardell Gray, and others, insofar as they were available, and would later be influenced by Sonny Rollins. By the mid-1950s LPs were becoming easier to obtain and with their capacity to allow musicians to take longer solos they became of key, if not always beneficial, importance in terms of how they affected British jazzmen. Long solos can often be boring.

The band that Hayes formed and took on the road faced the usual problem of having to cater for audiences that were not necessarily attuned to modern jazz. Spillett provides a useful list of the venues it appeared at during April and part of May, 1955, and as he remarks, it "wasn't exactly chock- full of outstanding jazz dates." Bassist Pete Blannin later recalled how the pressure was on to play for dancers rather than the probably small number of people who were there to hopefully hear some jazz. There were personal issues, too, that caused problems. Hayes was said to be self-centred and "liked to get his own way about everything," Blannin thought, and trumpeter Dickie Hawdon reckoned he was "a bit of a hooligan" and more interested in having a good time than in looking after the business side of running a band. But Hawdon also said that "It was a lovely shouting little band," and Jack Sharpe, who played baritone-saxophone, claimed that "Tubby's band on the road was an education I would not have missed for anything. One of the happiest periods of my life."

Besides touring with his own band Hayes continued to play in jazz clubs, often with Jimmy Deuchar, and to record for the Tempo label which, in the 1950s, offered opportunities for British modernists to show what they could do. Luckily, recent years have seen much of the Tempo catalogue re-issued by Jasmine and Properbox, and so allowed listeners to re-evaluate the music that players like Hayes, Deuchar, Dizzy Reece, Ronnie Scott, and others, turned out. It's true that the American influence is always noticeable, but even so many of the tracks are eminently listenable and a few can stand alongside most of what was being produced elsewhere at the time. I think it is correct to say that British rhythm-sections were sometimes a problem, and heavy-handed drumming can be heard on many records, just as I recall it could in the clubs. Dynamics were not always a major concern. And, with regard to Hayes himself, there were frequent complaints that he often played too much, too fast. I have to admit that my own reactions to his work did include this criticism. I listened in vain for the pauses and silences that can add tension to a performance. There are moments when what you don't hear can be almost as important as what you do hear. Hayes' boisterous personality seemed to incline him towards filling in every gap, rather like someone who wants to dominate a conversation.

The Hayes band eventually collapsed as a result of "the lack of suitable work, surfeit of unscrupulous promoters, and an ever-decreasing jazz content." There was also the rise of rock-and-roll to contend with. Younger audiences took to the music immediately. It was suitable for dancing and didn't involve musicians taking long, complicated solos. It also put the emphasis on singers. And from the point of view of anyone running a dance-hall or club it was cheaper to hire a three or four piece rock group than it was to bring in a nine-piece jazz outfit. Spillett does a neat job of explaining why audiences turned to rock-and-roll. Not all jazzmen were averse to jumping on the bandwagon and drummer Tony Crombie, an early activist in the bebop revolution, formed a group called The Rockets which was popular for a short period. Individual jazzmen also benefited by being brought in for recording sessions which required some brisk backing work. Hayes and Ronnie Scott, for example, were members of Art Baxter's Rock and Roll Sinners on at least one such occasion.

In 1957 Hayes and Scott formed what was one of the more-successful British groups, The Jazz Couriers, a two-tenor and rhythm outfit, with Hayes also sometimes playing vibraphone, and Jimmy Deuchar occasionally added to the line-up. There were questions raised about the group's overall approach and Spillett says that critics zoned in "on Hayes and Scott's propensity to cram their solos with endless streams of notes and the group's general preoccupation with appearing hip." But he qualifies such comments by pointing out "that the bustling energy of the Couriers' music came as a refreshing wake-up call to those who'd grown used to the more reserved charms of other local jazz units." That "bustling energy" is certainly what sticks in my mind when I think back to the late-1950s, though I also had some sympathy with those who found the "endless streams of notes" a little overwhelming. Even Ronnie Scott later acknowledged that he had doubts about his partner's technical proficiency: "There was always a but with me with Tubby. I don't know what you'd call it. It was like you turned a switch and bang, it was always there, a bit – mechanical."

His marriage having broken up Hayes's personal life was chaotic and sharing a flat with Phil Seamen, a noted junkie, and tenorman Bobby Wellins, who would soon have addiction problems of his own, wasn't likely to lead to it getting any better. When the Jazz Couriers finally called it a day in 1959 Hayes worked around the clubs with his own quartet and made a number of records. He appeared in the film, *All Night Long*, with Charles Mingus, Dave Brubeck, and others, and finally achieved his ambition of performing in a New York jazz club. His playing was known to American musicians who had worked in Britain, and Zoot Sims, in particular, helped to promote the idea of Hayes being hired to work at the Half Note. Sims, Al Cohn, and critic Dan Morgenstern, all spoke warmly of Hayes soloing. But returning to the limits of the British jazz scene was something of a let-down. It involved the usual visits to the remaining jazz clubs around London and trips to places like Liverpool, Leeds, Glasgow and Birmingham for one-night stands with his quartet.

The appearance by John Coltrane and his group in London in late-1961 certainly shook up the locals. I was at the concert in Kilburn on November 11th, 1961, and I'll not try to pretend that I was impressed or converted by Coltrane's work. I had gone there primarily to see and hear Dizzy Gillespie, who was leading the other group on the programme, and Coltrane's long solo on "My Favourite Things" frankly left me floundering. I remember someone in front of me arriving around twenty minute late for the start of Coltrane's performance and asking the person next to him what the first number was like. "This is the first number" was the cryptic reply. Spillett's description of how Hayes reacted to Coltrane that night reassures me that a non-musician like myself wasn't alone in finding Coltrane difficult to understand.

There were attempts by Hayes and his advisers to broaden the appeal of his music as The Beatles and other pop groups increasingly dominated the airwaves, though they were probably doomed to failure from the start. Spillett is interesting in his summary of how, by the mid-1960s, pop groups had not only taken over musically, but had also affected the lives of those who listened to them: "The Beatles were no longer simply a band, they were a way of life, a cult transforming the lives of those who followed them in the same catalytic way that Charlie Parker had once transformed young jazz musicians." I have my doubts about that, but they may be those of a jazz fan who found it hard to accept that pop music might have that sort of importance or influence.

Hayes continued to keep busy with both jazz and session work (he played flute on a Matt Monro record, to take one example of his non-jazz efforts) and he toured on the Continent and visited the USA again. But in London the outlets for jazz were drying up. He was drinking heavily and began to turn to hard drugs like heroin and cocaine for the stimulation he needed. Or did they offer an escape from the frustrations, both musical and personal, he felt? In addition, his health was in decline and he was diagnosed with a thrombosis which affected not only his legs but also his lung function. And the critical response to his music could sometimes be harsh. Brian Priestley, writing in *Jazz Monthly*, had this to say: "I'm bound to admit that I find it almost impossible to write objectively about Hayes's solo work simply because, after years of hearing him live and recorded, I seem to have acquired a built in resistance to the Instant Boredom he usually offers. No sooner does he start one of his marathons that I find I'm concentrating on the rhythm section, or reading the menu, or studying my fingernails."

There were problems in 1968 when his flat was raided by police and he was arrested and charged with possession of diamorphine. The details were widely reported in the national press. Tragedy was not far away, either, and Hayes's girlfriend, a singer named Joy Marshall, and like him a drug user, died from an overdose of barbiturates. The news hit him badly, because although their relationship had been stormy, and they were not a couple at the time of her death, the pair did have things in common beyond drug use and Hayes had been genuinely fond of her. He continued to work when and where he could, but collapsed in 1970 when appearing at a club in Birmingham. He was taken into hospital and placed under observation for what was referred to as an "unidentified infection." It had affected his heart, lungs and liver, and was probably caused by an earlier use of a dirty needle, though no-one seemed to be certain and it was suggested that an unclean razor blade could just as easily been the culprit. The infection had most likely been there for some time and was "triggered by Hayes's inconsistent lifestyle." He was hospitalised for fifteen weeks.

The remaining years of his life were not particularly happy ones. He was found to have a defective heart valve and needed an operation to replace it. When he eventually left hospital he spent some time recuperating and then returned to playing and worked with Bill Le Sage and Hank Shaw in a group called the Bebop Preservation Society. He also made a short tour of Scandinavia which included appearances in Gothenberg, Oslo, and Stockholm. Reports said that he'd stopped smoking, was drinking only moderate amount of light wine and beer, but still had problems when walking and had to amend the way he played to take account of his breathing difficulties.

Back in Britain in the early-1970s it was the usual round of clubs in pubs in Islington, Stockwell, Clerkenwell, and other London districts. As Spillett describes it: "The big names of the Brit-Bop generation – Stan Tracey, Phil Seamen, Hayes – had all now become fixtures on this scene, existing under the radar of a jazz press fascinated with the latest developments in fusion." But Hayes was not a well-man and when Phil Seamen died at the age of forty-six, his body damaged by the years of drug taking, he remarked to a fellow-musician, "It'll be me next." He continued to work, but by 1973 it was becoming obvious that he wouldn't be able to function much longer as a musician. Spillett's account of Hayes struggling and failing to get a sound out of his saxophone prior to going on stage at a gig in Brighton makes for harrowing and moving reading. He had to be admitted into hospital again as the replacement heart valve that had been fitted earlier was failing. An attempt was made to substitute another valve and it seemed to have been successful, but Hayes died in the operating theatre: "His blood pressure was too low and his body simply too worn down to be brought round."

How good was Tubby Hayes? He was clearly a major player on the British scene, though the consensus of opinion seems to be that he was more of an inspiration than an influence. Musicians who worked in his various groups spoke of his capacity to push them into playing better. But he didn't create a school of saxophonists playing in his style, perhaps because, like Hayes himself, younger jazzmen looked to the USA for their influences. There is, too, the accusation that he often played too fast for too long. In this respect, it could be that we may not have heard him at his best. There's a revealing comment by drummer Alan Ganley which is worth quoting in full:

"Sometimes on the stand it was like 'Look how fast I can play and for how long' which is open-mouthed stuff but not always as musical as he could play when he just relaxed and didn't bother about creating an impression. He was a showman, a natural showman, but when you'd get him in a situation where it was just a few guys hanging around and someone would just start playing, he could be much more relaxed. The best I'd ever heard him play would be at a party, an after-hours thing where he wasn't trying to impress."

Simon Spillett has written a book about Tubby Hayes that tells us a great deal about the man and his music, and about British modern jazz generally. It's closely researched, with ample notes and a useful discography. And it made me want to listen again to Hayes and all the other musicians we perhaps didn't fully appreciate in the 1950s and 1960s.

THE LONG SHADOW OF THE LITTLE GIANT: THE LIFE, WORK AND LEGACY OF TUBBY HAYES By Simon Spillett. Equinox Publishing. 377 pages. £19.99. ISBN 978-1-78179-173-8

UNDERGROUND LONDON
BEBOP AND BEYOND

In the early-1960s the term "underground" became so noticeable that it was difficult to think that what it was meant to describe – the publications, the people behind them, the activities they were involved in, and much more – really could be called underground in any meaningful way. Newspapers, glossy magazines, radio programmes, all highlighted aspects of the underground so that it was known about by many people and exalted or attacked according to where one stood on the question of its values, or lack of them. But ten or fifteen years before Beats and their supporters could be encountered around London, there was what might be described as a genuine underground to be found in Soho. It did attract some attention, though usually of a hostile kind.

My thoughts about that early underground were inspired by coming across an old copy of Raymond Thorp's *Viper,* an admittedly sensationalised account of how its author was drawn into drug addiction through his involvement in the London jazz club scene of the late-1940s and early-1950s. It's perhaps more accurate to say that he primarily got involved because of his liking for bebop, the music that had attracted the attention, and caught the imagination, of many young musicians in Britain, and especially in London. Not all of the jazz played in the clubs of the time was bebop, and the number of musicians who could play it effectively was initially very limited. Likewise, the number of enthusiasts who wanted to listen to bop was small. But both musicians and fans were often fanatical in their promotion of the music, and the fanaticism often led to them adopting a life-style that seemed to go with the intensity inherent in bebop.

I'm not about to suggest that *Viper* has any great literary merits. It hasn't and is now mainly of interest for its documentary qualities. It was, in fact, ghost-written, by a journalist named Derek Agnew. But that's not important, any more than the prose style which often runs to phrases like, "He was popping cocaine whenever he could get it, a really gone individual who played those keys in the craziest of ways." I doubt that anyone ever really talked like that, but it no doubt seemed authentic to readers who liked to view a strange world from the comfort of their armchairs. The main points of interest in Thorp's story are his experiences at the Club Eleven, a bop club that has a key place in the history of the music in Britain.

I'll get to the Club Eleven in due course, but it's of relevance to look first at Thorp's description of another club he frequented prior to the opening of Club Eleven. He calls it the Boogie Club, though I don't know if that was the real name, and describes the people who frequented it in the following words:

"And it was haunted by musicians on the dole, musicians wasting time and musicians smoking hemp, artists in blue jeans who had never painted, writers who couldn't write, philosophers who had never thought, jazz-hungry girls begging life to kick them, small-time crooks planning big-time jobs, women with empty heads but full figures and men with ideas about them, and a lot of other refuse from the pavements...."

It was at the Boogie Club that Thorp first came across marijuana, though in good story-telling fashion he claimed that he'd never before used drugs of any kind. But because of his need to be seen as someone who was "cool," and part of the crowd of musicians and enthusiasts he mixed with, he eventually succumbed and experienced his first "high." The description of it is suitably colourful, with a claim that it was like "jumping out of the rut and climbing on a rocket bound for heaven. Yes, heaven. I was up there, too. Up there sitting beside God on his throne, looking down. Lying on a star with my toes curling, laughing at a million miles of space." As the dealer who sold him the marijuana in the toilets of the Boogie Club said, "Best charge in town, man." It certainly must have been. It's impossible to know whether the words are Thorp's own or the ghost-writer's fanciful interpretation of his reminiscences of how he felt when he lit that first joint.

Looking back, Thorp recounts how he got interested in jazz by going to a concert by the Ted Heath big-band which, while out of necessity playing music with a broad appeal, did include a fair amount of jazz in its programmes and featured some capable jazz musicians. His next step was to visit the Feldman Club "in Oxford Street, not far from Tottenham Court Road underground station." The Feldman Club was an actual club, "a restaurant during the week and a jazz centre only on Sunday evenings." It had the reputation of being a well-run establishment and Thorp describes the atmosphere as "all very innocent." But it was at the Feldman Club that he heard about the Club Eleven in "Great Windmill Street - a few yards from Piccadilly Circus." It isn't far from Oxford Street to Great Windmill Street, but the distance between the situation in the Feldman Club and that Thorp was to experience in the Club Eleven was considerable. As one of his friends said when Thorp suggested going to the Club Eleven, "I don't like getting mixed up with those Soho types."

It might be useful at this point to provide a brief history of the Club Eleven. It was established towards the end of 1948 by a group of ten young musicians and an associate of theirs who agreed to manage its affairs. The musicians were all dedicated to playing bop and some of them had even worked as members of orchestras on cross-Atlantic liners in order to hear Charlie Parker, Dizzy Gillespie, and other bebop originators in the New York clubs. These musicians wanted a place where they could play what they liked without any concessions to commercialism, so it seemed logical to open their own club. Some of them, like Ronnie Scott and Johnny Dankworth, later became well-known, but others, such as the ill-fated Tommy Pollard, an early casualty of the drugs scene, and the Bird-influenced alto-player Johnny Rogers, slipped from sight as the 1950s progressed. It's a personal reminiscence, but I remember seeing Rogers in 1952 in a little club called Studio '51 which was in Great Newport Street, just off Charing Cross Road.

I think it's true to say that the Club Eleven attracted what might be best referred to as "underground characters." The musician and writer Brian Priestley put it this way: "There was a decidedly louche atmosphere at Club Eleven sessions, unlike the Feldman Club, which was family-run and quite decorous. The more night-time elements gravitated to 41 Windmill Street - showbiz types, Soho characters, dealers in this and that, military absconders." Another description of the club said it was "the wildest place in town" on a good night. The downside was that drugs were part of the scene and most of the musicians were using substances of one kind or another. The tenor-saxophonist Don Rendell, who played at the club, remembered that the smell of marijuana pervaded the atmosphere. And Tony Hall, who later recorded many British modernists in the 1950s, said that heroin was easily available and that several of the musicians were using it. It was inevitable that the club soon came to the notice of the police, and in April, 1950, it was raided and six musicians, including

Ronnie Scott, who was found in the possession of a small amount of cocaine, appeared in court and were fined. The club continued for a while, but the adverse publicity, and arguments among the musicians, eventually forced its closure. And one or two of the original founders of the club, such as the drummer Laurie Morgan, had become somewhat disenchanted with what they thought was the juvenile non-musical behaviour of other musicians.

Raymond Thorp had taken to the atmosphere of Club Eleven, and said: "I was at once at home with the relaxed feeling and 'gone' on the hot music. The musicians played what they liked as they liked – but it was mostly bebop and a lot more frantic than at Feldmans. There were no requests and no programme. If the music failed to please......well, you didn't have to stay. But there were hundreds like myself who liked the music. So we stayed while some left. And the more we stayed the more the Club Eleven crept into the marrow of our bones." Thorp began to socialise with people he met who were involved with drugs and sometimes minor criminal activity: "In the Club Eleven at least one pusher was always hanging around. If you could not find him there it was a certainty someone would be standing on the corner of Archer Street or sitting in the Harmony Inn waiting for business." Archer Street was something of an open-air hiring-hall where musicians congregated as they looked for jobs and the Harmony Inn a café popular with them and their hangers-on. Like the Club Eleven they were locations that were raided by the Drugs Squad.

Thorp soon began pushing marijuana himself in order to finance his own habit and his liking for new clothes and a life of hanging around the Club Eleven and similar places. And he was eventually arrested and charged with possession. It didn't deter him and in time he moved into pushing cocaine, thanks to a chance encounter with someone who had some but didn't know what it was worth. Thorp eventually started dabbling with heroin himself and was soon addicted. But I don't want to spend too much time on his account of how he survived, and what interested me most when I first read *Viper* were the references to the various characters he encountered in his wanderings from one shabby room to another. There was "Jeremy the Part. He was once an actor, took to odd philosophies, and was to be seen around Soho still living a part." And "Big David, and soon after him the man the whole of Soho knew as Jesus Christ."

He's described as "A short stockily built man with a great leonine head and a full growth of beard. He was a poet of some quality but like every viper idle to the core and incapable of doing anything with his talents." There are specific references to 1953 and 1954, so we can pinpoint the period he's talking about, and his account ties in with other books about 1950s Soho and its characters, such as the novels by Colin Wilson (*Adrift in Soho*) and Terry Taylor (*Barons Court, All Change*).

As I said earlier, *Viper* isn't a particularly well-written book and its main interest now lies in the fact that it provides information about Soho, the birth of bebop in Britain, and the sort of bohemia that existed prior to the arrival of the Beat Generation. In some ways I'm reminded of the kind of milieu that Kerouac describes in his New York section of *The Town and the City*, with its cast of would-be poets, jazz musicians, hipsters, hustlers, and others. Both settings refer to the "underground" of their period and place. There are differences, of course, but it is possible to identify some areas where there are similarities in terms of the kind of people attracted to a way of life outside the mainstream.

A final note about *Viper*. It is very much a book of its time in the way that it presents its story as a kind of morality tale that potential readers could use to justify their suspicions about bebop, bohemians, and ways of life outside their experience. When the drummer Dickie Devere died as a result of his addiction his father said: "I know it was modern jazz and heroin that killed my son. With modern jazz the brain can only go so far and then it has to be boosted up.....with drugs."

There are also numerous references to the role that "spades," the term in use for blacks (mostly West Indians), played in the 1950s club and drugs scene. And a few to Jews who were involved. Again, I can't help thinking that they were there to appeal to the suspicions, if not prejudices, of the general readers who the book would have been aimed at.

NOTES

Viper was originally published in 1956 in hardback by Robert Hale Ltd., London. The paperback edition was published as a WDL book in 1960.

The Colin Wilson and Terry Taylor novels mentioned were republished by New London Editions in 2011.

The novelist and short-story writer, Julian Maclaren-Ross, a well-known character around Soho in the 1940s and 1950s, wrote a satirical article called "Bop" (it's in his collection, *The Funny Bone, published by Elek Books, London, 1956*) in which he described a visit to a bop club. He refers to the customers wearing "existentialist clothes," meaning the sort of dress that he associated with jazz clubs in Montparnasse. But he also describes the males as wearing "drape suits with long jackets, mainly powder-blue."

Stephen Fothergill's *The Last Lamplighter: A Soho Education* (London Magazine Editions, London, 2000) has references to the Club Eleven, and the Harmony Inn, and places both in the context of the wider Soho bohemian scene.

There are good descriptions of the Club Eleven, the musicians who played there, and the atmosphere, in John Fordham's *Let's Join Hands and Contact the Living: Ronnie Scott and his Club* (Elm Tree Books, London, 1986).

There's a short-story called "Drummer Unknown" in John Harvey's *A Darker Shade of Blue* (Heinemann, London, 2010) which refers to a photograph taken in the Club Eleven. The narrator says, "I'm not usually one to cast blame, but after the influx of Americans during the last years of the war, hard drugs were always part of the scene. Especially once trips to New York to see the greats on 52nd Street had confirmed their widespread use."

If anyone wants to know more about the Club Eleven and the modern jazz scene generally in Britain in the late-1940s and early-1950s they are referred to the website Henrybebop.co.uk

The 2-CD set Soho After Dark (Giant Steps GSCR 038) is useful for musical examples of the period. But the best source for the music is a four-CD set, Bebop in Britain (Esquire CD ESQ 100-4), released by Charly records in 1991.

BOPPER

Most of you probably won't recall the time when be-bop was popular amongst jazz fans, and if you do you perhaps weren't all that involved. What I mean is that lots of people hung around the clubs, but not too many of them were really interested in the music. You can usually tell the handful who were even now, and I suppose there's some truth in the idea that if you were genuinely involved - either deliberately or intuitively, intellectually or emotionally - then you were never quite the same again. The attitudes stuck once you picked them up.

The interesting thing is that bop did catch on outside the big cities. Nearly every town had its bop club, and its small group of boppers, and if a lot of them were interested more in drinking and dancing, well, a few of us cared about the music. We studied the monthly record lists and bought the latest 78s - Parker, Howard McGhee, J.J. Johnson, Charlie Ventura, Tito Burns, Ronnie Scott. If a record had some connection with bop we bought it. And we'd sit around in each other's houses on Sunday, nodding our heads to an Afro-Cuban beat and peering across the room from behind dark-glasses. Around town, and at the dances or conceits where a name band was playing, we wore drape-suits and shirts with spear-point collars; knitted ties; slip-on shoes, sometimes with thick crepe soles. I even had a beret once, and later bought a tartan shirt because I'd seen a photo of Dizzy Gillespie and he was wearing one. Our hunched shoulders and refusal to even consider dancing completed the picture.

Johnny McKenzie was one of the boppers I knew. I'd met him when I walked into the toilets at the club whistling "Lemon Drop" or "Ornithology" or some such tune. He had a Lennie Tristano record under his arm and we argued about whether Tristano was going to be the new thing. I was crazy about Bird and Fats Navarro and Dexter Gordon, and all the other original wild bop musicians, and couldn't believe that anyone would ever replace them. Their sound was the sound of the time and when you're young you have a kind of religious belief in things only getting better.

Johnny played trumpet. He wasn't wonderful but he made it with the local bands and in London a few of the musicians let him sit in at parties and jam-sessions. The clique was small then and anyone

198

showing interest was accepted. He knew a few of the big names and a lot of the lesser ones, but I won't mention them. One or two were partly responsible for what happened later and it wouldn't be fair for them all to be connected with it.

If you look back in old newspapers of the period you'll read about a police raid on the Club Eleven in London, and the sensation it caused when some of the musicians appeared in court on charges of possessing marijuana. Well, it wasn't all that difficult to pick up the stuff in the provinces. Quite a few West Indians came down to our club and they smoked regularly, and in any case some of us used to go to Liverpool for the weekend and visit clubs there. I was too scared to try it, but Johnny did and we'd sometimes sit together, listening to records, and I'd wonder if he was hearing the same music. He'd finger the valves of his trumpet and blow into it softly, and his eyes would have a dreamy, far-away look. It didn't bother me a great deal, because I always was happy when people listened quietly to records. I got so many kicks from listening to the music that it never occurred to me to do anything else, even learn to play an instrument.

When he'd been to London Johnny would always come back with a pile of the new records, and a bunch of new stories about various bop musicians. He once told me about a club where the trumpeter was so stoned he sat in the audience listening to his own band instead of playing with it, and the casual way in which he mentioned the man's name was, of course, the point of the story. And he'd laugh about the parties he'd been to. There was one, thrown by a well-known drummer, where everyone got high and banged on pots and pans as a girl danced on a table and stripped.

It was during one of his London visits that Johnny started dabbling with heroin. He couldn't do all the things he wanted to with his trumpet, and I think he thought it would help him play the ideas he could hear in his head but couldn't get out of the bell of his horn. Smoking relaxed him but he still couldn't say what he felt, and his lack of technical skill held him back. I sometimes wonder, too, if other pressures didn't have a lot to do with it. The bop craze was losing some of its freshness and excitement and Johnny wasn't the only one who wanted to sustain the tension and the sense of belonging to a special group. Some musicians carried on for years playing the old bop standards and using the period clichés and mannerisms. And some of us kept on documenting the period, and maybe that's a way of trying to make time stand still?

At first no-one in our crowd noticed anything different about Johnny's behaviour. We wouldn't have known what it was all about even if we had. Hard drugs were outside our world, though we regularly read reports about this or that American musician dying from an overdose or being arrested for possession. Johnny still came to the club quite often, but spent most of his time with Hank, an ex-merchant seaman who'd once shipped out to New York just to hear the real bop musicians. I didn't like Hank. I felt uncomfortable whenever I spoke to him and I'd smile politely, or shrug, when he asked me questions in a hipster jargon, half of which I didn't understand. He had that effect of someone spreading tentacles to pull me into a world and way of life that was strange and dangerous. Most of us at the club thought we were hip because we dug Bird and Dizzy but Hank was the kind of hipster who was always involved in shady deals of one kind or another. He would get Johnny on one side and have muttered conversations with him, and they'd both leave the place early.

The club was closed down by the police shortly after Johnny and Hank took to hanging around together, so I didn't see either of them for several months. I met Hank in town that summer and he told me Johnny was living in London, taking care of his habit. He grinned when I looked puzzled, and said, "Oh, you know, like he's got to be where the stuff is." I must have seemed a bit shocked because Hank added, "He's all right, man, he's cool." He said it as if being an addict was something to be admired, and his tone implied the unspoken justification, "Well, Bird's on, isn't he?"

Coincidences come easily to me, probably because I move in a small circle and have a specific range of interests, and it's not surprising that I invariably meet people again when I think I've seen the last of them. I was in a club off Charing Cross Road a couple of years later when I noticed Johnny sitting at a table near the bandstand. He was thin and tired and even more preoccupied than when I first knew him. I asked him if he was still playing trumpet, and he said, "No, I haven't bothered much lately. It's different down here, I mean..." his voice trailed off and he looked around the room. I don't want you to think I'm trying to put over that inarticulate junkie image because it wasn't like that at all. He just wasn't interested in what I had to say and so couldn't be bothered explaining himself to me. If I'd had some contact with his world he'd have talked to me, and before I left we did manage to discuss records and musicians for a while. He didn't refer to our mutual home-town and I didn't bring up the subject either.

A year or so later I heard that he'd died. Of course, this was five or six years after I'd first met Johnny and the old crowd from the club had either settled or moved on. I only found out about his death when I met Hank at a concert in Manchester. When I muttered something about it being sad, Hank shrugged his shoulders and said, "Well, everyone has to pay their dues." The following week I went to see Johnny's parents and I sat with them for an hour or so. His mother asked if I wanted a cup of tea, and I couldn't help thinking of Johnny's stock response to the question. His eyebrows would lift slightly and he'd say, "Like you mean you drink tea, man?" There wasn't a thing I could really say to his parents. They were two middle-aged, working-class people who'd spent all their lives with the same routines, and it was hard for them to understand why their son had been mixed up with jazz and drugs and the police. They had a photograph of Johnny when he was sixteen and had his first drape-suit and crew-cut, and his mother kept looking at it and wiping her eyes. I had an uneasy feeling they somehow connected me with their son's death, and maybe they were right. I knew far more about his world that they ever would, even if I hadn't gone all the way into it.

All that happened over fifty years ago and my memories of Johnny are fragments which only come into focus when I play the old bop records. I listen to Charlie Parker and Dexter Gordon and can see Johnny's introspective smile and his way of rocking to and fro in the chair. And I hear discs by Howard McGhee or Fats Navarro or Dizzy Gillespie and I can almost hear that soft sound from the other side of the room as Johnny blows gently into the mouthpiece of his trumpet.

BORDER TROUBLE

WHEN I was about ten or eleven I used to hang around with a gang of kids from the nearby streets. We'd sit on the garden walls of the houses by the main road until the householders chased us away and then we'd drift across the road and throw stones at the kids in the streets there. Over the years the road had become a dividing line and we rarely crossed it without running into trouble.

There weren't any major economic or social differences in the two areas. The houses were pretty much the same - two up, two down, toilets in the back yards - and our parents probably worked side by side in the local factories. It sticks in mind that Catholics predominated on the other side but I don't recall that this was the main source of conflict.

Our gang had a few Catholics, misfits like myself (my parents weren't particularly religious - they did send me to Sunday School but that was so they could have a quiet hour after the heavy Sunday lunch - my father was a lapsed Catholic my mother originally from one of the minor Protestant sects) and even a Jew. But we would freeze out a kid from the other side of the road.

I remember one summer we carried on an intermittent war with the other side. I was beaten up on my way to the fish and chip shop, and a few days later got my revenge by helping to chase a couple of our enemies as they came home from school. Both sides were in strategically vulnerable positions. We had to cross into their territory to get to some of the shops and they had to pass through our streets to reach the Catholic school. By some kind of unspoken agreement, the local cinema was no-man's land and we never fought there. We all knew they'd throw us out if we got too rowdy.

The summer's skirmishing came to a head when both sides agreed to a pitched battle. The word had been passed around that day at school and after tea we got our sticks and dustbin lids, filled our pockets with stones, and gathered in groups. It was a warm evening and people, were sitting on their front steps. They shouted and swore at us as we moved towards the road banging on the dustbin lids and screaming. After a couple of probing attacks we advanced in a body towards the other side.

We chased away the handful of kids who threw stones at us and charged up a street towards their main force. They retreated and we followed until we passed an intersection. It was then that we discovered our bad planning. Another gang poured out behind us and we were trapped.

I saw one of my friends fall to the floor and another ran past me with blood pouring from his face. Someone hit me across the chest with a stick and I backed up against a wall, swinging wildly at my opponent. I glanced around and saw that most of our side were in full retreat so I threw my stick at the kid opposite me and ran past him when he ducked.

I was scared, it's true, but wasn't sure whether it was because the other gang might get me or because the stick I'd lost was the handle from my mother's brush. We poured back across the road and the pedestrians stared at the sight of 40 or 50 kids running and fighting and dodging in between buses and cars.

When we got back to our side we re-formed our battered lines and drove away the more impetuous kids who'd chased us. Then we stood, throwing stones and shouting insults, until a police-car came along and both gangs disappeared into the maze of streets on each side of the road.

Afterwards we sat on the wall trying to convince each other that we'd won because we had managed to get into their streets. But we all knew we'd taken a bad beating, our collective pride was hurt at being caught in such an easy trap. For days we watched in sullen silence as the Catholic kids walked through the streets to their school. We couldn't even raise the enthusiasm to chase them and if we catcalled they invited us across the road for another fight.

That was the last major battle I was in, although the war dragged on for some months. I had one or two brief scuffles and was once badly scared when I was caught alone in the enemy streets. My friends had dared me to walk that way to the cinema.

Shortly after the big fight, however, I started attending the local grammar school and so became a member of a group which was heartily despised by the kids on both sides of the roads. My former enemies would call me names but considered it beneath their dignity to bother chasing me, and my friends stopped saving a space on the wall for me in the evenings.

They were usually sitting there when I came home with my satchel and if I stopped to talk they shuffled uneasily and made veiled comments about snobs. After a few weeks of this I started taking a different route home.

LOVE FROM UNCLES BERT AND JOE

When I was nine I thought the sun shone out of Joe Stalin's pipe. That was in 1945, and I used to sit on the garden wall at the end of Larkhill Street with Roy Archer, Jackie Oldfield, Kenny Martin, Bob Sumner, and a couple of others whose names now escape me. We were solid socialists all, some with a liking for the Labour Party, and others like myself with a leaning towards the communists. It was my proud boast that I'd once seen Harry Pollitt plain. And one thing was certain. There wasn't a Trotskyist among us, and if asked, we would probably have said that Trotsky was the name of a Russian racehorse.

Those were days of innocence, but also days of hope. We knew what the war was being fought for; not only to defeat Hitler and Hirohito, but also to help build a new and better world. So, we did our bit, chalking slogans on walls. I can't claim that any of us were responsible for "Second Front Now" scrawled on a gable end. That had appeared a couple of years before when the comrades were convinced that Britain and America were deliberately holding back from such a policy in order to let Russia and Germany exhaust themselves. But I did write "Support the CP" on the side of an air-raid shelter when the 1945 election campaign began.

Mind you, I also compromised myself when I stood outside the local polling station collecting numbers for the Labour Party. The Labour Club was at the end of our street, and it was offering five shillings and a hotpot supper to anyone willing to help. I didn't then realise that this hankering after material comforts was what would eventually dilute almost to oblivion the socialist principles of our elders.

In 1945, though, things were still clear-cut. A friend's father had a picture of Stalin over the fireplace where other families hung photographs of the King and Queen. On VE Day, when the flags dangled out of upstairs windows, the row of Union Jacks was disrupted by a single red Hammer and Sickle. Uncle Bert had got his priorities right, if no-one else had.

He was, incidentally, the man who told me that Uncle Joe's Mint Balls were made from a recipe concocted by Stalin himself as an aid to nourishing the children of Britain. "There's a leader for you," said

Uncle Bert, "A nation at war, faced with the greatest threat in its history, and he takes time out to think of kids like you." I was impressed and for years after could never pass that factory in Wigan and its "Keeps you all aglow" sign without thinking of Stalin with a warm feeling of comradeship.

I've never been able to work out exactly when it all started to go wrong. I remember the newspapers beginning to talk about a Cold War. I heard murmurings on the radio about Czechoslovakia. And it was impossible to escape the Berlin Air Lift. By the early 1950s and the Korean War, the rot really had started to set in.

Intellectuals will tell you that the Communist Party commenced to fall apart in the mid-1950s when Hungary and the Krushchev revelations combined to disillusion many people, but I know better. The grass-roots mood had begun to change earlier than that, and communism, even socialism, went out of favour with the working-class before a shot was fired in Budapest or a bad word said about Stalin. The glorious Red Army didn't seem all that glamorous when Hitler was no longer around. A lot of party members simply slipped quietly away as conditions improved. I once asked a friend why her father had stopped being a member. "Well," she said, "it was the man going around selling rhubarb who used to collect the Party dues. And when people started to prefer buying from shops he stopped calling, and my dad's membership just lapsed." No rhubarb, no movement.

In 1954 I went into the army for a few years and when I came out in the late-1950s the old gang had dispersed. Two had left town, others had married, and one was in prison. I contacted a couple of them, but they were tied up with mortgages and careers and didn't want to know about matters beyond their immediate concerns. Whenever I called on an old friend, the television set winked away in a corner and the conversation was about wall-to-wall carpeting and buying a car.

In the end, and almost without realising what was happening, I found myself drawn into a similar way of life. Having a *Tribune* or *Daily Worker* around the house, and going to a few union meetings to discuss the next pay claim, didn't make me into a radical. I was as disillusioned and adrift as my old friends were. If we had a few drinks together I'd sometimes catch a flash of the old fire that had enlivened our street-corner discussions. Or I'd observe a wistful gleam in an eye at the mention of an old idea. We were more sophisticated and knew we were no longer dreaming, but that didn't hold back the occasional dream about dreaming.

I have to admit that I feel I betrayed my boyhood comrades. I should have held on to the dream and what we were in 1945. Oh, I know that Stalin turned out to be a monster, and that communism was shown to be fallible, but I'm not talking about those aspects of the times. To admire Russia and shout "Support the CP" were only symbols of other aspirations. We genuinely thought that there was a better world a-coming, and I doubt that any of us, no matter what our personal successes and current comforts, can honestly claim that it worked out that way.

We had a dream and we lost it. And whatever Roy Archer, Kenny Martin, Jackie Oldfield, Bob Sumner, and the others who names I no longer recall, happen to have become, I suspect they feel the same way. We sold out, comrades, and I've never forgiven myself for it.

ARE YOU SURE IT'S TONIGHT?

Sitting with another poet and the person who'd organised the event, I watched the third poet get up to read his work. We'd all had a few drinks, and he'd stumbled as we climbed the steps onto the platform, which was raised well above the audience, with the front row almost immediately below its edge. The poet smiled and launched into his first poem, advancing a couple of feet as he did so. They took him to the edge and he hung there, reading brilliantly but slowly leaning a little more each time he started a new phrase. He tilted over and the people in the front row slid down in their seats as he loomed above them. The organiser crept off his chair and tugged at the poet's jacket and he swayed back but soon began to go forward again.

You have the picture, I hope, and somehow the poet got through his reading without actually falling into the audience. Later, after we'd all done our bit and then made for the bar, I talked to a lady who had been directly below him: "It was wonderful," she said, "1 felt I was right there, in the poems." She almost was, I thought.

Just another night on the poetry reading circuit, though not all are as fraught with tension. Some are routine, it's true, but a lot have their little stories attached to them, and most poets will know about places where the given address doesn't exist, or the premises are closed, or someone says, "But that was last week. Didn't anyone tell you?" And which poet hasn't had the long wait for an organiser who arrives late and doesn't seem to know who you are or what day it is? I've been promised meals after tiring journeys and then given cold coffee and a stale sandwich. Being left high and dry in a strange town when a hotel booking hasn't been made has happened more than once, and on one occasion I was dropped at a railway station to catch a last train that had stopped running six months before. All in a day's work, though I've never been able to figure out why the worst organisers are often the supposed "professionals." There was the time I travelled half-way across England, alighted at a small, unmanned station in the middle of nowhere, and waited for the arranged lift to the reading. After an hour, I decided to look for a telephone, left a note pinned to the station door, wandered down country lanes in the pouring rain, and eventually found a call box. No answer from the contact number, so I went back to the station, waited another hour, and then caught a train home. I never did find out what had happened, and sometimes wonder if an audience is still waiting for me to arrive.

A poet can lose an audience, and an audience can lose a poet. We lost a poet once when we were told that a reading had been transferred to another location several streets away, but it wasn't surprising. We had to pass half-a-dozen pubs on the way, and the poet did like a drink or two and more. The same man had to travel from Liverpool to York for a reading, and thought he was having a heart-attack, so got off the train to die in Manchester. Some people think that getting off a train in Manchester is a form of death in itself, but we'll let that pass. After a few drinks he realised that he'd just been suffering from a monumental hangover, and he knew he was due in York, fifty miles away, so he hired a taxi and arrived half-way through the reading. "Do me a favour," he said to the organiser, "Pay the taxi-driver. I don't seem to have the right change." The organiser, thinking the poet had just come from the railway station, went outside and returned a few minutes later with a dazed expression on his face.

Poets often look on organisers like musicians view band leaders, as enemies to be outwitted, but having arranged a few readings over the years I have a certain amount of sympathy with anyone trying to get a group of poets out of a bar and onto a stage. I recall being asked to escort a notoriously hard-drinking poet to a reading in Glasgow, but he managed to slip away from me when we stopped at a pub, and I arrived alone, to be met by an agitated organiser saying I was to blame. As it happened, the poet turned up on a later train, very tipsy but still able to read, though he almost got us killed that night when, having been paid in Scottish bank notes, he hurled them into the air in a restaurant, saying they were worthless. A group of hard-looking locals at the next table took exception to this insult to their homeland and we left hurriedly.

But drink alone doesn't cause problems. The environment can have its effect, as when I toured the Lake District with another poet and a folk singer. The plan was to give a series of readings in local halls and to advertise them with lunch time appearances in the market-squares, performing from a small platform attached to the rear of a mobile book shop. A good idea, and I stood, spouting forth, not realising that the wind was carrying my words to one side, and to the audience I was simply a man opening and closing his mouth. They applauded all the same, probably thinking I was some sort of performance artist imitating a goldfish.

In Berlin I gave a reading in a small book shop with the audience sitting in two separate rooms. I had to stand in the doorway between them, trying to communicate with both groups. At a college near Blackpool I thought everything was going well until no-one came back after the interval. "It's not your fault," the organiser said comfortingly, "The Miss World competition is on TV and they've all gone to watch that." And readings in pubs have been interrupted when someone has decided to put a coin in the jukebox or turn on the radio for the football results. Readings in pubs can be good, though, with everyone relaxed and out to enjoy themselves, but the occasional heckler can get in the way. I watched with amazement in Ilkley as an irate poet brawled with a drunk who had been delivering a steady stream of supposedly witty comments.

There are stories that ought not to be told, of poets sneaking out of bedrooms they shouldn't have been in, and it's only right that we draw a veil over those. In any case, public escapades are more amusing than private ones. Who was the poet who fell asleep in the middle of his reading? And how about the poet who, standing in front of a lectern and gripping it tightly with both hands, slowly keeled over as he read, not missing a beat, until he and the lectern were lying side by side on the floor. The drink again, but I can't condemn him. I tried to keep up with his consumption of vodka and Guinness the next morning - "The ideal cure for a hangover," he said - and had to be put to bed mid-afternoon.

What of the long-suffering audiences, or are they? I sometimes think they expect to see at least one poet topple over, and are disappointed if they don't. And they continue to turn up, at least most of the time. I remember a reading in London where the poets outnumbered the paying customers and jokingly invited the audience to read to them. Now, as everyone knows, poetry audiences are mostly composed of people who want to be poets, so it wasn't surprising that they took the invitation seriously, pulled out wads of poems, and began reading. The "professionals" sat with glazed looks as they were bombarded with poems bad and worse and generally long. Which reminds me of a reading I gave in North Wales. Or almost gave, because the local poets had to read their work. Reasonable, you might think, and the guest poet rounds off. But they did warn me that

"John writes big poems and he has some personal problems, so we like to let him have his say," which he did, without stopping, until the organiser approached me, said, "Thanks for coming," and indicated that the evening was at an end.

Not quite as bad as the experience that a well-known English poet told me about. He was asked to read to a group in a distant place and made his way there. The organiser met him and explained about the local poets reading first.

The two of them then went to an upstairs room in a pub and the organiser read his work to the poet, muttered an excuse, and left the poet alone. He waited for thirty minutes and finally went home. Curiously, his cheque for the reading did turn up in the mail a few day later, but without any explanation.

And I suppose you could ask why, with such experiences behind me, I continue to respond positively when asked to give a reading. Well, it's useful to earn some money, and a lot of readings are well-organised, and I sell a few books and meet some nice people. It's also fun, and life might be boring without those wet nights when I arrive in a town I've never been to before, find my way to a small pub, and the landlord looks puzzled, and says, "Poetry Reading? Are you sure it's tonight?"

NOTES

ALAN ANSEN
Alan Ansen was very much alive when I wrote the review of *Contact Highs*. He died in 2006. I suspect that he will be fated to be a footnote in books about Auden, Burroughs, and the Beats. His book, *The Table Talk of W.H.Auden*, was originally published by the small Sea Cliff Press in New York in 1989, but was picked up and published in Britain by Faber in 1991. It's probably what he will be mostly remembered for.

BOB KAUFMAN
There are a couple of publications that appeared after my article was published, and which may be of interest:
Jazz – Jail and God: Bob Kaufman, An Impressionistic Biography by Mel Clay. Androgyne Books, San Francisco, 1987.
Cranial Guitar: Selected Poems by Bob Kaufman. Coffee House Press, Minneapolis, 1996.

BOPPER
This piece had a curious history. When it was published in *Jazz Monthly* its title somehow disappeared. In *The Little Word Machine* it was called "Johnny: A Memoir." When Appliance Books published it as one of their Ragged Edge Magsheets pamphlets it was finally given the title I'd originally had in mind when I wrote it.

LOVE FROM UNCLES BERT AND JOE
When this article was published in *The Guardian* I received a letter from an English couple who had lived and worked in East Germany for many years. They advised me to move there so I could experience "actual existing socialism." I had a brief correspondence with them and sent copies of some of my books, though I never followed their suggestion about leaving England and capitalism. But I always wondered if the feared East German secret police, the Stasi, had intercepted my packages and inspected them before passing them to their rightful recipients.

ARE YOU SURE IT'S TONIGHT?
The idea for this came about when I was in Jersey for a poetry event. Diane Moore, the organiser, was driving myself and Ann Born to a

reading and the conversation turned to funny encounters and incidents at poetry readings. Diane later decided to compile an anthology of reminiscences by various poets, including as well as Ann and myself, Dannie Abse, Alan Brownjohn, Carol Rumens, Michael Hamburger, and several others.

www.ingramcontent.com/pod-product-compliance
Lightning Source LLC
Chambersburg PA
CBHW030315290526
45785CB00001B/367